PRAISE

"Jesse Lee Peterson has rejected the poison of hate, blame, and victimhood in his own life, and has been encouraging men and their families to do the same for twenty-five years. *The Antidote* distills a quarter century of wisdom into one bold, powerful, and compelling book. I urge you to read it." —DAVID LIMBAUGH, *NEW YORK TIMES* BESTSELLING AUTHOR AND POLITICAL COMMENTATOR

"Jesse Lee Peterson is a courageous figure in today's race-baiting America. In *The Antidote*, he takes on racial myths and knocks them down and provides solid solutions in the process." —BEN SHAPIRO, *NEW YORK TIMES* BEST SELLING AUTHOR OF *BULLIES*

"Jesse Lee Peterson is one of the very few people I have ever met—and one of the very few writers I have ever read—who can truly be described as 'fearless.' Against the legion of race hustlers who have enslaved many of our fellow citizens in a pathology of dependence and rage, he speaks the liberating truth of forgiveness and love. *The Antidote* is a courageous book: typical of the man." —ANDREW KLAVAN, AWARD-WINNING AUTHOR, SCREENWRITER AND MEDIA COMMENTATOR

"The race-baiting policies of Obama and his cohorts has ruined lives, polarized the nation, and set race relations back decades. . . . In this extraordinary book, the Rev. Jesse Lee Peterson not only sketches out what went wrong and why the Left has failed black Americans, but he also sketches out a way forward: a path back to sanity not just for the black victims of political opportunism and ill-advised socialist policies, but for the entire nation. . . . This is an absolute must-read." —PAMELA GELLER, PRESIDENT OF THE AMERICAN FREEDOM DEFENSE INITIATIVE AND AUTHOR OF *THE POST-AMERICAN PRESIDENCY* AND *STOP THE ISLAMIZATION OF AMERICA*

the ANTIDOTE

HEALING AMERICA FROM THE POISON OF HATE, BLAME, AND VICTIMHOOD

REV. JESSE LEE PETERSON

REPUBLIC

BOOK PUBLISHERS

THE ANTIDOTE

Paperback edition published by Republic Book Publishers
Hardcover edition originally published by WND Books, Washington, D.C.

Book designed by Mark Karis
Photo design by Ryan Krebs, BOND Studios
Photography by Douglas Massey, BOND Studios

For inquiries about volume orders, please contact:
Republic Book Publishers
27 West 20th Street, Suite 1103
New York, NY 10011
editor@republicbookpublishers.com
Published in the United States by Republic Book Publishers
Distributed by Independent Publishers Group
www.ipgbook.com

Paperback ISBN: 9781645720355
eBook ISBN: 9781645720348

Library of Congress Cataloging-in-Publication Data For the Original Hardcover Edition
Peterson, Jesse Lee, 1949-
    The antidote : healing America from the poison of hate, blame and victimhood / Reverend Jesse Lee Peterson.
        pages cm
    Includes bibliographical references and index.
    ISBN 978-1-942475-00-2 (hardcover) -- ISBN 978-1-942475-01-9 (ebook)
1. African Americans--Social conditions. 2. African
Americans--Psychology. 3. African American young men--Social conditions.
4. Parent and child--United States. 5. African American families. 6.
African American neighborhoods. 7. Community life--United States. 8.
Anger--Social aspects--United States. 9. Blame--Social aspects--United
States. 10. United States--Race relations. 11. Peterson, Jesse Lee,
1949- 12. African American clergy--Biography. I. Title.
    E185.86.P527 2015
    305.896'073--dc23
                            2015015816

Printed in the United States of America

To my grandfather, Sabbath, and my grandmother, Rosa Lee. At a time when life was hard for you and those like you, you provided me with a living example of how to work, deal with people, and most of all, love. Your gift will always be a part of me.

CONTENTS

FOREWORD

Given the nature of my work as a nationally syndicated radio talk show host, and given the moral essence of my message, I have been able to meet some of the best people in America. By best, I mean good (as in kind, just, honest), intelligent, and wise.

Jesse Lee Peterson, whom I have known for about twenty-five years, is one of these. He is, first of all, one of wisest people I have ever met.

In prior eras, wisdom was far more valued than in our time. When I was in college, fools in my generation came up with the slogan, "Never trust anyone over thirty." That meant that wisdom no longer meant anything. In the past, the "wisdom of the ages" was the accumulated insights into life over millennia. It was believed that in order to lead a good life people needed to learn from the past—from those older than them and from those who had left us insights and have since died.

But if nothing and no one over thirty is to be trusted, wisdom no longer counts for anything.

So, when I say that Jesse Peterson is one of the wisest people I have ever met, it obviously means something only to those who value wisdom.

I do. In the short time I will spend on earth, I want to soak in every great insight and idea I can. Having Jesse Peterson in my life has therefore been a gift from God. Now, with this book, multitudes of people can receive his gift of wisdom.

In the thirty-three years I have been broadcasting, I have interviewed probably a thousand authors. I have interviewed virtually every major thinker who speaks English. Yet, a full hour that I interviewed Jesse

Peterson stands out as one of the most significant hours I ever broadcast. It was mesmerizing radio.

However, as good, kind, and wise as he is, he possesses one other trait that makes him particularly rare.

There are many admirable traits that a good person may possess—honesty, integrity, compassion, among others—but there is one trait that very few good people have. That trait is courage.

One of the great tragedies of the human condition is that all the goodness that people have in their hearts and express outwardly adds up to very little without courage. There were undoubtedly many good Germans. The reason the Nazis prevailed was that few had courage. The same holds true whenever evil takes over a society. It is rarely an absence of decent people that enables the triumph of evil. It is that few of those decent people have courage.

And here is where Jesse Lee Peterson stands out.

Jesse is fearless. Or to be more accurate, he does not allow fear to govern his behavior or speech. I have no idea whether or not he has fears. I only know that fear plays no role in his work. He answers to God and his conscience.

To be honest, I have a fear—that what I have written here will sound too good to be true. Can anyone be this extraordinary? The truth is that he is better than what I have written.

And now, thanks to this book, far more people will get to know this man—his autobiography is riveting—as are his brilliant, frank, and courageous insights into perhaps the most intractable problem in American life: the black underclass.

There are a number of excellent books about black America. But if you read only one book about what ails large segments of contemporary black America—and the only way to cure that ailment—this should be the one.

There is wisdom on every page. Jesse is unflinchingly honest, willing to openly confront painful realities despite a political and cultural environment that wishes to pretend otherwise, and either ignores or severely punishes those as candid as he is.

The Antidote should be read and much of it memorized by every American. Black America is its subject; but it is really about the nature of truth, of men and women, of fathers and mothers, about human weakness, about anger, and about redemption through letting go of that anger. It is, for those who still value it, immeasurably wise.

—DENNIS PRAGER

ACKNOWLEDGMENTS

First of all, I must thank God, my Father, for bringing me out of the darkness of anger and into the light of forgiveness and love. Words cannot express my gratitude.

I so appreciate WND Books for giving me the opportunity to write the book I've always wanted to write—a book that tells the truth, that provides the roadmap to rebuilding families, that lets the reader know there really is an antidote so they no longer need to hate, blame, or play the victim. I appreciate Republic Books for rereleasing the book.

I appreciate the undying love and support of Joseph and Elizabeth Farah, and of my friend David Kupelian, who originally contacted me to invite me, "in the event you have another book brewing deep down inside you, to let us know." How did he know?!

And thank you to Geoffrey Stone for guiding this vision from inspiration to reality.

I appreciate all the WND and Republic staff for being so kind. You have helped me create what I truly believe is a very special book. We are presenting a missing part of a great puzzle, which, once understood, will cause so many to be free. This gives me immense joy.

There are so many others I'd like to thank who have encouraged me and been my friend over the years, but there are far too many to name, and I don't want to offend or leave anyone out. Just know that I appreciate you more than you'll ever know.

1

DEATH ON CANFIELD DRIVE

I f he slept at all the night before—and that much is doubtful—Michael Brown woke up at his grandmother's apartment on the morning of August 9 angry. He did not know this would be the last day of his life. He probably didn't care.[1]

How do I know this? I know it in part by researching Brown's history, in part by observing his actions later that day, and in part by having been where Michael Brown was. When I was younger, anger drove me almost as hard as it drove him. Many of the same things that angered Michael angered me. For years, I drank deeply from a toxic spring of hatred. I consumed the poison. I wallowed in it. Thank God I lived long enough to find the antidote. Michael did not. The poison—not Officer Darren Wilson—killed him before he had a chance.

In 1999, when Michael was no more than three, his parents separated. Not much had held them together anyway. They had never married. By all accounts, it was a nasty split. Michael moved with his mother, Lesley McSpadden, to a new neighborhood and a new school.

Growing up, sometimes Michael would call his father and ask to be "rescued." That was not easy for his father to do. "And the two different families, we really didn't get along, so it was kinda hard for me to go pick him up," said Michael Brown Sr. in one of his more honest moments. "I had to have a family member go get him and bring him over to the house."[2] The tension unsettled Michael. How could it not have?

Lesley and Michael Sr. were still in their twenties when they split up. But in time, each would have a new partner and form a new family, or what passed for a family, in Ferguson, Missouri. The younger Michael did not meet his father's new wife, Calvina, until his mother threw him out of the house and dropped him off on his father's front porch. He was sixteen. For three months he stayed with his father and Calvina, sulking in his room and refusing to go to school.

Meanwhile, Michael's mother had hooked up with a fellow named Louis Head. The media routinely designated Head as Michael's "step-father," but a police report after Brown's death listed him as "McSpadden's Boyfriend." Whether husband or boyfriend, Head brought little to the relationship beyond a bad temper and a lengthy rap sheet. Michael would never feel comfortable in any of these households. This helps explain why he ended up living most of the final year of his life with his grandmother, Desuirea Harris. At least there he would not have to compete with a new spouse or a new boyfriend for a parent's attention.

No one talks much about the hostility between men and women that infects black families, but believe me, it is there. When their men walk out, as they do too often, women grow angry and bitter. "The women work," an older neighbor of Brown's said of the area. "The guys stay home, smoke dope and walk around harassing people. You can't say nothing to them. They'll cuss you out."[3]

Single black mothers often take their frustration out on the son who resembles the man who abandoned them. They turn the child against the father by saying the father is "no good," or "He doesn't love you." This constant disparagement makes the child feel unloved, and it destroys him emotionally and spiritually. A mother might curse her son, smack him, tell him he will amount to no more good than his old man. The boy cannot help but absorb that message. From all appearances, this seemed to be the kind of environment that produced Michael Brown. No wonder he needed to be rescued.

Later in life, these boys may tell the world how much they love their mothers, but many of them do not mean it. I certainly did not. When my mother separated me from my father, all I felt was anger; it was the sentiment I knew best. That anger was so consuming it took over my soul. I projected it everywhere, toward my mother and father, toward my teachers and friends, and especially toward white people. By having others to blame for the sorry state of my own life, I did not have to blame myself. Such was my life before I learned to forgive.

Eight days before he died, Michael Brown graduated from high school. The media treated his graduation as a bridge crossed, a sign of brighter things to come. This is the same story the media tell every time they choose to turn a violent lost soul into a victim. Michael knew better. He knew the graduation was a bridge to nowhere. He had attended a chaotic high school, learned almost nothing, finessed his way to a diploma through some half-baked alternative program, and entered the world unskilled, unready, unarmed. This is a story the media do not want to tell.

At eighteen, no longer in school, Michael did not see a life full of promise. He saw a life full of anxiety. For all of his heft—six foot four and nearly three hundred pounds—he was still a scared little boy. He could bluster all he wanted to, but inside he was feeling empty, angry, and unloved. He had no idea what he wanted to do or what he could do. As an adult, he had no idea what *to do*.

Without parents to give him direction along the way, he grew up feeling lost on the inside. Despite his size, he lacked the discipline to play football or any other sport. A good coach can sometimes turn a young man around. Michael never had such a coach. On the threshold of manhood, he had no idea of how a real man lived his life. Telling him to go out and find a job and perform well enough to keep a job was like telling him to grow a pair of wings and fly.

In an age when fatherlessness is epidemic throughout the culture, many white young men enter the world no better prepared than Michael. There is, however, a difference between those white teens and boys like Michael, a fatal difference. Michael had an excuse for his failings that they did not. Michael was black. From the time he was a little boy, the people around Michael were telling him that the white man kept the black man down. He heard this at home, among his friends, on television, at school, and maybe even at church. Barack Obama's mentor, Jeremiah Wright, was far from the only preacher preaching hate. This hatred may have made Michael's own failings seem less painful and less personal, but it was crippling him.

Just before noon on August 9, Michael and his friend Dorian Johnson, both high, walked toward a convenience store on West Florissant Avenue, a few blocks from the apartment where Brown had been staying. Once inside, Michael grabbed a pack of cheap cigars that dopers like to hollow out and fill with marijuana. They call them "blunts." On that day, Michael was feeling angry enough and entitled enough to take the cigars without paying. He was convinced that the white man had screwed him and owed him. I know the feeling. I've been there.

The merchant may not have been a standard-issue Missouri white man, but to Michael he probably was white enough. Michael had been told that these foreigners got help from the government to start a business, help that had been denied to the black man. How else to account for the man's success and that of others like him in a black neighborhood? Michael could not believe this dude would try to stop him as he left the store. He was likely sick of all the storekeepers spying on him, following him, doubting him, now even confronting him, Michael Brown, the biggest, baddest dude in his small southeast corner of Ferguson. They may have thought they were better than he was, but he would show them.

Without thinking of the consequences, Michael grabbed the fellow, shoved him up against a display case, and exited the store. *To hell with them all!* This was one angry young man. He and Johnson headed back down West Florissant on foot, then turned onto Canfield Drive, where his grandmother lived. Michael had just committed a crime that could have sent him to prison, but if he was worried, he certainly did not show it.

Michael walked down the center of Canfield Drive as if he owned it, flaunting the cigars as he walked. Johnson, half his size, walked in front, knowing Brown had his back. Michael had no fears of what Grandma might say or do. He knew there would be no repercussions even if word got back to her. (It is the rare grandmother willing or able to exert the force necessary to control a wayward grandson.) Michael could not have made a bolder statement of who he was and what he was about than he did that August day. He was showing his dominance. To the outside world, he may have seemed a loser. But on Canfield Drive, he was the alpha male. He was daring anyone to say otherwise. He expected no challenge.

And then, to Michael's surprise, Officer Darren Wilson drove by.

Earlier that morning, a local woman had called 911 when a gunman threatened her. That call, of a type much too common in this neighborhood, had drawn Wilson to the area. Another call followed from a frantic mother whose baby was sick. That call kept Wilson in the neighborhood and set up his tragic encounter with Michael.

Officer Wilson saw the young men walking in the middle of the street. At first, Wilson did not demand much. He just asked Brown and Johnson to get out of the street. With no respect for authority and even less for a white cop, Michael spat back, "F*** what you have to say" and kept on going. Shocked, Wilson decided to check Brown out more closely. It was then that he noticed the cigars and realized Brown was likely the guy who had just robbed the convenience store. Wilson called for support and backed down the street to cut the pair off.

At this point, I suspect, Michael stopped thinking altogether. I never lost it quite as he did, but I have gotten close. I know how it feels when all the suppressed rage against the white man explodes in a sudden burst of anger and energy. When Wilson tried to exit the car, Michael cursed him out once again, pushed him back into the car, reached through the open window, and started punching him in the head. Wilson would later describe Brown as having the face of a "demon." When Wilson reached for his gun, Michael grabbed for it. Two shots went off. One of them grazed Michael's hand. If Michael had not crossed a bridge when he graduated from high school or even when he robbed the convenience store, he had now.

There was no turning back. Michael was either going to die or go to prison. There were no other ways for the day to end. His first instinct was to run. This was what all boys everywhere learn to do when they get in trouble. But if not quite a man, Michael was no longer a boy. He had a reputation to uphold. He was not going to let this white man—cop or no cop—intimidate him in the middle of Canfield Drive, not after the gunshots had alerted the neighbors. They would be watching.

Incredibly, Michael made the conscious decision to turn around and confront the armed Wilson. Forget the "hands up, don't shoot" line that the media promoted and perpetuated. The myth would have insulted Michael. He was in no mood to surrender. A lifetime of slights and insults had enraged him beyond reason. He ignored Wilson's commands to stop and charged the startled officer.

Wilson fired repeatedly as Brown rushed him. As Wilson knew from experience, an angry, charging three-hundred-pounder is no more "unarmed" than a bull in a bullring. The initial hits to Michael's right arm scarcely slowed him down. The closer Michael got, the more accurate Wilson's aim grew. Finally, a shot to the top of Michael's head as he lunged toward Wilson ended the showdown on Canfield Drive.

The neighbors who had not seen the shooting already knew the story line. Two years earlier, the media had walked them through it in the shooting death of Trayvon Martin in Florida. There, they were told, this innocent little "boy," on the way back from getting his "brother" some Skittles and iced tea, was stalked and shot by a racist thug named Zimmerman, who, if he wasn't exactly white, was white enough.

The neighbors never learned just how closely Trayvon's life—and death—paralleled Michael's. When Trayvon was three, his father, Tracy Martin, had left home too. For the next twelve years, Trayvon spent most of his time at the home of Alicia Stanley, Tracy Martin's second wife. When Trayvon was fifteen, Tracy left Alicia for a woman named Brandy Green, and Trayvon lost his home again. The boy was shattered. Alicia had been his rock. "I'm the one that went to them football games," Alicia told CNN's Anderson Cooper. "I'm the one that was there when he was sick."[4] After the shooting, Alicia was treated as if she did not exist. The same was true for Brandy Green. For the sake of the cameras, Tracy had to be reunited with Sybrina Fulton, Trayvon's birth mom. It made for a better image.

Once he had to leave Alicia's home, Trayvon's life became unglued, and there was no one around to put the pieces back together. A conversation on Facebook between Tracy Martin and his sister-in-law Miriam showed just how unsettled Trayvon's life had become.

> TRACY: i need time to myself 2day!!!!!! my son think imma damn fool! this is the part i hate in our father to son relationship! when you start telling lies about nothing you gone walk you ass into an ass cuttin! be honest with your old boy [meaning, the father] and you wont have to get yelled at like a negro in the streets!

> MIRIAM: That's right and when you finish cutting his ass send him to home to Auntie & Uncle house so we can get on him too. You know how we do it.[5]

In the last two years of his life, Trayvon shuttled between one house and another—his mother's, his father's, his uncle's, Brandy Green's in Sanford. A few months before he died, his mother exiled him after he had been caught fighting at school. "She just kicked me out," he told a friend online. When the friend asked why, Martin answered, "Da police caught me outta skool."

His friend said, "U a hoodlum."

"Naw," replied Martin. "I'm a gangsta."[6]

No one in Trayvon's family knew him well enough anymore to even notice his anger or his outlets for it—drugs, burglary, guns, truancy, and street-style mixed martial arts. It was only George Zimmerman who got to see the real Trayvon Martin.

Zimmerman had alerted the police that Trayvon, who was high at the time, was wandering aimlessly in the rain. As neighborhood watch captain, Zimmerman tried to keep an eye on Trayvon after he took off running. But like Michael Brown, this now six-foot-tall street fighter had enough of running away. He circled back, sucker punched

Zimmerman, and was beating the life out of him, MMA-style, for nearly a minute when Zimmerman finally pulled his gun and shot him.

The evidence was never in doubt, yet the state prosecuted Zimmerman to satisfy the media, the politicians, and the race hustlers. Predictably, they all refused to accept the verdict when a mixed-race jury acquitted Zimmerman, sending the message to Michael Brown and people like him everywhere that "nothing had changed." Benjamin Crump, the Martin family attorney and later the Brown family attorney as well, had the nerve to say, "Trayvon Martin will forever remain in the annals of history next to Medgar Evers and Emmett Till, as symbols for the fight for equal justice for all."[7] Crump was one of many to compare Martin to Till, a fourteen-year-old Chicago boy lynched in 1955 in Mississippi for whistling at a white woman. Evers, a brave civil rights leader, was shot in the back by a racist assassin in 1963 Mississippi. Martin was shot in the chest while bashing in the head of a neighborhood watch captain who had done nothing but look at him suspiciously.

Michael Brown and his neighbors knew the Trayvon story by heart. The media told it and retold it at every opportunity. The people in Ferguson just didn't know the story they were being fed about the little boy with the Skittles was false. They had heard all their lives that the white man had it in for them. When Dorian Johnson said the cop had shot Michael in the back or shot him as he was trying to surrender—whatever—they were prepared to believe him. Those who knew Brown well were probably not surprised. They might have thought he had it coming, but they were not about to share that thought with the media. Because of their anger against white people, they would pretend Brown was a good guy killed because he was black. Sad but true, the hatred of white folks runs deeper than whites want to believe. It creates a kind of community among the haters.

Within a half hour of Brown's death, an activist was rehearsing the neighbors in the "hands-up, don't shoot" gesture. Those half dozen or so neighbors who saw what really happened chose not to talk to the media. They knew that "snitches get stitches." Later, though, they did have the courage to talk to the grand jury. It made all the difference. At least it should have.

Brown's death, like Trayvon's, could have been a teachable moment. The media might have said that when a child is shuttled between relatives all his life, when he is trapped in a series of failing government schools, when he is instructed in ways big and small about the evils of the white man, bad things happen. But this was not a story the media wanted to tell any more in 2014 than they did in 2012.

The reporters and editors preferred to tell a story that would make them feel better about themselves. In their version of events, a racist cop shot a poor young black boy, a "gentle giant" with dreams of college, despite his willingness to surrender. To tell this story, the media had to ignore Wilson's account, Brown's life history, the convenience-store video, the brave grand jury testimony of eyewitnesses on the scene, and all the forensic evidence. Still, by projecting racism onto white people— Officer Wilson or cops in general—the media could assert their own moral superiority.

This narrative suited the race hustlers as well. They needed to keep black people angry. They wanted them to believe that the white man was out to get them, that nothing had changed in the last fifty years, and that if it weren't for Al or Jesse or whoever, things would be much worse still. Said attorney general Eric Holder of Michael Brown's death, "There is [an] enduring legacy that Emmett Till has left with us that we still have to confront as a nation."[8] The media played right into his hands.

Politicians like Holder love the bogus narrative. As they interpreted events, local police were as racist as they always had been. The federal government still needed to intervene to punish wayward cops and remind them that "black lives matter." Of course, black lives matter to politicians—especially in election years.

Brown's family needed the bogus narrative more than anyone else. It got them off the hook. It freed them to play the victim. For all the abuse a mother might throw at her son, she will almost always defend him blindly from accusations of wrongdoing, no matter how legitimate, especially if white people are doing the accusing. McSpadden was no exception. "I know my son far too well," she said on *CBS This Morning* after the grand jury decision came down. "He would never do anything like that. He would never provoke anyone to do anything to him and he would never do anything to anybody." As to the undeniable video of Brown attacking the store clerk, she offered, "If something happened in that store—and that's a big if—that could have been dealt with."[9] Sure, mama, "a big if."

Trayvon's mother, Sybrina Fulton, sent McSpadden a letter of encouragement. "Trayvon was not perfect," she wrote. "But no one will ever convince me that my son deserved to be stalked and murdered. No one can convince you that Michael deserved to be executed." Fulton preferred to blame both of these deaths on "senseless gun violence."[10] Neither mother would take any responsibility for the self-destructive anger that consumed both their sons. It was so much easier to blame guns, the police, the white man.

On the night of the grand jury announcement clearing Officer Wilson, Brown's mother stood atop a car outside the Ferguson police station, yelling incoherently to a large crowd of protesters. Once the decision not to charge Officer Wilson was broadcast, she began weeping uncontrollably. New husband—or whatever (the police report showed that they were not married)—Louis Head and others embraced her in a show of solidarity. Then Head turned toward the mob and repeatedly yelled, "Burn this b***h down!" McSpadden and Head took no responsibility for the rioting and looting that ensued.

Michael Brown Sr. meanwhile appeared on CNN and called Officer Wilson a "murderer." He also said that if his son had been white, Wilson would have said hi and kept on driving. With these kinds of parents as role models, Michael Brown didn't have a chance. The apple doesn't fall far from the tree, and bad parents raise rotten children. Michael Brown is dead because his parents failed him, and because he failed himself. Recently I received an e-mail from a father whose son was killed under similar circumstances. He wrote after hearing me on *Kilmeade & Friends*, a Fox News radio program. "Rev. Jesse," he said, "when I heard you on the radio, I needed to tell you I agree. It is tough to say and come to the realization your child is to blame. One day—maybe tomorrow, maybe next year, when all the dust settles—Mrs. Brown in a very private moment will say to herself, 'Michael killed Michael.'"

With the race hustlers and the media egging them on, the members of Brown's family did not have the cohesion to pull together in the face of tragedy. The various couplings and uncouplings had created much bad blood over the years, and that blood boiled over in an ugly incident on West Florissant two months after the shooting. According to the police report, Pearlie Gordon, the mother-in-law of Michael Brown Sr., was selling "Justice for Michael Brown" merchandise when twenty or thirty people pulled up in cars, jumped out, and rushed them. At the head of the cavalry was McSpadden. "You can't sell this s***," she told Gordon.

Gordon explained who she was—namely, the mother of Brown's wife, Calvina—and told McSpadden that unless she could document a trademark on the Michael Brown name, she was going to continue to sell her wares. McSpadden's mother then piped up, "You don't know my grandson like that. I'm gonna tear this s*** down," and she proceeded to do just that. Someone then hit Gordon in the back of her head, and the people with McSpadden, Louis Head included, began wrecking the booth. "That's Calvina's mom. Get her ass," McSpadden yelled, then ran up and punched Gordon. Others did the same. McSpadden's posse made off with fifteen hundred dollars in merchandise and four hundred dollars in cash and fled the scene before the police arrived.[11] Although no one much wanted Michael around when he was alive, apparently everyone wanted a piece of him when he was dead.

2

THE ALCHEMISTS

The unraveling of Michael Brown's family speaks volumes about the state of the black family in general and, by extension, the black community. For a half century or more, black people have labored under the spell of what I will call the "alchemists." The practice of alchemy came into Europe by way of the Islamic world in the twelfth century. The most common goal of the alchemist was to transform a base metal, such as lead, into a "noble" metal, like gold. Although many alchemists likely meant well, there was something godless and unnatural about the whole process, not to mention flat-out materialistic. The goal was, after all, to skip the hard work that the acquisition of gold usually required and create gold out of nothing.

So it is with today's "civil rights" movement. Although some of those involved mean well, the field is dominated by hustlers, media hacks, politicians, community organizers, and the like, who scheme to create wealth without sweat. Like President Obama, these modern-day alchemists promise to "fundamentally transform" America.[1] The transformation they promise, however, produces only fool's gold—unearned benefits, such as welfare, food stamps, payouts from lawsuits, and maybe one day even "reparations." Worse, to secure these counterfeit goods, recipients have to sacrifice something of infinite value: the sanctity of the two-parent family. It is a devil's bargain.

To make this experiment work, the alchemists have created an ungodly and unhealthy environment, one in which the white population is made to feel guilty and the black population is made to feel angry. If the alchemists have to lie to keep black people agitated, so be it. They have been doing just that for the last fifty years. Those lies have filled American blacks with the venom of hate and are slowly poisoning the nation at large.

As bleak as this all sounds, an antidote exists, thank God! If I could summarize that antidote in two key concepts, they would be "forgiveness" and "truth." The one follows the other as day follows night. Forgiveness and truth saved my life, saved my son's life, and have saved the lives of any number of young men we have counseled at BOND, the organization I founded in 1990 to help rebuild men and families— particularly the black family.

Before discussing the antidote in any detail, I will share with you how the black community in America has come to need an antidote so desperately. In doing so, I will tell my own story and the parallel stories of many young men and women, most of them black, and show the pattern of behavior that has undone black America.

This pattern is so obvious I am still shocked almost no one talks about it. It is this simple: children, black or white, when deprived of fathers, grow up angry at their parents. White children displace their anger in many different directions. Black children, for the most part, channel theirs in a single destructive direction—toward and against white people. The alchemists encourage them to do this, enable them, and even reward them. This anger fuels the system and pays the alchemists' bills.

The antidote, however, lies within reach. Some people accept it in a spontaneous moment of pure grace when they realize they are ready to accept the pain that comes with self-knowledge. Others struggle for years before accepting it. In either case, with the antidote comes courage. What I discovered is that when God took the anger out of my heart, He also took the fear. I know that telling the truth makes enemies, but my message is right and just, and I have no desire to modify it to please others. I am reminded of what abolitionist William Lloyd Garrison said when asked to soften his attack on slavery:

I am aware, that many object to the severity of my language; but is there not cause for severity? I *will* be as harsh as truth, and as uncompromising as justice. On this subject, I do not wish to think, or speak, or write, with moderation. No! no! Tell a man whose house is on fire, to give a moderate alarm; tell him to moderately rescue his wife from the hand of the ravisher; tell the mother to gradually extricate her babe from the fire into which it has fallen;—but urge me not to use moderation in a cause like the present. I am in earnest—I will not equivocate—I will not excuse—I will not retreat a single inch—AND I WILL BE HEARD. The apathy of the people is enough to make every statue leap from its pedestal, and to hasten the resurrection of the dead.[2]

The alchemists have worked their magic well. They have transformed the golden promise of the civil rights era into the grim urban reality of today, and they promise more destruction still. If we are to stop them, we cannot equivocate. We cannot retreat. We must be heard.

3

BEFORE THE FALL

Over the years, because of the positions I take, many a critic has questioned whether I am an "authentic" black man. If they really want to know the answer to that question, I would invite them to come back with me to the plantation where I grew up outside Eufaula, Alabama. For the record, Eufaula was the name of one of the Creek tribes that inhabited the area before white settlers bought them out and encouraged them, sometimes a bit aggressively, to find lodgings west of the Mississippi. The settlers liked the location on the Chattahoochee River, some forty miles south of what is now Fort Benning, Georgia.

As a young boy in Jim Crow Alabama, this was all the world I knew. I lived with my grandmother and my cousins in a tiny, tin-roof house on the plantation that my grandfather oversaw. Although most families followed traditional lines in those days, my grandparents clearly did not. My grandfather, in fact, lived down the road with his wife. In our house, my male cousins and I slept in one bed in the living room, and my female cousins slept in another bed a few feet away. My grandmother claimed the other bedroom. We had a fireplace to keep the house warm and a wood-burning stove in the kitchen to cook the food. The wind sometimes whistled through the cracks in the house's cardboard-thin walls. As for the "bathroom," there was no bath. No shower either. No running water—no "room," for that matter. As most people in that time and place did when nature called, we braved the elements, day or night, and made our way to the outhouse.

In the mornings, I would get dressed, feed and milk the cows, eat breakfast, and catch the bus at 7 a.m. for a ride to the Rebecca Comer Vocational High School in Springhill. Sometimes during the school year I would stay home to help with the plowing and the planting, the picking of cotton, and the harvesting of crops. Now, if that is not an "authentic" black experience, I am not sure I know what is.

Boxing great Joe Frazier faced many of the attacks I have—and then some—when he squared off against Muhammad Ali. Young whites, who embraced Ali only after he resisted the draft, somehow painted Ali as the authentic black champion, this despite the fact that Ali had two white great-grandparents and grew up with both parents in a middle-class Louisville neighborhood. With Ali's encouragement, the media painted Frazier as an Uncle Tom, a white man's black man. These taunts stung Frazier worse than all the punches he ever took.

"[Ali] set out to cut me down, and hurt me," Frazier wrote in his autobiography, "the only way he knew how—with his lying, jiving mouth."[1] Frazier knew he'd led a "blacker" life than Ali. The twelfth child of a one-armed sharecropper, he had darker skin, proud Gullah roots, a black manager and trainer, and an integrated management team. "I grew up like the black man—he didn't," Frazier told *Sports Illustrated*. "I cooked the liquor. I cut the wood. I worked the farm. I lived in the ghetto."[2] Frazier could never understand why the media had turned on him. "He had a white man in the corner and those rich plantation people to fund him," Frazier wrote of Ali. "A white lawyer kept him out of jail. And he's going to Uncle Tom me?"[3]

At the time, I knew even less about how the greater world worked than Frazier did. I went to the same homey, little school for grades K through 12. My schoolmates had a way of reminding me that I was born with a cleft palate that was not quite properly repaired. Kids are like that everywhere. Other than the teasing, school was something of a sanctuary.

At home I knew something was missing: namely, a mother and father. As I would learn later, when my father found out my mother was pregnant, he didn't believe that the child was his and refused to marry my mother. She knew otherwise and held a grudge against my father long and deep.

It was not until shortly before her death that she forgave him, and only then after our long talks about forgiveness. Still, there was no doubting her powers of persuasion. She found another man to marry before I was born. Soon, they started having children of their own. Although my stepfather treated me well enough, he knew and I sensed that he was not my real father. When he and my mother moved to Indiana, they thought it best to leave me behind with my grandmother.

When I was six, my grandmother finally told me who my real father was. Occasionally, she would allow him to sneak around and see me. When he did, it was as if God Himself were coming to visit, like a light unto my feet. Other than those infrequent visits, though, there was a void where my father should have been. Thankfully, I had a grandfather who helped fill that void. He taught me to work hard and to be patient and strong. If he assigned me a chore, like plowing a field, there would be hell to pay if that field went unplowed.

Phil Robertson of *Duck Dynasty* fame, who came of age in the rural South in the same time frame I did, was taken to task for saying of the blacks he knew in Louisiana, "Were they happy? They were godly; they were happy; no one was singing the blues."[4] Critics accused him of endorsing Jim Crow, but I knew what he was saying. Out in the country, you had little sense that things were not as they were supposed to be. White or black, you worked; you prayed; you lived your life. My grandparents carried themselves proudly. I never felt as if I had to prove myself to anyone else. When we went to the store, white people were nice to us. We were nice to them.

It was only when I went into town and saw the separate water fountains and sat in the balcony of the movie theater that I knew something wasn't right. Once the North left the South to its own devices a decade or so after the Civil War, local and state governments began to impose a series of absurd and self-defeating laws. Governments have a way of doing that. These laws required businesses and other establishments to have two different entry doors, two sets of seats, two pairs of bathrooms, two sets of schools, two of all sorts of things, one of each being entirely unnecessary. This was expensive for the businesses and the taxpayers and irritating for black people. At the time, though, I was not angry about it. Compared to the wrongs at home—the absence of a father and a distant mother—Jim Crow was not that big a deal.

Of course, the school I attended in Springhill was all black, but I had little sense at the time that this was somehow wrong. Today, we think of all-black schools as being inferior by definition, and not just inferior but disorderly and even dangerous. The Rebecca Comer Vocational School was none of those things. Other than the one fight I got into myself in the tenth grade, I don't recall seeing another one. That fight was so scandalous that my grandmother knew about it before I got home. And if I thought I whupped the other guy, she evened the score. We respected our teachers at Comer, and we respected each other. If we got crosswise at school, we knew that there were parents at home—or, in my case, grandparents—ready and willing to straighten us out.

This was a limited world and sometimes a menacing one, but the blacks who survived it were decent, God-fearing people with much promise. Six million strong, they headed north to fill the jobs made available first by World War I and then by World War II in America's great cities. Unlike most of the world's oppressed, they did not have to ask anyone's permission to go. Many drove their own cars. They had such a good reputation as workers that their white employers were panic stricken that they were leaving. Some even followed them north to try to lure them back.

These determined black migrants brought their values with them. Census records show that they were more likely to be married and raising their children in two-parent families than the urban norm. They also had lower levels of unemployment, higher rates of workforce participation, higher incomes, less poverty, and less welfare dependency.[5]

After World War II, when the social barriers started to fall, these people had the potential to make America's cities livelier, more dynamic, and more prosperous than they had ever been.

Then the alchemists began to work their dark magic.

4

FALL FROM GRACE

D o you know how you can tell you are in a black neighborhood even if you see no one in the streets? Sad but true—you can tell by the iron bars on the windows and doors. Those bars aren't there because the residents think they look good. In fact, with enough of them in place, they make a neighborhood look like a zoo. And they aren't there to keep out white people. White people don't break into black homes. No, the sorry truth is that the iron bars are there to protect black people from other black people.

In one of his rare honest moments, Jesse Jackson summed up the situation much too well. "There is nothing more painful for me at this stage in my life," Jackson admitted in 1993, "than to walk down the street and hear footsteps and start to think about robbery and then look around and see it's somebody white and feel relieved."[1] I know exactly how Jackson feels. The difference is that I am not going to apologize for feeling that way. There is too much at stake, namely, the soul of the black community, which is dying, if not dead: ashes to ashes, dust to dust. A fire still burns in those few who cling to the values of old, but our days as a people of character, self-respect, and unshakable spirit appear to be over.

To test this thesis, visit any street in America named Martin Luther King Jr. Boulevard or Drive or Avenue. After Dr. King's death in 1968, civic leaders sought to honor him by naming the most prominent black commercial thoroughfare in his honor. More than seven hundred cities did just that. Today, virtually every one of these streets is a disaster. For a retail operation to have an address on Martin Luther King Jr. Boulevard is the kiss of commercial death.

I just barely remember a time when the black community was still alive and seemingly well. By the time I was six or so, both my mother and my father had moved to the Gary, Indiana, area. I started visiting Gary in about 1960. At that time the city had nearly two hundred thousand people. Close to half were black. The downtown was busy and alive with people of all colors. The predominantly black neighborhoods had lively commerce up and down the main streets: grocery stores, barbershops, beauty salons, movie theaters, candy stores, restaurants, funeral homes—a little run-down maybe, but friendly and functional just the same. Merchants of other races had shops in the black neighborhoods as well. The Chinese had restaurants and laundries. Italians had pizzerias. Jews had delicatessens, even jewelry stores. Unemployment was low. Most kids had a father at home. Crime was not much of an issue. Churches were everywhere and well attended, and back then a black church was where you went to overcome sin, not have it winked at.

If anything, older cities throughout America, north and south, had even more lively black commercial centers. Some were so vibrant that they attracted a steady stream of white customers, especially for their music but also for their restaurants and theater. Harlem comes to mind. So too do Kansas City, Memphis, Chicago, and St. Louis. When singer Sam Cooke moved to Los Angeles about a decade before I did, he found its commercial heart at Vernon and Central "as glamorous as any white-folks' neighborhood."[2] Local historian Michael Betz described it as "a self-sufficient community with two black-owned newspapers, banks, insurance companies, churches and civil rights organizations."[3] What particularly attracted Cooke was a music scene as dynamic as any in America.

The cities in the South and Mid-South had an odd advantage early on in that segregation forced blacks to create their own enterprise from top to bottom. Even in the Deep South the free market trumped Jim Crow. Little was done to discourage blacks from owning and creating their own businesses. A black man might be forced to sit in the balcony of a first-run movie theater, but it was possible he had more money than all the white people in the orchestra seats below. He might have even owned the theater, but the laws of the land would have still told him where to sit. To be sure, the end of segregation threw a wrench into some black commerce, but it was not responsible for the unraveling that followed. I watched this unraveling without fully understanding what I was seeing during my summers in Gary.

The alchemists inevitably blame what happened to black America on the economy. You know; the steel mills closed in Gary. The car companies left Detroit. Something else shut down somewhere else. Blacks were the last hired, first fired. Unemployed, they could not support their families. The families turned to welfare, and poverty led to crime. Blah, blah, blah. This, of course, is all backward. The black community in Gary was collapsing during the 1960s while jobs went begging in the steel mills. I know this firsthand. In 1968, as an inexperienced eighteen-year-old, I got a well-paying job at Inland Steel without half trying.

In reality, the collapse had almost nothing to do with the economy. When I first arrived in Gary about 1960, the participation of black males in the labor force was equal to or greater than that of whites nationwide and likely in Gary as well. This was true for every age group, including teenagers, as I can attest from my own experience. In the age before an easy "disability" check, when black men lost jobs, they tended to find a new one quicker than white men did.[4]

During the 1960s the unemployment rate fell steadily throughout the decade for all races. By 1969 the national unemployment rate had reached 3.5 percent. It has not been lower since.[5] Yet in that same decade, even controlling for population growth, violent crime more than doubled in the nation, as did property crimes. In Indiana, the increases were even more extreme. The violent crime rate nearly tripled during that decade. The robbery rate more than tripled. The forcible rape rate nearly quadrupled. Disproportionately, blacks were both the perpetrators and the victims, but whites were victimized often enough to get the message. Even if the media lied to them, whites understood the way crime worked. This is one reason why they fled Gary and other cities. Blacks understood this as well, which is why they put bars on their windows and watched the city melt right in front of their faces. It was only when I visited my mother in Gary that I began to see a glimpse of a new black America that I had not seen in Alabama. At the time I had some sense of what was happening, but it would take years before the larger picture came into focus.

If there was one thing obviously missing from the lives of my Indiana peers, it was respect. In Alabama, our elders demanded respect, and we gave it. Knowing its value, we gave respect to one another as well, and we respected ourselves, not perfectly, of course, but as well as growing boys could. By the mid-1960s, the welfare culture had settled into Gary, and respect was breaking down. In Alabama I was the rare black kid not to have a father in the home, but in Gary I was close to the norm. If nothing else, I had an active stepfather. Many boys had neither. Other boys had fathers who took no interest in their lives.

These kids had little respect for authority and even less for each other. You did not need many of them on the block to change that block's culture. There were some scary guys in Gary back then, and their bad behavior forced other kids to adapt. I kept my distance as best as I could, but their world was my world as well. There was no easy escape. I began to wonder how white people must have felt. They saw what I saw, and they had options.

In 1967 my Alabama grandmother tried to discipline my increasingly ornery self, so I took off for Indiana and stayed for the eleventh grade at Thomas A. Edison High School. It proved to be the worst year of my life. I had never lived among black kids that were so violent. I had not grown up like that. Innocent rube that I was, I felt the way a white person might have felt in the same environment. The black students seemed perpetually at war with whites, with Hispanics, and with each other. These kids were so out of control that I would walk home through the snow—there was a lot of it in Gary—rather than ride the school bus. On the positive side, I made my first white friends that year.

They tended to be nicer to me and more respectful. Their parents were kind to me as well. Hanging out with them seemed as natural to me as hanging out with my black friends in Alabama.

As a side note, there was one very large and highly disciplined two-parent black family in that Gary neighborhood. Even in the 1960s, I could see that the children in this family had the ability to go places. So occasionally I would go over and watch them rehearse or perform in talent shows. Their family was hardly a perfect one—no family is—but there was no denying that the parents gave their kids the skills and the work ethic to succeed, and succeed Michael, Marlon, Tito, Jermaine, Jackie, Randy, Janet, and LaToya Jackson most certainly did. What their parents did not give them was a faith strong enough to endure the assaults of an increasingly godless popular culture, but even the best parents sometimes lose that battle.

In November 1967, the troubled year I spent at Edison High, Gary was the first major city in America to elect a black mayor, Richard Hatcher by name. You'd have thought his election would ease the anger of the black students and inspire them to do better, but in fact, it had the opposite effect. It empowered the black kids to act out even more, giving them permission to ramp up their attacks on non-blacks. I know a lot of white people took comfort in Obama's election, thinking it would convince blacks that all was well. But from what I'd witnessed in Gary, I knew that was not going to happen. As we have seen, and will explore later, the alchemists have exploited Obama's presidency to aggravate the black sense of grievance, and violence has followed.

Hatcher's election made no difference, at least no positive difference, on Gary's future. The new mayor proved to be as willfully blind to the real source of his city's problems as were the white politicians before him. The only thing the lot of them were good at creating was excuses. Today, Gary is a rotting shell of what it once was. Median home prices on Martin Luther King Drive are in the forty-thousand-dollar range. In the last fifty years, the city has lost more than half of its population, and the alchemists, black and white, are still making excuses about why their magic isn't working. In 2011, Gary elected its first black female mayor, and true to form, this Harvard-educated lawyer won't even mention the problem at hand. "Gary is open for business" is her message.[6] Sure it is. It's just that no business owner on his own dime will go near the city, and if he did, he would have a hard time finding people to work.

The community was ill at ease, as was my own soul. In Gary, my mother remained as bitter as ever toward my father. Making matters worse, I looked just like him. When relatives commented on the resemblance, it would anger my mother all the more, and she would direct that anger toward me. She did her best to keep my father away from me, and that made me all the angrier toward her. The problem of the black community, I would one day come to see, was my problem magnified by the thousands—no, by the millions.

5

THE ROAD TO DAMASCUS

I n the summer of 1967, after my junior year in high school, I flew for the first time ever. That first flight has to be exciting for anyone, but when your life is pretty much limited to a plantation in rural Alabama and your first flight takes you to Los Angeles, it's like a trip to a brave new world.

My mother's baby sister had moved to Los Angeles some years before with her husband and family. She had three children under foot by that summer and asked me to come out to babysit. I flew out there and was overwhelmed by the sights and sounds of Southern California— the freeways, the palm trees, the coastal breezes. As far as I could see, even if I did not see much that summer, California was, as advertised, the golden center of the universe.

I returned to Alabama to finish my senior year in high school, but I knew I was not going to stay any longer than I had to. I lived with an uncle that year and took advantage of his absence one night to introduce my girlfriend to the wonders of lovemaking with Jesse Hollywood. Sure enough, she became pregnant. I had grown up thinking that I would get married young and have ten children, but California beckoned. I promised that as soon I got a job in LA, I would send for her and marry her, but her mother had no use for me or my dreams. She persuaded her daughter to marry another man to give the baby a name. My boy came into the world under circumstances almost identical to my own, and he would be subjected to many of the same tensions. This all worked out much better than I deserved, but more on my son later.

After graduating high school I headed back to Gary and got a job at Inland Steel to make some quick money for airfare. The work at the steel mill was hot and brutal. Given the choice, I'd pick cotton any day. As soon as I saved enough money for a one-way ticket to LA, I was out of there. The year was 1968, the same year Hollywood star and future governor Arnold Schwarzenegger first arrived in Southern California. "It is so warm," he wrote a friend back home. "In Graz [Austria] I am always cold. Here is where I will stay. The sun shines."[1] I could not have said it better myself.

In California, I felt a sudden surge of freedom that people from all over the world felt when they arrived. Other than my aunt and uncle, no one knew me. The traditions of the old South, good and bad, were behind me. I could re-create myself almost any way I wanted. I got a job at Better Foods on Western Avenue. I bought my first car. I saved my money and got my own apartment. I started taking classes at Los Angeles Community College. I even dated a white girl, which, truth be told, was one of my major reasons for attending community college in the first place.

On the down side, I started learning how to project my anger. Although I still thought of myself as a Christian and was not tempted to join his organization, I started listening to Louis Farrakhan. An angry and eloquent man, Farrakhan preached the hatred that was at the core of the Nation of Islam (NOI) with a passion few others could match. As we shall see, the NOI was created as a place for the black man to store and nurture his hatred of the white man. Many blacks who have chosen to follow a more traditional Islamic path sign up for the same reason. It legitimizes their hatreds.

Farrakhan had no tolerance for those who dissented. When Malcolm X turned away from the Nation's explicit message of hate, Farrakhan turned on Malcolm X. "The die is set and Malcolm shall not escape,"[2] he said in a speech in February 1965. Days later Malcolm X was murdered in the Audubon Ballroom in Harlem. At the time I knew none of this. Back then, Farrakhan's message worked as well on me as it did on any troubled young black man. I believed those lies. They stoked my repressed anger and gave it a target. In Alabama, I had been taught not to hate. In California, my attitude was changing gradually from love to hate. Hate of the white man in particular gave me a satisfying way to explain all my other failures. I was not alone in this. Hate was destroying South Central the way it was destroying Gary.

The economy had nothing to do with it. The Los Angeles area was booming when I got there. It would not hit an economic snag until the 1990s when the fall of the Communist empire depressed the need for production from the area's many defense plants. And yet what I saw happening in Gary was happening in Los Angeles. Young men were not working. Young women were on welfare. Boys were growing up in homes without fathers. They were taking their anger into the street and finding the family life they craved in their increasingly violent gangs. The commercial heart of South Central was on life support. This same pattern was happening in every major black community in America, and in every city the alchemists desperately sought some unique local reason to explain why their twisted chemistry wasn't working.

Fatherlessness was taking its toll on more than just South Central. Charles Manson arrived in Southern California just before I did. The fatherless product of a seriously screwed-up home, Manson nurtured the suppressed anger of a colony of lost youth. They too came from broken homes. In 1969, the year California introduced no-fault divorce, Manson turned that anger outward in a pair of brutal mass murders that shocked affluent California into a state of high and understandable anxiety.

In South Central, the violence was less spectacular but steadier and deadlier. The same year as the Manson killings, a pair of sixteen-year-olds, Raymond Washington and Stanley Tookie Williams, launched a lethal neighborhood association called the Crips. So violent were the Crips that unaffiliated gangs in the area felt the need to band together to protect themselves. And so began the incredibly pointless war between the Crips and the Bloods. More young Americans, virtually all of them black, would die in this war than died in both Gulf wars combined.

I should add that South Central, at least when I arrived, did not look like a "ghetto" is supposed to look. My aunt and uncle, like many people in the neighborhood, perhaps most, had their own home and took care of it. The neighborhood was not crowded or noisy or poor, at least not in material things. When my aunt arrived, it was still peaceful. In 1953, the year both Washington and Williams were born, the state of California had only 276 homicides, and South Central was scarcely more dangerous than any other parts of town.[3] That would soon change.

In 1979, Washington was shot dead, and Williams killed four innocent people, which led to his eventual execution by lethal injection. That year, nearly three thousand Californians were murdered, ten times more than in 1953 and a stunning six times more per capita. South Central was now at the epicenter of that violence. The question black leaders and the media refused to ask was, what happened between 1953 and 1979? The answer should have been obvious. As it happened, moved largely by guilt, the Feds in 1960 changed the Aid to Dependent Children program to the Aid *to Families* with Dependent Children, or, more realistically, Aid to *Moms* with Dependent Children. A working dad at home just got in the way of the gravy train.

In 1964, the Feds sweetened the pot for abandoned moms with food stamps, and in 1965 with Medicaid. Soon afterward, public housing honchos decided fixed rents were unfair and moved to a policy where folks paid just a percentage of their income. This made fathers all the more useless and encouraged everyone to cheat on his or her reported income. Before my eyes I could see that housing projects, which were once safer and better maintained than the neighborhoods around them, were becoming a blight on those very neighborhoods. Without white guilt, these "reforms," such as they were, would not have come to pass. The alchemists exploited that guilt. The hard core knew what they were doing. They knew that a dependent population would forever owe them their votes and gratitude. Like savvy dope dealers, they were creating junkies, and they were pleased with their creation.

At the time, if anything, I was part of the problem. I may have stayed away from the violence, but there were few other vices I failed to explore. Like so many lost souls in Southern California, I worked a series of miscellaneous jobs just to make enough money to keep my car running, buy my intoxicants, and party. The people I partied with were all black. They were as rootless and unfocused as I was. For our lack of success, we always had the white man to blame, and we did so often. If we needed inspiration, there was always some outside source—a Farrakhan, say, or a Jesse Jackson, or a TV series like *Roots*—to remind us how the white man put us down and kept us down. My friends would taunt white people, yell at them, and insult them in ways big and small. Although it made them feel good in the moment, nothing in their life changed. Nothing in my life changed either.

Just like my friends, I absorbed the sense of anger and entitlement that Jackson and the others were feeding me. At work, whenever I wanted to move up, if my bosses did not promote me, I assumed the only reason was because I was black. I would argue with them when it suited my purposes. This did nothing to improve my chances, but it made me feel righteous at the time.

During the mid-1970s, I worked in a hospital X-ray department with a white woman for a boss. One day I got it into my head that she was harassing me because of my color. What else could it have been? Weak performance? Bad attitude? No, of course not. So I called her out. I called her racist this and racist that. I knew that I could get away with it because there were no witnesses. She apparently did not know how the game was played. So she got me fired. I, of course, hired a white lawyer. I got my job back with back pay for the time I wasn't at work. After that—no surprise here—she did not bother me anymore. Many black people in America have a similar story to tell, but when they tell it, they are still convinced they were harassed because of their color and deserved their settlement.

I drifted like this for twenty years. I was miserable. I had no purpose. I even ended up on welfare for a while. I told the authorities I could not work because of my drug use. They gave me a stipend, no questions asked, and put me on food stamps. Thanks! That was just what I needed—dependency on top of my anger! I was still living alone and going downhill slowly. My anger only increased, and I continued to project it outward. It was easier than examining its source.

One day I exploded. I was on Pico Boulevard. The traffic was sluggish—what else is new? I was bitter about my life and the world in general. When a white woman in front of me did not run a yellow light as I expected her to, I leaned on the horn, and she threw me a finger. That happens a lot in LA, but at that moment, so deep was I in denial, I convinced myself she'd flipped me off because I was black. I became so enraged I lost all sense of where I was and what I was doing. Looking back, I can hardly believe what happened next. I got out of my car, leaned into her window, spit on her, and called her every vile racial slur I could conjure in my demented state.

As I write this, I'm reading an account from today's news that shows how widespread the anger I felt is. The incident took place in Austin, Texas. A young black man, enraged that a white woman with a toddler on board was shooting video of his erratic driving, leaped out of his car, spit on her windshield, raised a right clenched fist, shouted "black power," and called her a "white bitch." It is for that young man and others like him that I write this book. I know where he is coming from.[4]

Not too long after my own road-rage incident, I had an unusual and entirely unexpected experience. I was standing in front of a mirror getting dressed, and by some unknown impulse I found myself asking God to let me see myself—not on the exterior; I knew what I looked like on the outside. I wanted to see what I looked like on the inside, and in a flash I was able to do just that. What I saw wasn't pretty. In fact, it was downright hideous. I looked in that mirror, and now there was something dirty and dark in front of me. I understood that something was me. I was repulsed.

If I ever doubted that a person could have a divinely inspired, life-changing experience, as Paul did on the road to Damascus, I no longer did. On the spot, I started praying and asking God for clarity, and He provided it. He showed me just how consumed I was by the anger toward my mother that I had been suppressing since I was a boy. That anger was holding me back, twisting and darkening my soul. In a moment I understood how wrong and self-destructive it was to hate my mother.

It was this hatred that people like Farrakhan and Jesse Jackson fed on. I did not realize it at the time, but Farrakhan, Jackson, and I had something very fundamental in common: our fathers refused to accept responsibility for us at birth. Former Atlanta mayor Andrew Young knew Jackson as a young man when both worked with Martin Luther King Jr. He attributed much of Jackson's bad behavior to the nature of his upbringing. "Growing up as a child, seeing your father in another family, there is almost an irrepressible need for the support from the father that you never got as a child," wrote Young. "And I think one of the strains in our relationship and one of the strains in his relationships with others is that that suddenly seeps in."[5] I suspect that the mothers of Farrakhan and Jackson never forgave the men who rejected them. I know the sensation. As I've mentioned, my mother forgave my father only shortly before she expired. Nowadays, unfortunately, such rejection is commonplace. At the time the three of us were born, it was a source of great embarrassment and lingering resentment.

This revelation came at a providential moment. My mother was soon to visit her sister in South Central. When she arrived, I knew I had to apologize to her in person for harboring the hatred that I had. I have never been as frightened as I was on the drive to my aunt's house. I was literally shaking and sweating. All the early fear I felt as a child came surging back.

Upon seeing my mother, however, I found the grace to do what I needed to do. Instantly, God took away my fear and anger and gave me peace. My mother seemed relieved and started crying. She said she was sorry for taking out her anger for my father on me, and explained that her mother had done the same thing to her. It was a moment I will never forget.

I was thirty-eight at the time and was working as a medical transcriber at Hollywood Presbyterian Hospital. I'd also started my own janitorial service, but these were just jobs. I had at this point no career, no vision, and little faith. That was about to change. I realized then that blacks were not suffering from racism, but from denying the real source of their frustration. In denial, they chose to believe the lies they were told about white America.

When I let the anger toward my mother go, my anger toward white people slipped away as well. I called a friend, and he let me use his place to share what I learned with my friends and his. Once I opened up, several others did as well. They were suffering much of what I had been suffering. We continued our meetings and gave our small community a name, the Brotherhood Organization of a New Destiny—BOND. Only a fool would have believed we would still be going strong twenty-five years later, but I was that fool.

At the time, no one knew better than I did how unlikely a leader I made. I had little education beyond high school. I was nervous, and between my cleft palate and Alabama accent, very difficult to understand. When I listen to my old tapes, even I have a hard time understanding what I was saying. Still, for all my shortcomings, I realized BOND was my mission, my calling. I had a message of hope and love to communicate, and I was determined to do it.

One avenue that I thought had potential was radio. I bought an hour of airtime each week on a local South Central station, and I began to reach out beyond my immediate circle. My message was simple and straightforward. It was time for blacks to stop blaming others for their failures and to look within. People started listening. Not all of them agreed. Many of them took to calling the station, threatening me and threatening station management. Friends told me to watch my back, but I was no longer afraid.

As I saw it then and still do, blacks in America were as enslaved to anger and government dependency as our ancestors were to their "owners." The difference is that our ancestors knew they were slaves and desperately yearned for freedom. Too many blacks today refuse to recognize their bondage. Toward those who offer freedom, they react violently. Although the white station manager appreciated what I was saying, the threats of violence forced him to cancel my show, even though his was a Christian station. That cancellation, however, attracted media attention, and Jesse Lee Peterson, an indifferently educated, barely understandable cotton picker from rural Alabama, found a national audience—proof, if any were needed, that God does work in mysterious ways.

6

THE CHAINS OF BLACKNESS

As a seven-year-old, I wanted nothing more in the world than a little red wagon. I wanted it as badly as Ralphie wanted his Red Ryder BB gun in *Christmas Story*, maybe even more. Poor as we were, I never got my hopes up. When Christmas came around, I tried to put it out of mind and enjoy the season.

There was much to enjoy. At school we would sing Christmas songs. Although we did not have much in the way of snow to go dashing through, my favorite carol was always "Jingle Bells." At the Nero Baptist Church on the neighboring plantation, we sang Christmas carols and hymns in the weeks leading up to the big day. At that age, my grandmother made me sit next to her. She wanted to be able to give me that "look" if I got too fidgety, and Lord knows, what a look she could give!

On Christmas Eve I could only dream about what presents I might get, but I knew what I would find on the dinner table: sweet potatoes, fried corn, potato salad, a chicken that had been running around the henhouse just a few days earlier, a big slice of ham from one of our pigs that had sacrificed his all for our Christmas, and, best of all, those wonderful homemade cakes and pies. There would be lots of neighbors there too, and aunts and uncles and, in a good year, maybe even my mother and stepfather down from Indiana.

The year I was seven was the best year of all, for when I cleared the sleep from my eyes, I saw that bright, shiny little red wagon! I had it outside before I even got my winter shoes on—didn't wear any in the summer. In the days to come, I would pull my friends around, pull my little cousins, pull loads of wood and loads of dirt. I would pull everyone and everything until the wheels fell off. That wagon meant everything to me. When I think of Christmas, I still tear up thinking of that wagon.

In our world, we never thought of Christmas in terms of black or white. We thought of it in terms of Jesus Christ. No one tried to deny us Christmas or tell us we could not celebrate it. It was a day that unified all of Alabama, all of America. Looking back, I am sure there were thousands of boys that morning, from sea to shining sea, singing Christmas carols, eating pumpkin pies, and pulling their friends around in their little red wagons.

Then came 1966. A Maryland-born thug with a trumped-up African name—Maulana Karenga—concocted a new "tradition" for black people, with a name as phony as his own: Kwanzaa. Today, the Official Kwanzaa Website is all about Karenga.[1] Click just about any link, and it will take you to some Karenga promotion—the "Founder's Welcome," his biography, his books for sale, his "Message" from past years, and, of course, the donation page. One name you won't find on the web page is Jesus Christ.

In the opening sentence of his most recent Founder's Welcome, Karenga reminds readers that Kwanzaa is an "African American and Pan-African holiday." The thing is, the ethnic group composed of African Americans/Pan-Africans contains literally thousands of different cultures with little in common save their "blackness." What Karenga offers them as a bond is a jerry-rigged holiday as cold and loveless as the lump of coal everyone's mother promised if the kids misbehaved before Christmas. As to Kwanzaa's famed "Seven Principles"—or seven "values of African culture"—they owe less to anything African than they do to Marxism.[2] "People think it's African, but it's not," Karenga said of his holiday in an unusually honest interview quoted in the *Washington Post*. "I came up with Kwanzaa because black people in this country wouldn't celebrate it if they knew it was American. Also, I put it around Christmas because I knew that's when a lot of Bloods would be partying."[3]

Karenga makes for an unlikely Santa Claus. He was born Ronald

Everett in 1941. A sharecropper's son from Maryland, he moved to Los Angeles about ten years before I did and even attended the same community college. In the early 1960s Karenga founded a militant black power organization called the United Slaves, or US for short. In one of its less inspired moments, the FBI quietly supported Karenga's people in the hope that they would undermine more popular outlaws, like the Black Panthers. In a typical confrontation, the US and the Black Panthers fought to see who would control a new black studies program at UCLA. The US more or less prevailed when two of its members shot and killed two Black Panthers on the UCLA campus in 1969.

In 1971, the increasingly paranoid Karenga turned on two black women in his own organization. He thought they were trying to kill him. According to the *Los Angeles Times*, the women were whipped with an electrical cord and beaten with a karate baton after being ordered to remove their clothes. One woman had a hot soldering iron placed in her mouth, and the other had her big toe tightened in a vise. Karenga meanwhile put detergent and running hoses in their mouths and hit them on the heads with toasters.[4] September 11 mastermind Khalid Sheikh Muhammad got off easy compared to these ladies. He only got waterboarded. The jury found Karenga guilty of felonious assault and false imprisonment, and he was off to prison. This story is conspicuously absent from the official Kwanzaa website.

In prison, Karenga had no moment of awakening, no hint of forgiveness or redemption. If anything, his philosophy hardened. It was the same old anticolonial, anti-American, socialist mumbo jumbo that was all the rage in black power circles. He just found ways to make it more marketable through concoctions such as Kwanzaa. He also wormed his way back into academia, eventually emerging as chair of the Africana Studies program at California State University in Long Beach, which tells you just about all you need to know about certain institutes of higher learning. From that perch, Karenga would tell whoever was listening that to make America "a just and good society in a multicultural and global context," it was important first of all to reject "the right-wing insistence on morality."[5]

Apparently, it was not enough for blacks to have their own Christmas. Now they had to have their own morality. Unfortunately, too many of them already do, Karenga included. Visit a prison or a shelter for battered spouses or an inner-city abortion clinic and you will see what happens when people practice their own morality. In reality, Karenga was just trying to give political cover to bad behavior. To this day, if forced to discuss his own criminal past, he will refer to himself as "a political prisoner." In his world, black people can do no wrong. Only white people can.

Fortunately, most blacks were smart enough to see through Kwanzaa. The bogus holiday has been kept alive by well-placed whites too frightened to tell the truth and black politicians too eager to exploit their fears. One of those politicians is Barack Obama. In December 2014, Obama issued his formal Kwanzaa greeting. He listed the seven crypto-Marxist principles of Kwanzaa—unity, self-determination, collective work and responsibility, cooperative economics, purpose, creativity, and faith—in the expressed belief that families were gathering "all around the world . . . to light the Kinara today."[6] If any black family anywhere was lighting a Kinara, I do not know that family. I don't even know what a Kinara is. I have some friends who like the idea of Kwanzaa, but as far I know, none of them has ever gotten around to celebrating it. Kwanzaa flatlined some years back and now, if you've noticed, exists only on media life support. Today, the average black kid is more capable of naming Santa's reindeers than he is the seven principles of Kwanzaa, and that is just as well.

As the Kwanzaa experience shows, fixating on blackness narrows horizons. It does not expand them. At their heart, creations like Kwanzaa or black studies programs or Black History Month provide no value for black Americans or anyone else. In reality, black history is American history, and any attempt to detach the two separates blacks from their country and empowers useless black "leaders" like Karenga. These programs are more about hating white people than they are about loving black people.

The goal of "traditions" like Kwanzaa is to encourage black students to feel alienated from America, resentful of its great achievements, and hostile to the white people largely responsible for making them happen. The same is true of the designation "African American." The alchemists switched to this phrase in the 1970s not to emphasize the "American" part but the "African" one. Before that change, black people, like white people, were simply American. Yes, if asked, a person of Irish descent might have said he was Irish-American, but that was not his primary identity. He would not get upset if you referred to him as simply American.

Black people had fought hard for the right to be taken seriously as individuals. There is a memorable scene in the 1967 movie *Guess Who's Coming to Dinner* in which the Sidney Poitier character turns to his father and says, "Dad, you're my father. I'm your son. I love you. I always have and I always will. But you think of yourself as a colored man. I think of myself as a man."[7] Now the alchemists were asking for me to be called "colored man" once again. They just dressed up the terminology as African American.

If Obama were serious about "the tight tapestry of this nation,"[8] he would do away with Kwanzaa, Black History Month, and the term *African American* by executive order. That would be no big deal for a man who, with a stroke of the pen, made five million illegal aliens legal.

Trust me, though. The thought won't cross his mind. Leaders like Karenga—and, yes, Obama—use blackness as a chain to bind blacks to their agenda. To make black anger seem righteous and justified, they fail to acknowledge the suffering of others. I doubt, for instance, that Karenga's United Slaves had any regard for the Slavs, who lent their name to create the word *slave*. You can bet that these white ethnics from Southeastern Europe did not do this by choice. It is just that they were frequently taken captive by warring neighbors, some of them Islamic, and sold into slavery.

How many black kids know this or that any other people were enslaved other than their ancestors? How could they? The whole thrust of black education today is to make blacks feel uniquely victimized. As they did with the bogus anti-American, anti-Christian story told in *Roots*—both the book and the TV series—the alchemists have been transforming fiction into "fact" to turn young blacks against their faith and their country.

Blacks, however, have not been alone in their suffering. Neither were Slavs. For a thousand years the English oppressed and starved the Irish in their own home country. Millions of Irish left the country simply to survive, many of them as indentured servants or as prisoners with no other crime than debt. The Japanese raped and pillaged the Chinese, and we did not treat the Japanese or the Chinese particularly well here in California. The Germans slaughtered Jews. The Turks slaughtered Armenians. Arab slave traders captured and sold black slaves to Spanish and Portuguese traders, who brought them to the Americas, North and South. American Indian tribes owned black slaves into the twentieth century. ISIS and Boko Haram murder and enslave Christians to this day.

These massive historic injustices, past and present, pale in the face of what is happening to black people in America—or so you would think if you only follow the mainstream press. The sad truth is that no people anywhere are encouraged to ignore their blessings and nurse their grudges the way black Americans are. I could cite a thousand examples of how this plays out, but let me cite one recent example from my neck of the woods. It started when the Glendale Police dared to pull over a car driven by the twenty-year-old son of Taraji P. Henson, star of the hit TV show *Empire*. When Henson learned what happened to young Marcell, she went public with her outrage.

"My child has been racially profiled," she told *Uptown* magazine. She claimed that Marcell "did exactly everything the cops told him to do, including letting them illegally search his car." Proof of the cops' evil intent was that "they didn't give him the ticket for what he was pulled over for." Henson was so upset by the incident and another alleged one on the University of Southern California campus that she decided to send Marcell back to her native Washington, DC.[9]

Henson made an odd choice in trusting her son to Washington.

Marcell's father, William Johnson, had been knifed to death by a black couple on the streets of that city when Marcell was eight. Johnson never married Henson, and he was not living with the boy and his mother at the time he was killed. This may have lessened the trauma for Marcell, but it might also have further deformed the relationship between him and his mother.[10]

In fact, Marcell lied to his mother. As the police dash cam video showed, he drove through a lighted crosswalk with a pedestrian in it. The officer could not see that the driver was black when he gave chase. Nor could he have been more polite. Marcell volunteered that he had "weed" in the car. After failing to produce his medical marijuana dispensation, he allowed the officer to search the car. The officer "didn't give him the ticket for what he was pulled over for" out of kindness, not racism. As he explained, that ticket could have cost Marcell his license. Other than these minor details, it was just another incident of the "man" hassling an innocent young boy because he was black. When the *Los Angeles Times* went public with the dash cam video, Henson had to say something. To her credit, or more likely to her publicist's credit, she apologized to the Glendale Police for overreacting. Had it not been for that video, Marcell's account of the incident would have stuck.

In a way, Marcell was just playing the role the alchemists have assigned him. The "authentic" black person is expected to remain angry and resentful and to project that anger toward whites. No one will tell Marcell how privileged he was to get his own Honda Civic at seventeen years of age, or how fortunate he is to live in the freest and most prosperous country in the world. All his leaders can instill in him and others like him is a sense of bitterness and covetousness that reaches down to the very young. In Africa, in the Caribbean, in South America, even in Alabama, you see black kids with beautiful, unforced smiles. In America's inner cities, you almost never see that. This is not a result of slavery. This is the result of a civil rights movement gone bad.

The young will learn to smile only when they learn to appreciate the great traditions they inherited not just as black people, but as Americans.

Take the development of jazz, one of the twentieth century's great art forms. I read about it on a web page titled "Culture & Change: Black History in America."[11] No doubt, blacks contributed greatly to its development, and that is a good thing. This history traces the roots of jazz to blues. "The blues evolved from hymns, work songs, and field hollers—music used to accompany spiritual, work and social functions," writes the author. "Blues is the foundation of jazz as well as the prime source of rhythm and blues, rock 'n' roll, and country music."

This is all largely true, but it misses the point that the author could—and should— make: only in America could this music have come together. If blues evolved from hymns, where did blacks learn the hymns? Not in Africa. They learned them in Christian churches here in America. If blues influenced country music, so too did the folk music that Scotch-Irish settlers brought from the British Isles. Their music, in turn, influenced black musicians. I see on this site a picture of Louis Armstrong playing the trumpet. There were no trumpets in black Africa unless the British brought them.

Imagine if Italian kids in America were forced to learn their history the way black kids are. They would be reading books about Joe DiMaggio and Joe Torre and ignoring Babe Ruth. They would be singing Frank Sinatra songs in class and tracing them back to Italy, ignoring the people who wrote them, like Irving Berlin. They would learn about how Marconi invented the wireless radio but would not know—or care—who Thomas Edison was. As for the Mafia, that would be off-limits. In today's ethnic studies classes, students only learn the good things about their subculture and the bad things about everyone else's. Multiculturalism today means "I'm okay; you're not."

The message should be, "Look what we have accomplished as Americans." That is a great unifying message, and it gives any ethnic group in America more pride of ownership in more great enterprises than would be possible anywhere else in the world. By contrast, "blackness" puts our imagination in chains and ghettoizes our dreams.

7

THE ONE-DROP LEGACY

In teaching black kids to disown America and distrust white people, black studies programs are teaching them to hate themselves. For if not American, what are these kids? They are certainly not African. And unless they just arrived recently from abroad, they are almost certainly part white, and maybe more than just a small part. In the past, it was Southern racists who focused on color at the expense of character. Today, it is the alchemists. In either case, the only things this kind of focus creates are confusion and contempt.

The case of radical activist and current black hero Malcolm X is instructive. For all of his claims to blackness, he had a white grandfather. His mother, as he said, "looked like a white woman." This caused Malcolm any number of emotional problems. The fact that he had reddish-brown skin and reddish hair made him the apple of his dark-skinned father's eye and elevated his status among other blacks, blacks being more color-conscious than even whites are. Said Malcolm, "I was one among the millions of Negroes who were insane enough to feel that it was some kind of status symbol to be light complexioned."[1]

If you grow up dark-skinned, as I did in rural Alabama, you have no doubts about your identity. You know who you are, and you don't think twice about it. Like many light-skinned blacks, though, Malcolm was anxious about his identity as a black man. To compensate, he became aggressively "black." After a stint in prison, he joined the openly racist Nation of Islam (NOI) and preached hatred of whites—"a race of devils"—for twelve years in much the same style as Louis Farrakhan has done, but he did so even more aggressively. "I was a zombie then—like all Muslims," Malcolm said about his life in the NOI. "I was hypnotized, pointed in a certain direction and told to march. Well, I guess a man's entitled to make a fool of himself if he's ready to pay the cost. It cost me twelve years."[2]

Zombie or not, Malcom X has a devoted fan in none other than former attorney general Eric Holder. When asked on his departure from office what book he would recommend to young people, Holder volunteered Alex Haley's book, written in collaboration with Malcolm. "I would hope that I say this not to every African-American of his age but for every American," said Holder, "that you read *The Autobiography of Malcolm X* to see the transition that that man went through, from petty criminal to a person who was severely and negatively afflicted by race, to somebody who ultimately saw the humanity in all of us."[3] In Holder's view, Malcolm's 1964 break from the NOI and the final year of his life, from 1964 to 1965, atoned for the many years of bad behavior and justified his being considered a role model.

In 1963, Malcolm X began to tell his life story to Haley. In that telling, however, Malcolm showed no sign of remorse for his crimes and the racial hatred he had perpetuated. Worse, he had even less interest in telling the truth than he did when he was with the NOI. He made the incendiary claim, for instance, that his father, Earl Little, "was . . . to die by the white man's hands."[4]

According to Malcolm, members of a white racist group called the Black Legion murdered his father. He claimed they beat him to death and then laid his body across streetcar tracks in East Lansing, Michigan, Malcolm's hometown. A streetcar did run over Little and kill him. One insurance company ruled his death a suicide. Another ruled it an accident. The police believed it to be an accident too. So did Malcolm before he started inventing the racist twist to the story. In 1963, while visiting Michigan State in East Lansing, Malcolm "described Earl's death as accidental." So wrote black historian Manning Marable in his excellent biography of Malcolm X. It was not until 1964, Marable added, that Malcolm "cast his father as a martyr for black liberation."[5] In short, it was only during the last year of his life that Malcolm X shifted the blame for his father's death to the white man.

In his *Autobiography*, written during that last year as well, Malcolm claimed that white vigilantes burned down his family's house on two different occasions, once before he was born and once when he was old enough to remember. "My father . . . shouted and shot at the two white men who had set the fire and were running away," he told Haley. "Our home was burning down around us. We were lunging and bumping and tumbling all over each other trying to escape."[6] There was no reason to believe that either account held any more truth than the story of his father being killed by the Black Legion. The first incident Malcolm said he learned from his mother, but she would spend much of her life in a mental institution. The second incident allegedly occurred when he was a toddler.

In telling these stories during the last year of his life, Malcolm was doing what many black leaders would do for the next fifty years. He was inventing stories of racial abuse to intensify the distrust his followers felt toward white people. When blacks read the *Autobiography*, it makes them angry. When they see the movie Spike Lee made from the book, they get angrier still.

If Malcolm X had seen the light the way I had, if he had looked within and forgiven those who wronged him, he would have had a different story to tell. Even in that final year of his life, however, Malcolm made very little progress. True, he left the NOI to become an orthodox Sunni Muslim. True too, he saw the possibility of fellowship with white men. But he held out the olive branch only to those white men who saw the world the way he did. "We are interested in practicing brotherhood with anyone really interested in living according to it," said Malcolm at his last speech, this time before fifteen hundred coeds at Barnard College.

The question is, how did Malcolm X see the world? In his Barnard speech, Malcolm preached the same kind of anticolonial, socialist claptrap that people like Karenga or Jeremiah Wright preach today. "We are living in an era of revolution," said Malcolm, "and the revolt of the American Negro is part of the rebellion against the oppression and colonialism which has characterized the era."[7]

Malcolm X faced dangers, but not from white people. Four days before the speech, his New York City home was firebombed. This was real. The culprits were designated assassins from the NOI. Three days after the Barnard speech, the NOI would finish the job by sending a hit squad to shoot and kill Malcolm while he was speaking at the Audubon Ballroom in Harlem. Malcolm had his flaws, but cowardice was not among them.

In the final year of his life, Malcolm X made one convert whose fame would outshine his own. Under Malcolm's influence, Muhammad Ali, born Cassius Clay, also made a great show of his blackness, but to prove his blackness, Ali had to disown his white great-grandparents. So he lied about them. "If slaveholder Clay's blood came into our veins along with the name," he said, "it came by rape and defilement."[8]

Here, Ali was just echoing the NOI boilerplate. Malcolm X had also insisted his white blood came through rape. "I learned to hate every drop of that white rapist's blood that is in me," he told biographer Haley.[9] I don't know if Malcolm was telling the truth, but I know Ali wasn't. Ali's mother, Odessa Clay, was born a Grady. Her grandfather was an open-minded Irishman who married her grandmother Dinah after the Civil War. There's no evidence anyone was raped. Odessa's other grandfather, Tom Morehead, had a white father and a black mother. He had fought on the Union side in the Civil War.

Whatever the source of Malcolm X's white blood, we do know that he had the kind of relationship with his parents that breeds anger. "They seemed to be nearly always at odds," said Malcolm of his parents. "Sometimes my father would beat [my mother]." On the night of his father's death, his parents were "having one of their arguments." He attributed the tension to "Black Legion threats,"[10] but that does not ring true at all. He likely blamed his mother for driving his father out of the house on that fateful night—the father may well have committed suicide—and he would later learn to project that same blame toward white people.

In the Little household, Malcolm's mother supplied nearly all his beatings. After his father's death, when Malcolm was six, her mental health quickly deteriorated, and she was institutionalized. In the years that followed, Malcolm lived with relatives and in foster homes, and he did not seem to have ever forgiven his mother. He certainly never visited her. Still, like so many black men, the mama syndrome had a hold on him. He claimed in his *Autobiography*, "I have rarely talked to anyone about my mother, for I believe that I am capable of killing a person, without hesitation, who happened to make the wrong kind of remark about my mother."[11] This love-hate relationship extended to his father as well. Earl Little rarely beat his son, but Malcolm attributed this to his light complexion.[12] In rejecting the family name Little, he severed his emotional tie to his father.

Muhammad Ali was a confused young man when Malcolm put his spell on him. There was a price Ali had to pay to join the NOI, however, and that was to betray Malcolm X when the NOI turned against him. This is a story that no one tells during Black History month. That betrayal "hurt Malcolm more than any other person turning away from him that I know of," Betty Shabazz, Malcolm's wife, told Ali's biographer, Tom Hauser. The reason was that Malcolm alone among the NOI crew had backed Ali before he became champ. When the death threats against her husband grew serious, Shabazz begged Ali to call off the dogs. "You see what you're doing to my husband, don't you?" she told him. Ali raised his hands in the air and said, "I'm not doing anything to him."[13] Pontius Pilate could not have said it better.

During his zombie years, the easily influenced Ali did what his masters at the NOI told him to do. He ducked the draft. He denounced America. He humiliated Joe Frazier, and he reveled in his own imaginary blackness at Frazier's expense. But Ali was not as jaded as many of his colleagues. He came from a solid two-parent family, had a good relationship with his parents, and loved his mother. He was not by nature an angry person. During his ten years with the NOI, he played at hating the white man, but he never felt it. When he left the nation, he became himself again—charming, friendly, open-minded, but still easily influenced. He even attended the 1984 Republican National Convention as a Reagan supporter. Still, the damage he inflicted on Joe Frazier during those years would never heal.

As Ali's life showed, there is nothing simple about race in America. Golfing great Tiger Woods was once asked by Oprah Winfrey whether it bothered him to be called African American. "It does," he said. "I'm just who I am, whoever you see in front of you." As a kid he had invented the term *Cablinasian* to describe his racial mix of half Asian (Chinese and Thai), one-quarter African American, one-eighth Native American, and one-eighth Dutch.[14] For this he caught hell from many black leaders, who called him a "race traitor" and insisted that he identify himself as "black." Such are the chains of blackness.

In 1997, President Bill Clinton wanted Woods, who had just won the Masters Tournament, to participate in a tribute to Jackie Robinson on the occasion of the fiftieth anniversary of Robinson's breaking baseball's color barrier. Unlike many people, however, Woods did not see himself as the "Jackie Robinson of golf." There had been black pros before him who'd actually broken barriers, and he was not one of them. Woods knew he did not deserve the comparison to Robinson. Then just twenty-one, he had suffered no greater racial slight in his young life than the occasional odd look. When he turned down the president's request, the alchemists promptly turned on him. In a typical attack, Maureen Dowd of the *New York Times* headlined her column on his refusal "Tiger's Double Bogey."[15]

Just as white racists in the past decided who was white and who was black, the alchemists do the same today. They are the ones perpetuating the infamous "one-drop" rule that classified as legally Negro any person with so much as one drop of "black blood." Although criticized by the left, Woods was fulfilling the legacy of Martin Luther King Jr. He was asking to be judged not by the color of his skin but by the content of his character.

Actress Halle Berry took a different route. Although she was raised by her white mother, Berry imagined herself the Hollywood equivalent of Jackie Robinson in accepting the best actress Oscar in 2002 for her role in *Monster's Ball.* "This moment is so much bigger than me. This moment is for Dorothy Dandridge, Lena Horne, Diahann Carroll," said Berry, citing black actresses who had come before her. "It's for the women that stand beside me, Jada Pinkett, Angela Bassett, Vivica Fox. And it's for every nameless, faceless woman of color that now has a chance because this door tonight has been opened."[16]

In fact, Hattie McDaniel had won the best supporting actress Oscar sixty-five years earlier for her portrayal of Scarlett O'Hara's mammy in *Gone with the Wind.* Sidney Poitier had won a best actor Oscar thirty-eight years earlier for his role in *Lilies of the Field.* Berry did not open any doors. The fact of the matter is that there are many more whites in America—and in Hollywood—than blacks. Berry could not have played the roles of eight of the previous ten female winners—*Shakespeare in Love,* for instance—any more credibly than Gwyneth Paltrow could have played Scarlett O'Hara's mammy.

Berry has done okay by white America. Before she was old enough to drink, she had won the Miss Teen All American contest, the Miss Ohio USA contest, and the right to represent America in the Miss World contest. To appear topless in a previous film, she earned an extra $500,000. For her role in a subsequent film, she earned $17.5 million. For all her talk of blackness, Berry has lived a pretty white life. The first two people she thanked at the Oscars were her Italian-American manager—"the only father I've ever known"—and her white mother. She made the news in 2012 when the white father of her child got into a brawl with her white husband, sending them both to the hospital. Clearly, the reason she has played the race card over and over was to intimidate white Hollywood into giving her better parts. In the process, she has stoked the anger in the hearts of black women and helped drive the races further apart.

Instead of fretting about how imperfect their lives are, I challenge black Americans to get over their "blackness" and start building character. Over the past fifty years, blacks have been seduced away from character and truth. Their "leaders" have convinced them that their struggle is a *physical* battle with whites and that America is a racist nation. The truth is that there is good and bad in every race, and every human being is engaged in a *spiritual* battle of good versus evil.

Blacks in the United States are the freest and wealthiest group of blacks anywhere. If black America were a country, it would be the sixteenth wealthiest nation in the world. Blacks who are caught up with their skin color and think they need a Black History Month foolishly believe they are righting past wrongs. The sad truth is that they're wasting their time and building false pride.

8

THE FORBIDDEN FRUIT

n 1868, William Edward Burghardt Du Bois was born in Massachusetts to a free and prosperous black family with white ancestors on
either branch of the family tree. As a boy, Du Bois attended integrated
public schools and did well. His white teachers encouraged him along
the way, and his largely white church congregation raised money to
send him to college. At Fisk College in Nashville, he encountered the
culture of the South and understandably wanted no part of it. He would
eventually graduate cum laude from Harvard College. After studying
in Germany on a scholarship designated for black students, Du Bois
returned to Harvard, where he got his PhD in 1895.

Du Bois was first exposed to socialism while in Germany, and like
many a naïve young scholar, he bought in. More than a century ago,
just as today, socialist theory appealed to the sense of superiority of the
highly educated. It tempted Du Bois and others with much the same
lure the serpent presented to Adam and Eve in the garden. "Ye shall be
as gods," said the devil. Du Bois took his bite at the apple and bit hard.
He wanted to be a god. What Harvard man hasn't?

In 1903, William Du Bois, now known as W. E. B. Du Bois, presented his emerging socialist ideas in a manifesto of sorts called "The
Talented Tenth." Like most Socialists, he began with the assumption
that he knew better than others how the world should be organized,
and he was not afraid to say so. "The Negro race, like all races, is going
to be saved by its exceptional men," wrote Du Bois. "The problem of
education, then, among Negroes must first of all deal with the Talented

Tenth; it is the problem of developing the Best of this race that they may guide the Mass away from the contamination and death of the Worst, in their own and other races."[1]

In the eyes of Du Bois, I would be one of the "Mass"—one of those cotton-picking blacks from the South waiting to be uplifted by light-skinned, wellborn people like himself. I might even qualify as being among the "Worst"—one of those malcontents either too dumb or too sullen to buy the magic beans that Du Bois was selling. His language offended me when I first read it, and it offends me now. Today, I hear that same language all around me, from President Obama on down. The modern "civil rights" leaders are, one might say, the illegitimate children of Du Bois, who himself was a founding member of the NAACP. They look down on people like me. I find their condescension more insulting than even white racism.

Unable to motivate the sluggish ninth-tenths of the black population with a positive message, Du Bois and his descendants have relied on racial and political agitation to achieve their ends. He wrote in his 1903 manifesto, "For three long centuries [white] people lynched Negroes who dared to be brave, raped black women who dared to be virtuous, crushed dark-hued youth who dared to be ambitious, and encouraged and made to flourish servility and lewdness and apathy." There is, of course, truth to what Du Bois wrote. Alchemists almost always build their narrative around a kernel of truth, but what Du Bois introduced in his finger-pointing essay was the license for blacks to be permanently outraged. He was not telling black people what they could accomplish. He was focusing them instead on whom they should hate. This is commonplace today, but then it was revolutionary.

Just forty years earlier, hundreds of thousands of young white men died to end slavery. Virtually every nation in world history had slavery, but no people ever sacrificed so much to end it. They got no credit from Du Bois. He also refused to acknowledge that it was the white man who introduced America's blacks to the greatest gift they could ever receive, the saving grace of Jesus Christ. This counted for nothing in the socialist playbook from which Du Bois was reading. This was the same playbook that would be refined by the likes of Lenin, Che Guevara, and Saul Alinsky and serve as inspiration for both Barack Obama and Hillary Clinton.

In many ways, Barack Obama represents the fulfillment of Du Bois's dream, the half-white, elitist, Harvard man who knows how to use black people to achieve his ends, even if it means their debasement in the process. *Newsweek's* Jonathan Alter summed up the Obama delusion in his book *The Promise.* "Obama's faith lay in the cream rising to the top," wrote Alter. The reason why: "He himself was a product of the great American postwar meritocracy."[2] Alter might as well have said "the Talented Tenth."

Although Obama was elected on the promise of moving beyond "a black America and a white America and Latino America and Asian America" to create a "United States of America,"[3] he has done just the opposite. Whenever the opportunity has presented itself, he has stoked the hornets' nest of racial unease to remind blacks that even though there is a black president, white racism is still the order of the day.

I knew what a charlatan Obama was when I heard his offensively titled "A More Perfect Union" speech to try to explain away his relationship with the Reverend Jeremiah Wright. In the speech, Obama described Wright's recent provocative remarks as "a profoundly distorted view of this country—a view that sees white racism as endemic, and that elevates what is wrong with America above all that we know is right with America."[4] This description of Wright was fine. What was not fine was Obama's fake disgust. He had been sitting in this man's church for the last twenty years. The man married him and Michelle and baptized their children.

Wright had been preaching the hate that Du Bois introduced a century earlier. He was not alone in this. Today, black preachers are more likely to address the sins of the white man than they are the sins of their own congregants. That was certainly the case at Wright's church, and Obama never saw fit to protest until his election was jeopardized.

He did not protest until then because he agreed with Wright. If proof be needed, he named his 2006 book, *Audacity of Hope*, after Wright's sermon "Audacity to Hope." In his memoir, *Dreams from My Father*, Obama described the sermon in great detail, and did so with complete approval. He even quoted some hateful Wright lines, such as "White folks' greed runs a world in need," as if they were perfectly legitimate.[5] And this sermon, he boasted, was his blinding moment on his own perverse road to the anti-Damascus.

To escape the fallout from the Wright tapes, Obama compared the half-crazed Wright to his white grandmother, who once expressed unease after being hassled by a large black man, and former vice-presidential candidate Geraldine Ferraro, whose comment that Obama would not have ascended so quickly if he were white was to Obama a sign "of some deep-seated racial bias."[6] Grandma was right to be afraid. Ferraro was right about Obama's ascent. Comparing them to Wright was outrageous.

Then, to excuse Wright's anger, Obama, like Du Bois, recalled for the thousandth time all the injustices that blacks have suffered and still suffer "under the brutal legacy of slavery and Jim Crow": inferior schools, legalized discrimination, failed welfare policies, lack of basic services.[7] He then blathered on about how he was uniquely capable of bridging the divide between black and white, meaning not a word of it, knowing that for the next however many years he would continue to remind blacks of how they were screwed over by the white man and to reap the political rewards from their anger.

Ferraro, of course, was on the money. Obama owed his success to the fact that he thought and talked just like a white elitist but looked like a black man. "I mean, you got the first mainstream African-American who is articulate and bright and clean and a nice-looking guy," said future vice president Joe Biden. "I mean, that's a storybook, man."[8] Unlike me, and most other black Americans, Obama had no slaves in his family tree, just slave masters. Whatever the legacy of slavery and Jim Crow might have been, he did not suffer a bit because of it. Instead, he enjoyed the fruits of affirmative action that were allegedly designed to lift up the nine-tenths but that have been used instead to enrich the one-tenth.

Once elected, Obama did not hesitate to play the race card when it suited his purposes. In July 2009, for instance, black scholar Henry Louis Gates, a Harvard man and Talented Tenth designee like Obama, was returning to his house in Cambridge, Massachusetts, from an overseas trip. Unable to open the front door, he and his driver forced it open. Not knowing Gates, a neighbor called 911. Sgt. James Crowley took the call and, upon arrival, requested politely that Gates step out-side. When he did, Gates tapped into the well-rehearsed anger that the Talented Tenth have mastered. "Why?" he shouted. "Because I'm a black man in America?"[9]

An angry Gates threatened Crowley and did not heed the officer's warnings any better than Michael Brown would heed Officer Wilson's. He left Crowley little choice but to arrest him on a disorderly conduct charge. Feeling the heat from Washington, the district attorney dropped the charges, but Officer Crowley surprised the media by refusing to apologize as a good white man is expected to do in the face of black rage, even if manufactured. His bosses backed him up.

About a week later, a reporter at a press conference asked Obama what he thought about the Gates incident. Obama admitted he did not know all the facts, but he knew enough about America's "long history" of racial strife to proclaim, "The Cambridge police acted stupidly." Obama had failed to do his homework. Crowley fit no one's stereotype of the nasty, racist white cop, not even Obama's. In fact, he was an Obama supporter and a model officer. A black police commissioner had chosen him to teach the department's course on racial profiling.[10] Crowley's failure to buckle forced these facts into light and caused Obama to host a bizarre "Beer Summit" with Crowley and good-old-boy Joe Biden to keep the police unions in his corner, at least through the 2012 election. After that, as was evident in the fallout from the Ferguson incident, Obama could not have cared less.

Obama had another chance to show that he was serious about

creating "one America" after the shooting death of Trayvon Martin in Sanford, Florida, in February 2012. As February turned to March and Obama said nothing about the shooting, black activists probed his weak points. "Obama is perfectly willing to give a sermon to black men on Father's Day about what they need to be doing," wrote blogger Yvette Carnell, "but totally incapable of advocating for a black boy who was murdered in the street while carrying only Skittles and iced tea."[11]

In an election year, Obama had to be careful. He needed to stoke the base without alienating his blue-collar white supporters. On March 23, four weeks after the shooting, Obama finally weighed in. "Obviously this is a tragedy," he said. "I can only imagine what these parents are going through. When I think about this boy I think about my own kids and I think every parent in America should be able to understand why it is absolutely imperative that we investigate every aspect of this and that everybody pulls together, federal, state and local to figure out exactly how this tragedy happened."

Of course, Obama had to know by this time that the six-foot Martin had attacked the pudgy Zimmerman, who was nearly half a foot shorter and no match for Martin's mixed-martial arts skills and his seething anger. He also had to know the eyewitness testimony supported Zimmerman's version of events. He even may have known that Zimmerman was an Obama supporter and a civil rights activist, but if he knew, he did not care enough to be straight with America. As a black president, he could have put a lid on this simmering stew pot in a way that a white president could not have. He chose to do the opposite. He chose to stir the stew. "But my main message is to the parents of Trayvon—If I had a son, he would look like Trayvon."[12]

"Education must not simply teach work—it must teach Life," Du Bois said. "The Talented Tenth of the Negro race must be made leaders of thought and missionaries of culture among their people."[13] That is just what Obama was doing. The individual black man did not need to know the facts of the Zimmerman case. Obama would tell him what to think. He was a Harvard man, after all. Du Bois's warped ideas were winning out. Blacks were allowing themselves to be led about by leaders whose main purpose was fomenting political and racial agitation.

It did not have to be this way, and almost wasn't. When Du Bois emerged on the national scene, he knew that to advance his own philosophy, he would have to discredit the working philosophy of that era's most prominent black leader, Booker T. Washington. Unlike the wellborn Du Bois, Washington was born a slave to a woman named Jane in Virginia five years before the beginning of the Civil War. At war's end, the nine-year-old Washington got a job as a salt packer. When his mother and stepfather moved to West Virginia, he went to work in the coal mines and worked hard enough and smart enough to catch the attention of the mine owner and his wife. She encouraged him to pursue his education, and at sixteen Washington headed off to the Hampton Normal and Agriculture Institute in coastal Virginia.

At Hampton, Washington worked as a janitor to pay his room and board. Given all the rooms he had to take care of, Washington had to work late into the night and yet still get up at 4 a.m. to make sure the heating fires were lit. "I gladly accepted [the job]," Washington wrote in his classic autobiography, *Up from Slavery,* "because it was a place where I could work out nearly all the cost of my board."[14] Although the work was hard and taxing, Washington stuck to it.

It was at Hampton that Washington learned the enduring value of work, not just for the money part of it, but for "the independence and self-reliance" that a job well done afforded him. Washington's mentor at Hampton was a former army lieutenant colonel named Samuel Armstrong. In one of life's odd coincidences, Armstrong, the son of a missionary, went to the Punahou School in Honolulu, the same one from which Barack Obama would graduate. Unlike Obama, Armstrong volunteered for the military as soon as he graduated from college. The year was 1862, and the Civil War was raging around him. At Gettysburg, in fact, Armstrong was among those gallant men defending Cemetery Ridge against Pickett's famous charge.

His valor did not go unnoticed. Armstrong, who himself was white, was given command of the 8th Regiment of United States Colored Troops. He and his soldiers earned a fair share of glory during the Siege of Petersburg, as they were among the first troops into the city once resistance was broken. This experience left Armstrong with a deep respect for his black soldiers and a lasting interest in the progress of black Americans. It also led him to establish the Hampton Normal and Agricultural Institute in 1868 when he was not yet thirty. Washington would describe Armstrong as a "great man—the noblest rarest human being it has ever been my privilege to meet."[15]

Armstrong believed that character and morality mattered, and he reinforced those virtues in his students. He also believed that a practical education would give his students a foothold in society and the foundation for later entrepreneurial efforts. This was the philosophy that Washington took with him when, as a twenty-five-year-old in 1881, he headed south to Alabama to serve as the first principal of what was then known as the Tuskegee Normal School. It wasn't much of a school when Washington got there, but with the practical skills the students learned in class, they helped build a larger facility and later other buildings as part of their work-study program. By the turn of the century, the facilities and farms of the Tuskegee Institute covered roughly four square miles.

I learned about Washington while I was still in high school. One of my male teachers shared Washington's views on education and took us, when I was a senior, on a field trip to the Tuskegee Institute, only about an hour away. For us, passing through the gates of the Institute was like entering into the garden of Eden. I had never seen such beautifully manicured lawns and tasteful architecture. I would learn later that the original architect was the first black graduate of MIT, but at the time all I knew was that someone did a heck of a good job putting the place together.

Looking back, I never thought, *Wow! Black people did this!* I did not think that way because I lived in a world where black people did everything. I had no reason to believe that black people could not create an environment this attractive.

We spent the weekend on campus. Our teacher taught us about

Washington and his legacy, and I was all eyes and all ears. Although I, like other blacks my age, would soon be instructed that Washington was an Uncle Tom and a throwback to some dark past, that lesson never sank in. I had seen too much when I was young to dismiss what I knew. The Nation of Islam never built a Tuskegee. An army of Jesse Jacksons would not even know how to lay the first brick.

In September 1895, Washington, not yet forty years of age, spoke to a largely white audience at the Cotton States and International Exposition in Atlanta. The invitation was a breakthrough in itself, especially in a Southern state like Georgia. Washington thanked the organizers for making it possible. "It is a recognition that will do more to cement the friendship of the two races than any occurrence since the dawn of our freedom," said Washington, and he was not exaggerating. The speech that followed would stand as Washington's manifesto, the one that Du Bois had to undercut if his vision was going to prevail.[16]

Unlike Du Bois, Washington felt no need to list the injustices blacks had suffered in America. Given that everyone in attendance, white and black, knew them, Washington refused to "permit our grievances to overshadow our opportunities." He also acknowledged the false steps that his fellow liberated blacks had made after the Civil War. He referred specifically to those black politicians more intent on grabbing a seat in Congress or the state legislature than in mastering the skills needed to succeed in the real world. Then, as now, as Washington pointed out, "stump speaking had more attractions than starting a dairy farm or truck garden."

For all the "sins" the South had committed—and Washington used the word *sins*—one they had not committed was denying black citizens "a man's chance" to compete in the commercial world. As Washington saw it, blacks shared the responsibility for not succeeding as well as hoped. In making the "great leap from slavery to freedom," too many of his brethren had not bothered to master the trades needed to get ahead. "No race can prosper till it learns that there is as much dignity in tilling a field as in writing a poem," said Washington. "It is at the bottom of life we must begin, and not at the top." For a self-appointed member of the Talented Tenth, like Du Bois, these were fighting words.

Washington encouraged the white members of the audience to help blacks get a foothold in the economic life of the South. A student of the free enterprise system, he understood that black success would not limit white success but enhance it. The black one-third of the population, he argued, would "contribute one-third to the business and industrial prosperity of the South." Given this understanding, he appealed less to his listeners' sense of charity than to their self-interest. Washington's assessment of the way the economy worked was accurate and specific: "You will find that [independent blacks] will buy your surplus land, make blossom the waste places in your fields, and run your factories."

If white Southerners did as suggested, Washington promised that they and their families would "be surrounded by the most patient, faithful, law-abiding, and unresentful people that the world has seen." Although "surrounded" by blacks, white Southerners need not fear being forced to integrate their institutions. As Washington phrased it, "The opportunity to earn a dollar in a factory just now is worth infinitely more than the opportunity to spend a dollar in an opera-house." Washington felt that social interaction would come in time, but he saw no reason to press, and I am sure the audience was relieved he did not.

For the next century and more, Washington's bottom-up vision of black American progress would war with Du Bois's trickle-down vision. Until about 1960, Washington's vision prevailed, slowly and imperfectly, but steadily. The mass migration of blacks to Northern cities helped considerably, at least in the short run. In the cities, blacks had more opportunities for education and employment, and most took advantage of it. According to a report prepared by the United States Commission on Civil Rights in 1986, the economic status of black men in the United States showed "substantial long-run improvement" during the war years and for the next three decades. Between 1940 and 1980, for instance, the real earnings of black men increased 340 percent versus 164 percent for white men. The growth was strongest during the first three of those decades.[17]

Du Bois was blind to the progress around him and was sure he knew better than the average black man did what was best for the black man. In 1912, for instance, Du Bois advised his fellow black citizens to vote for the Democrat Woodrow Wilson for president.

This was one of Du Bois's first major political mistakes. Although the most progressive of the candidates running in 1912, Wilson, even progressives admit, was "a real racial reactionary who turned the clock backwards."[18] He signed a bill banning interracial marriage in the District of Columbia. He signed another bill segregating streetcars in the District. Some of his hard-core racist appointees segregated their departments. This included the post office, which was a major employer of blacks even then. Wilson's predecessors Grover Cleveland and Theodore Roosevelt had appointed blacks to political posts, but Wilson ended that practice too. Even then, certain politicians were talking a good game to get black votes, but once elected they sent blacks to the back of the bus.

Then Du Bois got serious. He started studying Karl Marx and visiting Communist countries. That included four trips to the Soviet Union. In October 1961, during the first year of John F. Kennedy's presidency, Du Bois showed his hand. He applied for admission to the Communist Party of the United States. By the time he got his official party card, Du Bois had to know about the terror-famine of the early 1930s in which the Soviets deliberately executed or starved to death millions of small farmers to force them off their land so the farms could be "collectivized." He had to know too about the "Great Purge," which was taking place in 1936 when he was visiting Russia. During this terror, hundreds of thousands of people that Joseph Stalin distrusted were executed. Many more were sent to the gulags. Except for these occasional road bumps, Du Bois was "convinced that socialism was an excellent way of life." As to the millions killed or exiled in the Soviet Union, the Soviets were doing what they had to do. "For Russia," Du Bois wrote in his application to become a Communist, "I was convinced she had chosen the only way open to her at the time." The Talented Tenth always knows better.

Communism "will make mistakes," Du Bois continued, "but today it marches triumphantly on in education and science, in home and food, with increased freedom of thought and deliverance from dogma. In the end communism will triumph."[19] This was all so easily disproved, even in 1961, that only a member of the Talented Tenth could possibly believe it, but believe it he and his comrades did, and they began to subject America to their alchemy.

In the 1970s, the earnings growth began to falter, especially among young black men. One symptom of the impending decline was black participation in the work force. Up until 1960, that participation was robust. After 1960, black male participation fell much quicker than that of whites, even when the variables of schooling and age were held constant. For younger men, "increased involvement in crime and imprisonment and a decline in marriage possibly underlie the decline in work attachment," wrote the authors of the Civil Rights Commission report with unusual candor. For older men, much of the decline was "attributed to the liberalization and rising benefit levels of Federal disability programs (supplemented by food stamps and other benefits)."[20]

Without even looking closely I could see what was happening in the neighborhoods of South Central. State and federal officials were all but encouraging people like me and my friends to abandon our kids. They may not have done this intentionally, but they did so just the same. Regretfully, I speak from experience. In my senior year, as I said earlier, I impregnated my high school sweetheart. Of course, I should have done the right thing and married her, but California beckoned, and I knew the government would take care of her. The state would not give my son a father to look up to, but it would make sure he and his mother would be fed and sheltered, and at the time, that was enough to clear my still-unformed conscience. My relationship with my son would turn out better than I had any right to think it would, and I am grateful for that, but it is hard not to look back at those years without cringing.

Farrakhan and Jackson and those clowns were telling me that since the white man screwed me over, it was time for him to pay me back—

reparations for slavery in all but name. Many academics were thinking much as they did. In 1966, two of them, Richard Cloward and Frances Fox Piven, formally drafted a plan that would have a real impact for the next fifty years.[21] It should not surprise anyone that the two taught at Columbia, the same university that produced Barack Obama.

In the spirit of W. E. B. Du Bois, Cloward and Piven knew better than the people themselves what was good for the people's long-term welfare. True, Cloward and Piven were white, but Du Bois was a fool to think that the white Talented Tenth would yield to the black Talented Tenth. Given white control over most academic institutions and political parties, black socialists had to secure white favor to get whatever goodies white socialists were willing to hand out. In time, this would lead black leadership to betray black citizens on critical issues like abortion and marriage, but that was all down the road.

In the 1960s, the marching orders came from white alchemists like Cloward and Piven to overwhelm the system. If enough people signed up for welfare and other benefits programs, their collective demands could break the system and force a social revolution. Since so many of these programs had been targeted at blacks, and since blacks were relatively easy to organize given their shared institutions and compressed neighborhoods, alchemists used the black poor as their battering ram against the free-enterprise system. The Ku Klux Klan could not have devised a better strategy to kill the soul of the black community.

In 1950, five out of every six black children were born to married parents. By 1990, that number had dropped to a disgraceful two out of six. Federal welfare reform halted the slide in the 1990s, but Obama and pals have undone all those reforms. In California, where I live, the state's overly generous welfare payments assured that behaviors would not improve. The legislature persisted in providing lifetime welfare benefits at a rate unmatched by any state in the Continental 48. Not only did this strategy corrupt California's black population, but it is now working its black magic on immigrants, many of them here lawlessly, from Mexico and Central America.

As Booker T. Washington warned in his Atlanta speech, if blacks were not allowed to secure a trade and earn their self-respect, "We shall prove a veritable body of death, stagnating, depressing, retarding every effort to advance the body politic." Anyone who has visited South Central lately—or any American city, for that matter—knows that Washington's worst fears have come true.

Drive down just any major street in a black neighborhood and you will see the same thing—boarded-up storefronts, the occasional liquor store, a Vietnamese nail salon every few blocks, the occasional convenience store run by a frightened family of immigrants, a run-down beauty parlor, and maybe a big drug chain, like Walgreens or CVS, sitting there like a colonial outpost of some greater civilization. The thriving black commercial centers of yesteryear are no more. In Los Angeles, Hispanics have taken over the commerce in the inner city, even at the intersection of Florence and Normandy—the epicenter of the Rodney King riots.

The young people who might have started a business or built one never learned the needed skills. Their educators from the Talented Tenth pushed them through school whether they learned anything or not. If they were halfway bright, they used affirmative action to push them through colleges a notch above their level of competence. There, to protect their self-esteem, as often as not they majored in useless subjects, like black studies or sports management or gender studies.

In the world of the educators, credentials mattered more than skills. At W. E. B. Du Bois High School in Baltimore, for instance, the school motto is "Every Student College Ready." The problem, of course, is that the motto is both unrealistic and untrue. Although Du Bois is a better-than-average Baltimore high school, only half the seniors who take the English proficiency test pass it, and the other half leave school without language skills or any skills of value. Worse, in every inner-city school, boys are overrepresented among the discards.

Those who have watched the powerful Baltimore-based HBO series, *The Wire*, know how many of these discarded boys will end up:

namely, either in prison or dead. Many more will shuffle between low-end jobs or the unemployment line or disability checks, mooching off their mothers or their girlfriends. We see these lost souls everywhere we turn in the inner city. One reason we see them on the streets is because they don't have the wherewithal to own a car, the first step toward a middle-class life in every city but the densest few, like New York. In Los Angeles, if you don't have a car, you don't have a future.

The look is the same everywhere. When I was a boy, young black men prided themselves on looking sharp. Today, they all too often look like clowns, their pants drooping halfway to their knees, their shirts loose and oversized, their two-hundred-dollar Nikes extravagantly colored and unlaced. Just by the way they dress, they disqualify themselves from many a likely job. Plus, as someone told them in some self-esteem course somewhere along the way, they are too good for entry-level work, a "McJob" in street language. According to a Pew study, in the last fifteen years alone, the share of sixteen- to twenty-four-year-olds saying they didn't want a job rose from 29 percent to 39 percent. Although not broken out by race, young blacks likely score even higher than 39 percent.[22] It is discouraging to think how these young people will make it through the next fifty of their so-called productive years.

I was fortunate to grow up when and where I did, under the educational influence of Booker T. Washington and not W. E. B. Du Bois. On the plantation, especially with a strict taskmaster like my grandfather, I learned how to get up early in the morning, get to work or school on time, use tools, perform useful work, and finish a project I'd started. I was not alone in this. At my last high school reunion, I saw that just about everyone I went to school with had a decent job and a home of his own. Even during my own wayward years in Los Angeles, I always had skills enough to get a job and work ethic enough to keep one. At the BOND school we try to instill these basic understandings into our students along with a core education. In addition, in the Booker T. Washington tradition, we teach tangible skills, like carpentry.

It pains me to drive by construction sites and see few, if any, black workers. These jobs pay well not only in money but in self-esteem. Young men with hands-on skills are always in demand, and not just on work sites. Their families appreciate them, and their women appreciate them even more. Unfortunately, the reason I don't see young blacks on work sites is because too few of them have the skills or the work ethic needed. Employers wish there were more of them. The government even rewards employers for hiring black workers. They just can't find them.

For the most part, whites and Hispanics, especially those from rural areas, have been spared the W. E. B. Du Bois legacy. They have not been taught that manual labor is a shameful thing. They are also likelier to have had a father figure in the house or nearby who could show them and teach them basic skills. In one of life's great ironies, the birth mother of Apple founder Steve Jobs insisted that his adoptive parents have advanced academic degrees. When the parents she had picked out chose a girl baby instead, Paul and Clara Jobs stepped up. The fact that Paul Jobs was not a college graduate deeply upset the birth mother, but what Paul Jobs did have was a garage full of tools. He was a tinkerer and inventor and instilled the love of the same in his adopted son. The result is the Apple empire.

Pediatric neurosurgeon Dr. Ben Carson may not have had a father in the home, but he had a mother who insisted he read. And unlike many of his peers, who were reading books in school about how the white man enslaved his ancestors or stole America from the Indians, Carson was reading about real, tangible things, like "people in laboratories, pouring chemicals from a beaker into a flask and watching the steam rise, and completing electrical circuits, and discovering galaxies, and looking at microcosms in the microscope."[23]

Carson's mother worked two or three jobs as a domestic just to stay off government support. "She felt very strongly that if she gave up and went on welfare," said Carson, "that she would give up control of her life and of our lives." She also taught her sons the value of hard work, thrift, and self-reliance. In an interview with the Academy of Achievement, Carson tells of how his mother would take him and his brother out into the countryside on a Sunday, knock on a farmer's door, and ask, "Can we pick four bushels of corn, three for you and one for us?" That was not something kids learned at W. E. B. Du Bois High. They were not learning practical things at Carson's Detroit high school either. The classes were too disruptive. So Carson started working after school in the biology lab, helping the teacher set up experiments. He did much the same with his physics and chemistry teachers.

This hands-on experience helped lead him into the field of medicine, where he became one of the leading pediatric neurosurgeons in the country. "I like to do complex things," says Carson. One of the most complex operations he performed—and he was the first person in the world to do it successfully—was to separate Siamese twins joined at the brain. You can't fake that kind of skill. In the world of pediatric neurosurgery, there is no such thing as affirmative action. Social engineers don't mind entrusting the safety of poor people to under-qualified firefighters or the minds of public school students to under-qualified teachers, but they are not about to entrust the lives of their own children to under-qualified surgeons.

In reading about Carson's upbringing, I discovered that he and I shared a life-changing experience. Like me, Carson was driven by anger. He does not explain the source of it, but I suspect it derived directly or indirectly from the absence of a father in his life. His parents divorced when he was eight. In the ninth grade, he tried to stab someone with a camping knife, and might have succeeded had the kid's belt buckle not gotten in the way. The incident shocked him. He could see where his anger was taking him. So he locked himself up in the bathroom and started praying. "Lord, I can't deal with this temper," he said. Then he picked up a Bible and started reading from the book of Proverbs. "That was the first day that I started doing it," says Carson, "and I've been doing it every day since." I know just how he feels.

Carson explains how soul-deadening anger can be. He did not cite the Du Bois crowd as the ones doing the stoking, but he knows the consequences of being stoked. "If people can make you angry, they can control you," said Carson. "So, why do you want to give up control to every little insignificant person walking along?" Having conquered his anger, Carson set out to be the kind of man and father he wanted to be. "The American dream to me means that you have the ability to determine where you're going," he said. "And I am so grateful that I was born in America."

My regret is that Ben Carson did not run for president in 2008 and spare the nation eight years of Barack Obama. Carson is a spiritual heir of Booker T. Washington, but Obama had no use for Washington. He traces at least some of his development to Du Bois. As a father-less teen in Hawaii, Obama too was consumed by an anger he could not identify. In a 1995 speech he admitted to feeling directionless, "without father figures around to guide me and steer my anger."[24] Although he had no roots in the American slave experience, his leftist mother reminded him frequently that the white man had oppressed the black man in Africa as well. When Obama's father came to visit the ten-year-old Obama in Hawaii, he came to Obama's class and reinforced the message, telling the students "of Kenya's struggle to be free, how the British had wanted to stay and unjustly rule the people, just as they had in America; how many had been enslaved only because of the color of their skin, just as they had in America."[25]

Later, a black friend steered Obama, now an angry teenager, toward white oppression as the explanation for his unhappiness. His Communist mentor, Frank Marshall Davis, reinforced that message. To affirm this "nightmare vision," Obama began to read Du Bois, among other angry black authors, but finally he was put off by Du Bois's bitterness. Obama could not quite accept "withdrawal into a smaller and smaller coil of rage" as the price of being black. He turned instead to Malcolm X, a man who indulged his own bitterness for twelve years, not as a slave, but, as I mentioned earlier, a "zombie." Malcolm was referring to his twelve years in the racist Nation of Islam. In the last year of his life, he broke away and aligned himself with the larger Islamic world. "His repeated acts of self-creation spoke to me," wrote Obama in *Dreams from My Father*, but Obama was still unsure of how he wanted to re-create himself. In his book, Obama followed this moment of reflection with the frequently told story of how his grandmother reacted badly to a shakedown by a large black man. "I knew that men who might easily have been my brothers could still inspire their rawest fears," he writes.[26]

To talk through this incident, at least in his book, Obama went to visit his mentor, his own personal Du Bois, Frank Marshall Davis, a card-carrying member of the Communist Party USA, and a pornographer to boot. After reciting a few of the injustices his black ancestors suffered, Davis told Obama, "What I'm trying to tell you is, your grandma's right to be scared. She's at least as right as Stanley [Obama's grandfather] is. She understands that black people have a reason to hate. That's just how it is. For your sake, I wish it were otherwise. But it's not. So you might as well get used to it."[27]

The book largely tells the story of Obama's search for identity. The problem is, the various sources of wisdom that he turns to inevitably assure him that it's okay to hate. While Ben Carson and I were turning to God and asking Him to relieve us of our anger, the only "god" Obama found was in Rev. Jeremiah Wright's church. There, during Obama's fake epiphany, Wright claimed to be preaching "hope," but what he was really preaching was hate. "Reverend Wright spoke of Sharpsville and Hiroshima," writes Obama, "the callousness of policy makers in the White House and in the State House."[28] The Sharpeville massacre, where white police shot and killed numerous black protesters, occurred in South Africa thirty years before Wright's 1988 sermon. "Hiroshima," of course, refers to the dropping of the atom bomb on a Japanese city fifteen years before Sharpeville. What the two incidents have in common is that white men killed people of color. To Wright it did not matter that the then ruthless Japanese military had invited their own destruction not just by bombing Pearl Harbor but by their hair-curling brutality against the neighboring Chinese.

Obama writes earlier in the book, "In talking to self-professed nationalists like Rafiq [a Nation of Islam follower] . . . I came to see how the blanket indictment of everything white served a central function in their message of uplift; how, psychologically, at least, one depended on the other."²⁹ Although he seemed to reject Rafiq's strategy, Obama found a father figure in Wright, who was doing exactly the same thing. The bottom line is that Obama never really learned anything, never came to grips with his own internal strife. He found no peace in Christianity because the Christianity he halfheartedly adopted had nothing to do with Christ and everything to do with Jeremiah Wright.

Obama's real religion was socialism. He spent his early adulthood not learning an extraordinarily useful skill, as Dr. Carson had, but rather "organizing" his community along the Cloward–Pivens/Saul Alinsky model. Unfortunately, those being "organized" learned nothing useful to improve their own skill sets or character. Instead, they were bundled into an angry mass and used to break down the system—except, as always, the system won out in the end.

9

TARNISHED ANGELS

omedian Richard Pryor, who lived in Los Angeles when I did, had a revelation very much like my own, and he had it roughly at the same stage of his life. He was thirty-nine when he saw a twisted and deformed apparition of himself. He asked that image if he was the devil. "Yes," said the apparition. "I'm you."[1]

Pryor and I responded in different ways. I opened my heart to God and turned my life around. Pryor doused himself with 150-proof rum and set himself on fire. It was no accident. It was an act of self-obliteration. Although he joked about the incident after he recovered, he suffered third-degree burns over more than 50 percent of his body. Truth is, he never really did recover. Worse, he learned little from the experience. Richard Pryor was an angry, tormented soul. His story is worth telling because so many black lives are lived as destructively as Pryor lived his own, but few others are documented well enough to be instructive.

Born in Peoria in 1940, Pryor had a hustler for a father and a hooker for a mother. Both abandoned him when he was a boy and left him in the care of "mama," a grandmother who ran a bordello and beat him as she saw fit. At the age of seven, Pryor was sexually abused by an adult male repeatedly over a period of time. This happens all too often in homes without caring parents. The abuse alone was enough to cripple Pryor. Coupled with abandonment, it was all but fatal to his emotional development. Although I too was raised by a grandmother and can empathize with Pryor's pain, my problems were slight compared to his.

Pryor was a brilliant comic with great powers of empathy, but he never learned to live the way an adult male should. "There was absolutely zero he could teach me about living," said Franklin Ajaye, a successful black comedian in his own right. "I could learn from his comedy, but I didn't see anything about how he lived his life that I wanted to emulate. Zero." Said Jennifer Lee, his live-in white girlfriend, whom he beat on a nearly daily basis, "I've never met a man who needed love so badly and resisted it so much."[2] Lee would write a book about Pryor and title it, appropriately, *Tarnished Angel.*

If it had not been for his attraction to white women, Pryor might have become a Black Panther, a terrorist group with whom he openly sympathized. His alienation ran that deep. Instead, he projected his anger and self-loathing into his comedy. He had a gift for making his white fans feel uncomfortable without pushing them over the edge. He fed on their guilt. They in turn felt they deserved the discomfort, thinking it was their fault Pryor suffered as he did. His hip black fans meanwhile enjoyed his boldness and his edginess. They liked the way he put the screws to the man. Career alchemist Cornel West, a socialist academic, called Pryor "the freest black man America has ever had" and compared him favorably to Malcolm X and Martin Luther King.[3]

Pryor, however, knew he was not free at all. He was a prisoner of his own dark past. Toward the tail end of his career, he made an autobiographical film called *Jo Jo Dancer, Your Life Is Calling.* In the film he retraces the steps of his childhood. He sees his mother turning tricks. He hears his father say about him, "This boy ain't sh** and his mama ain't sh** either."[4] To the end, Pryor saw himself the way his father saw him.

When his grandmother died, Pryor, then a superstar, collapsed in grief. "Everything I've had and everything I've got is gone,"[5] said Pryor, who compensated for her loss by plunging deeper into drug use. You don't need to be a psychiatrist to see that Pryor was an empty shell of a man. And you don't need to be a sociologist to see that his failures were not the fault of white America but of a deformed, godless family life.

Few black men born in 1940 experienced anything like the family trauma Pryor did. For black men born in 1980, this kind of trauma was close to the norm. That was the year Rob Peace was born in Orange, New Jersey, a run-down enclave bordering Newark. His mother, Jackie, was a responsible workaholic who refused to marry Rob's father, Skeet Douglas, a smarter-than-average street hustler and drug dealer. She also refused to live with him after Rob was born for fear of the influences Skeet would bring to bear on his son.

Unlike many such mothers, Jackie read to her son at every opportunity and got him interested in books. Skeet objected. He worried that Rob would grow up too soft for the world they inhabited. The parents, almost never together with their son, pulled him in two different directions. They fought often and loudly for his soul. On the surface at least, Rob Peace took after his mother. He was hardworking, responsible, and an impressively good student. "But still," as Jeff Hobbs writes in his excellent book on Peace's life, "she saw the anger in him, a gradually thickening shade just beneath the sometimes impenetrable veil of his eyes." That anger hardened when Skeet was sentenced to life for murdering two sisters just as Peace was to start fourth grade at a private school his mother could barely afford. Peace helped out as best he could. Writes Hobbs, "He aggressively assumed the role of husband to his mother,"[6] not exactly the healthiest role for a ten-year-old to play.

In the ensuing years, Peace's progress through life testified to the way the white world welcomes ambitious young black men. He won a scholarship to St. Benedict's Prep in Newark, an excellent Catholic school with a largely black student body. There Peace starred in the classroom and in water polo, not your typical inner-city sport. A wealthy benefactor took an interest in Peace and paid his way through Yale, where he bypassed the African studies trap and majored in molecular biophysics and biochemistry. On the side, he worked in a cancer and infectious disease laboratory. It was at Yale that Peace roomed with Hobbs, a white kid from an affluent family who would chronicle his life.

That life was "short and tragic" because Peace never got over his anger. He learned instead to displace it. "I hate all these entitled motherf***ers," he said in Hobbs's presence, referring to virtually all his fellow Yale students, Hobbs included. That hatred helped ease any guilt about selling them marijuana at prices he could never get on the street. It also enabled him to join with his fellow black students in staging their own graduation. More destructively, his "vast reservoir of anger"[7] blinded him to the fact that his father, as Hobbs makes clear, was rightly convicted for killing two women. Peace preferred to blame the white establishment for Skeet's continued imprisonment.

Anger has a way of crippling people in ways that are rarely talked about. For all Peace's talents, for all his prospects, he never got traction in the real world once he moved beyond the discipline of prep school and college. He returned home and resumed the drug trafficking that was so easy and profitable at Yale. In the mean streets of Newark and the Oranges, he found a less dependable clientele and much rougher competitors. They saw him as a soft target and murdered him before he even thought to look in the mirror and see what was missing.

Despite his Catholic education, Peace had no God in his life. In his otherwise insightful book, Hobbs fails to comment on this. That much said, his book forced even the *New York Times* to acknowledge how the "'crippling emotional trauma" of fatherlessness coupled with the "rage of generations"[8] caused Peace's demise. Hobbs avoided the "institutional racism" charge the media usually fall back on to explain black failure.

Once the scales fell from my eyes, I could finally see how many young black men were as badly damaged as Peace and Pryor. When we launched BOND to address the problem, I thought that, though blacks had fallen far, there was a great chance for us to climb back up. But now, at the end of Obama's divisive presidency, I am not so sure. I find myself wondering if the battle has been lost, before I remind myself we have to fight on regardless.

I recall the conclusion I came to a few years back after much soul-searching, an internally tumultuous and spiritually troublesome exercise. At the time, I saw the death of Jesus Christ. I saw the death of the black soul. I saw the miraculous resurrection of Christ. And therein, I saw the glimmer of hope. Richard Pryor, by contrast, played the resurrection for cheap, self-indulgent laughs. In one autobiographical screenplay, he set a scene in a cathedral. There, he encounters Jesus on the cross, and Jesus begs Pryor to help him down. Pryor obliges Jesus and is helping him out of the church when several monks see what is happening, beat Pryor up, and nail Jesus back on the cross. As Jesus cries out in agony, Pryor vows to tell the world what he saw, to which a monk replies, "Who's going to believe you, nigger?"[9]

Today, too many young black men, like Peace and Pryor, have turned their backs on God. Like them both, they wallow in their anger and assume the role of "nigger" as a perverse badge of honor. But God is the one force in the universe that cares not at all about their color. If they can learn to see past their anger, they will see that the only hope for themselves and for the black community is a resurrection of miraculous proportions. Blacks of today must atone for the sins of our fathers to command the mercy and love that would precipitate such a resurrection.

A daunting task this is. Whereas Christ died with a holy nature, the black soul has died in the gallows of weakness and immorality. Seventy percent or more of black babies today are born out of wedlock. This has created an epidemic of fatherlessness. The black woman carries no respect for a man of such weakness and harbors a festering hatred for this man who bedded and then abandoned her. Have you heard me say this before? Do I speak too bluntly? This is as it has to be. Let me repeat the words of William Lloyd Garrison, "I *will* be as harsh as truth, and as uncompromising as justice. On this subject, I do not wish to think, or speak, or write, with moderation."[10] Our subject, I would insist, is as serious as Garrison's.

There is a vicious cycle at work here. A man is attracted to a woman who has a spirit similar to his mother's, but he leaves her upon sensing this is the same spirit he resented growing up. The father's absence makes the mother the most influential figure in the family. But her anger toward the man who left her is so great that she cannot easily be a positive influence. The black youth is victimized by his mother's dominant hatred. With no father as a figure of guidance and respect, the child yields readily, as Pryor did, to the force of darkness. Said Pryor at one point in rejecting help, "I don't see any need to be in reality because I've seen how ugly the world is."[11] This was said by an enormously wealthy, much-loved man decades after the legal playing field had been leveled. Ugly?

In the past, when a child was born into dire circumstances, he often compensated with a desperate drive to succeed. He innately felt that he must work hard, harder than all those around him, just to be able to survive. Too many young black men today feel none of this. Their focus is on the next 40-ouncer, the next blunt, the next hit. Meanwhile, young black girls do as their mothers did and adopt the same vicious, emasculatory techniques. Thus a cycle perpetuates. With few strong examples of God's commandments playing out in the black community, that community veers toward destruction. Not all blacks are like this, but the cycle I describe, sad to say, is an accurate representation of the evil that has taken hold of black America. It would not surprise me if God were tempted to pull the plug on our people as He did in Noah's time.

The penance that the black community is going to have to pay to regain God's favor is incalculable. God ordained a spiritual order of God in Christ, Christ in man, man over woman, and woman over children. Black men have lost their connection with Christ, and women have exploited that weakness to become the head of the temporal realm. This is a violation of God's established order and will never work. It is because black men refuse to be strong and speak against this that God has seemingly let the black community go. We are so far lost that it is going to require a huge step up by black men to regain God's blessing.

Just a few men stepping up will not absolve this sin for the black community. Many will have to sacrifice to rediscover our once-sacred relationship with Him. We all know by now that few, if any, of our leaders will lift a finger to this end. Most have made it clear that they are content to watch us slide further downward, all the while taking satisfaction in their growing power and wealth.

When Barack Obama first emerged, I saw the possibility of expanding the discussion. Here was a black man who may have grown up in a dysfunctional white home but who married a black American woman and seemed to be a good father to his two daughters. As much as I distrusted his politics and his long-standing relationship with the hateful, hypocritical Rev. Jeremiah Wright, I thought Obama might still present a useful example to the many shattered souls within the black community.

Obama's Father's Day sermon in June 2008 at the twenty-thousand-member Apostolic Church of God in the South Side of Chicago renewed my hope. His message was strong. The *New York Times* summed up the message in its headline, "Obama Sharply Assails Absent Black Fathers."[12] Obama preached, "If we are honest with ourselves we'll admit that what too many fathers are is missing—missing from too many lives and too many homes," and the almost entirely black congregation called back its approval. Surprisingly, Obama zeroed in on the heart of the problem. "You and I know how true this is in the African-American community." Obama even addressed the unfortunate results of this disorder, telling the congregants that boys who grow up in fatherless homes are "twenty times more likely to end up in prison." Of absentee fathers, Obama said words that I might have said myself: "They have abandoned their responsibilities, acting like boys instead of men."[13]

The response in the church itself and in the black community afterward was highly positive. Women, in particular, seemed to appreciate his remarks, and some of those posting online compared Obama favorably to Jesse Jackson, who himself was one of those absent fathers. Despite his own prominence as a preacher and role model, despite his own anguish at being born out of wedlock, Jackson had very publicly fathered a so-called love child. He was not at all pleased by the comments of the upstart Obama. Not long after Obama's speech, Jackson's true feelings "slipped out" on a hot mic before a TV appearance. "I wanna cut his nuts out," Jackson said to the fellow next to him. "Barack—he's talking down to black people—telling niggers how to behave."[14]

Jackson would make a halfhearted apology, but much of the left-wing media supported what he said. "Jackson Gaffe Turns Focus on Obama's Move to the Right," read the headline of Britain's left-leaning *Guardian*. As the *Guardian* article spelled out, Obama's comments on individual responsibility irritated alchemists like Jackson, who "hold government policies to account for the impoverishment of African-American families."[15] In any case, Obama got the message. He never told "niggers" how to behave again.

10

BLOODY SHIRTS

The civil rights movement is dead. As blue-collar philosopher Eric Hoffer once said, "Every great cause begins as a movement, becomes a business and eventually degenerates into a racket."[1] The civil rights movement has been a racket for many, many years.

I had the good fortune of remembering the movement when it was still alive. As a boy growing up in Alabama, I watched the pioneers of that movement earn their freedom. Alabama was ground zero in the real civil rights movement. Selma was only three or so hours away from where I grew up. I was fifteen when the famous march happened there, and I was old enough to know what was going on. At school we followed it closely. These seemed like decent people doing the right thing. Unlike Barack Obama, I do have a claim on Selma.

I have more of a claim on Clayton. As a high school student, I participated in a sit-in with my classmates at the Barbour County Courthouse in Clayton, Alabama. It was a very heady experience. I would like to tell you it was as scary as Selma, but it wasn't even close. We sang, "We shall overcome" on the courthouse steps and felt righteous about it. For their part, the townspeople generally ignored us. At the time, it felt like the right thing to do. In the South, blacks were still being denied some basic civil rights, like voting and attending public universities.

I must say, though, that I had a different take on the sit-ins taking place at lunch counters throughout the South. As much as I admired the courage of those sitting in, I was not sure why they would want to patronize a private business that did not want them. I also wondered why the owners should have to serve people they did not want to serve and wondered where all this would lead. Even then, I thought the civil rights movement was drifting away from a real expression of freedom toward coercion. This much became obvious on the day the civil rights movement died.

It did not die on April 4, 1968, the day Martin Luther King was shot in Memphis. It died the next day, April 5, 1968. While we school kids in Alabama sat in class almost too sad and shocked to talk, Jesse Jackson had the presence of mind to fly to Chicago and hire a public relations agent. The agent took the allegedly grief-stricken Jackson from interview to interview in a chauffeur-driven car so he could raise money for his Chicago operation.

Among Jackson's appearances was one on the NBC *Today* show. There he appeared in a shirt that he claimed was smeared with King's blood and boasted on national television, "He died in my arms."[2] This was a total lie. Jackson hid in the bushes on the floor below King's room at the Lorraine Motel in Memphis after he heard the shot ring out. He came upstairs only after the danger had passed. Andrew Young and Ralph Abernathy were the ones who tended to the dying King. "People freaked out and did strange things. Jesse put his hands in the blood and wiped it on the front of his shirt," remembered Andrew Young.[3] Said Abernathy of Jackson, "He was young and overly ambitious with a big ego."[4] King never trusted Jackson, and he had good cause, but no matter. From that day forward, Jackson made himself the public face of the American civil rights movement. In a way, that bloody shirt was the perfect symbol of the lie the movement became. It represented not sacrifice but self-aggrandizement at the expense of a people looking for genuine leadership. In the wake of King's death, Abernathy took over the Southern Christian Leadership Conference (SCLC), but Jackson had the charisma that Abernathy lacked. And he had the shirt. Through deceit and outright thuggery, Jackson consolidated his power, intimidating his would-be rivals and threatening the media.

In 1971, when a black reporter for the *Chicago Tribune*, Angela

Parker, reported on Jackson's alleged theft of funds from the SCLC, Jackson chastised her from his pulpit and his supporters picketed her home and terrorized her with threatening phone calls. Jackson's henchmen threatened another black reporter, Barbara Reynolds, after she wrote an honest biography of Jackson's tainted rise to power. And after black journalist Milton Coleman reported on Jackson's anti-Semitic slurs, Louis Farrakhan threatened him on Jackson's behalf.[5]

This was the same Louis Farrakhan, by the way, who said of the so-called Million Man March he organized in 1995, "The basic reason that this was called was for atonement and reconciliation."[6] Yeah, right. In fact, the march was a shameless display of power. Only a fellow believer would have bought into Farrakhan's message. One such believer was Barack Obama. He was there. So was Martin Luther King III. So were many Christian pastors. Seeing the pastors there did not surprise me. In my frequent debates with them on my radio show and in public forums, I know that many of them have lost their way. Unable to challenge me on facts, they accuse me of being judgmental, or worse. Every now and then, a pastor will lay a "house nigger" on me or an "Uncle Tom," but at least I didn't "Tom" for Farrakhan at the "Million Man March."

In December 2001, I got to see the "civil rights" movement, now deep into its bloody shirt phase, in action. The occasion was a meeting at the Los Angeles Chamber of Commerce, sponsored by Jackson's Rainbow/PUSH Trade Bureau. It was a classic Jackson shakedown, this time of the Toyota Motor Corporation. Recently, Toyota had run an ad that showed a black man with a gold Toyota SUV embossed on a front tooth. The ultrasensitive Jackson, the same one who referred to New York City as "Hymietown,"[7] claimed to be offended. "The only thing missing is the watermelon," he said in response.[8] To appease Jackson, Toyota was prepared to spend millions on its 21st Century Diversity Strategy, much of which would go to Jackson and his cronies. This meeting was a show of their submission.

My PR director urged me to attend, and he and I grabbed seats in the front of the room. Jackson dominated the pageant that followed.

From his position onstage, he asked the businesspeople in attendance, mostly black, to raise their hands if they belonged to his "trade bureau" and identify themselves and their businesses. Those who did not raise their hands were made aware that they could get their share of the goodies by purchasing a membership. Of course, Jackson did not say exactly "get your share of the goodies," but that is what the business-people were thinking. I think the phrase Jackson used was "open doors." The Toyota vice president onstage, Irv Miller, looked thoroughly whipped. It was his doors that were being opened. Jackson promised other corporate doors would follow. He mentioned BMW to whet the audience's appetite.

To show he meant business, Jackson introduced a Rainbow/PUSH member who was being promoted to head Toyota's supplier develop-ment program. It was this man who would monitor Toyota's "progress" in purchasing supplies from female- and minority-owned businesses. In other words, he was Jesse's gatekeeper, and everyone knew it. Why "minorities" and women needed Jackson's help nearly forty years after the passage of the Civil Rights Act was explained only in absurd clichés.

Toward the end of the presentation, a Jackson associate gave a fiery speech about how much Jackson had done for blacks and how much he had sacrificed to do it. Then Jackson's posse went from table to table collecting membership checks from those not yet signed up and contributions to Jackson's sixtieth birthday bash from everyone but the foolhardy.

After the strong-arming, Jackson launched a question-and-answer session. I should add at this point that once I opened my heart to God's love, He drove away all my fear. I say this to explain how I could walk into a lion's den like this one and confront the beast. "As the president of a nonprofit conservative organization," I said to Toyota's Miller, "I'm concerned that our young people will be locked out of any training pro-grams offered by Toyota because of our conservative beliefs. How can we work directly with Toyota instead of having to go through Jesse Jackson or anyone else, because we don't agree with *anything* they're about."

Although I asked the question respectfully, I could hear rude remarks and derisive laughter even as I was speaking. When I finished, all hell broke loose. Several of my fellow black citizens leaped out of their seats, shouting profanities. Among those doing the leaping was Judge Greg Mathis, the star of his own reality TV show and a longtime Jackson supporter. In fact, Mathis headed the Michigan operation of Jackson's 1988 presidential campaign. "You've been watching too much TV," Mathis shouted. "You've been watching too much O'Reilly." Fox News' Bill O'Reilly had been openly criticizing Jackson's tactics.

"Well, at least I don't watch your boring show," I said. At that point, Carl Dickerson, cochair of the event, began attacking me personally, calling me "stupid," among other unkind things. Then Jackson jumped into the fray, calling me and other black conservatives "parasites who want to pick apples from trees they didn't shake."[9]

It went downhill from there. A security guard tried to remove us, but we wouldn't leave. Jackson's son Jonathan and two of his buddies then stood in front of us until the forum ended and attempted to block us when we went to leave. I could hear Jackson yelling behind them, "Get his ass out of here." Mathis then joined in again, saying I needed to leave "before you get your ass kicked." Then, when we tried to leave, Jonathan cursed me and struck me in the shoulder. Jesse Jackson then walked over, joined in the cursing, and incited the crowd to do the same. As I testified at the ensuing trial, I felt like I was at a Klan meeting. With assistance from the Washington-based Judicial Watch, we took the Jacksons to court in Los Angeles in 2006. Although the jury ruled for the defendants on some counts and deadlocked on another, this was the first time Jackson was ever made to answer for his bullying tactics in public.

Such was the state of the civil rights movement as we moved into a new century. It had stagnated or worse from the moment Jesse Jackson spirited away Martin Luther King's blood. Incredibly, for the first forty or so years after King's death, this shameless huckster served as the presumed go-to leader of black America. He and lesser black "leaders" were continually inventing new rights so they could exploit white guilt and extort new benefits that only black people could enjoy. Why it was that only black people needed "leaders," no one seemed to ask. It was only natural, then, that when Barack Obama first emerged on the national stage, it was assumed he would be the new leader, the black Moses, the one to lead us poor, ignorant souls to the Promised Land.

That designation, however, left no place for Jesse Jackson. In his veiled threat to emasculate Obama, Jackson nailed him where he was most vulnerable, his shaky hold on his racial identity. Growing up in Hawaii, all Obama knew about black America was what he saw on television, which meant he knew nothing about the "niggers" Jackson threw in his face. Jesse Jackson did not share this weakness. For all of his faults, he had firsthand experience with the civil rights movement. Obama did not. He had to fake his roots.

A commemoration of the Selma march caught then candidate Obama at his phoniest. If he knew anything about this history, he ignored it and made up his own. As Obama told the story in his fake black preacher voice, the march at Selma inspired a whole chain of events that led to his nearly miraculous birth. The Kennedys were moved by the march to start an airlift for African students. His Kenyan father came to Hawaii, where he met his white mother, who was stirred sufficiently to overcome racial barriers and marry Barack Obama Sr. "They got together and Barack Obama Jr. was born." Said Obama in conclusion, "So don't tell me I don't have a claim on Selma, Alabama. Don't tell me I'm not coming home to Selma, Alabama."[10]

He didn't, and he wasn't. In reality, Obama Sr. came to America five years before the march, during the Eisenhower presidency. By the time of the march, Obama Sr. had long since left Hawaii to get his Talented Tenth stamp at Harvard. While real black people were staring down real white state troopers in Selma, little Barry was playing in the Hawaiian surf with Gramps. At Selma, Obama did not even seem to care that people knew he was lying. The reason was simple. He knew that a whole lot of influential white people would go along with him whatever he said.

Although Obama could fool his fans with his Selma lies, he could not fool the Jesse Jacksons of the world. They had him over a barrel, and he knew it. If Obama ever really believed in "one America"—and that is doubtful—he was afraid to prove it. After the Jackson blowback from his Father's Day speech in Chicago, Obama chose to blame the white man rather than to look within. Jackson owned him.

By the time Obama returned to Selma in 2015 to help celebrate the fiftieth anniversary of the march, the civil rights movement had degenerated into a noisy scrum of special-interest knockoffs. In his speech, Obama went through the whole laundry list of left-wing causes and tied them all to Selma. "Women marched through those doors," he said. "Latinos marched through those doors. Asian-Americans, gay Americans, and Americans with disabilities came through those doors."[11] It disturbed me to see him push gay rights in Selma or to single out those ethnic groups that Democrats were courting, even those here illegally, and ignore all others.

I was not the only one disturbed. "I marched with many people back in those days and I have reached out to some of my friends who marched with me, and all of them are shocked," said Rev. William Owens of the Coalition of African American Pastors. "They never thought they would see this day that gay rights would be equated with civil rights. Not one agreed with this comparison.

"The LGBT community hijacked our movement, a movement they know nothing about," Owens continued. "President Obama is delusional to compare our struggle with the struggle for marriage equality. Gays have not had fire hoses or dogs unleashed at them. They have not been hung from trees or denied basic human rights."[12]

Unfortunately, many black Christians cheered Obama when he made the comparison. A generation ago they understood the difference between discrimination based on something unchangeable, like skin color, and something as fashionable as sexual orientation. No one ever told gays they could not vote or sit in the front of a bus or drink out of a particular water fountain. Other than maybe Michael Jackson, no black person ever decided he was not going to be black anymore.

There is, however, one real point of comparison between the gay rights movement and the corrupted civil rights movement, and that is the condition of its victims. In a heartfelt 2015 plea to the gay community, Heather Barwick explained what it was like to be raised by two lesbians after her mother left her father when she was a toddler. "It is a strange and confusing thing to walk around with this deep-down unquenchable ache for a father, for a man, in a community that says that men are unnecessary," she writes. "There were times I felt so angry with my dad for not being there for me, and then times I felt angry with myself for even wanting a father to begin with. There are parts of me that still grieve over that loss today." The anger that children feel upon being abandoned is a universal phenomenon. "A lot of us, a lot of your kids, are hurting," added Barwick, now a married mother of four. "My father's absence created a huge hole in me, and I ached every day for a dad."[13] Not many men or women are able to shed their anger and voice the truth the way Barwick has. The alchemists encourage black people to do just the opposite—ignore the truth and channel their anger toward white America.

At Selma, if Obama wanted to address those whose rights were still being violated, he might have mentioned unborn babies. MSNBC's Melissa Harris-Perry mentioned the unborn only to celebrate their deaths. The biracial Harris-Perry was thrilled to see so many abortion supporters marching in their pink shirts. "We saw an enormous contingent of Planned Parenthood go past," she gushed, "folks who are clearly out here, marching because they believe that reproductive rights continue to be threatened in this country, and particularly in the South."[14] As many as half a million black babies are killed in the womb each year—roughly three times the rate of white babies. This is a symptom of an ongoing war between men and women in which women lack confidence that the men will provide for these children once born, and men lack the authority to protect their chidren's lives in the womb. Harris-Perry thought this borderline genocide worthy of applause, and Obama remained silent. Some black lives apparently don't matter at all.

11

FEAR AND LOATHING

In the pre–Civil War era, blacks knew slavery was wrong. They resented it and, as best they could, they resisted it. Privately, they condemned it and mocked those who passed themselves off as their "masters." Today, the alchemists have set up a new slave system. Instead of controlling people by force, these leaders—with a major assist from the government—control by dependency and addiction.

Unfortunately, most black people accept their state of dependency. Some applaud it. They call their new masters "civil rights leaders" and ask for more of the same. With the aid of the media, these leaders convince blacks that color trumps character and that white people, especially Republicans, hate them for their color. If need be, the leadership even manufactures incidents, as this chapter will show, to reinforce their fear and loathing of white people. The leaders of a movement built on the myth of the bloody shirt have no qualms about telling new lies to keep black people frightened and angry.

To get a compressed sense of how so-called civil rights leaders use fear to manipulate those in their way, we need only to look at the San Francisco of the 1970s. At the Peoples Temple, the mostly black congregation was taught that all white people were bad—well, not all white people exactly. The Temple's top dog, Jim Jones, "their father," was good, better than good. So was his white inner circle, the ones he sexually exploited and rewarded with favors.[1]

Jones was a communist. He made no bones about it. In his memoir, he told of how he chose Christianity as a means to a communist end.

"Free at last, free at last," he led his temple comrades in prayer. "Thank socialism almighty we will be free at last." A charismatic leader and fake Christian, Jones preyed on his congregants' insecurity and convinced them that only through him, the father, could they find safety and salvation.

With the surefire twenty-five hundred votes he could deliver, Democratic politicians, black and white, couldn't care less whether Jones was a Marxist or a Martian. They all came courting—House Speaker Willie Brown, Mayor George Moscone, famed gay San Francisco supervisor and icon Harvey Milk, even Rosalynn Carter, Jimmy's wife. "I figured if these people—if anybody should know, they should know," testified one black survivor as to why he stuck with Jones. Moscone appointed Jones to the Human Rights Commission in 1976 and then to the chairmanship of the San Francisco Housing Authority. That same year, the *Los Angeles Times* named Jones "humanitarian of the year."

In the next two years, Jones worked overtime doing what today's alchemists do a little more slowly. He stirred his followers' anger and stoked their fears of white people to the point where more than a thousand of them were willing to follow him blindly to the jungles of South America. There, when American authorities began to question Jones's actions, like kidnapping and rape, he persuaded his followers, the great majority of them black, to kill themselves before evil white Americans had the chance to do the same. More than nine hundred people ended up drinking cyanide-laced Flavor Aid (a product similar to the better-known Kool-Aid). Kool-Aid became the perfect metaphor for the toxins alchemists have been encouraging black people to consume for the last half century.

With their parents dead and their names unknown, authorities dumped the remains of some 250 of these children into a mass grave at the Evergreen Cemetery in the middle of Oakland, the victims of the greatest concentrated slaughter of children in the nation's history. Many more tears have been shed over Michael Brown than all these kids combined. Almost no one knows they are there, and the alchemists refuse to tell their story because Jones's story is their story told in fast-forward.

In Oakland, the killing has continued ever since, and the victims have been as ignored as the kids in the Evergreen Cemetery—unless, of course, their deaths can be exploited to satisfy the alchemists' ambitions. Oscar Grant got a lot of attention when a white BART police officer accidentally shot and killed him on January 1, 2009, at the now infamous Fruitvale Station. There were huge demonstrations after the shooting. The officer was sent to prison for involuntary manslaughter, and a highly sympathetic movie was made of the incident. After the Michael Brown shooting in Missouri, protesters in Oakland shut down the city on several occasions. But as to the hundred or so black people killed by other black people each year in that fallen city—crickets.

Funeral assistant Todd Walker was brave enough to point this out. He had the sad occasion to do so. His fourteen-year-old nephew, Davon Ellis, a football player and honor student, was gunned down on the Oakland streets almost three years to the day after Trayvon Martin was killed. "These are babies killing babies, and people are just sick and tired of it," Walker told *San Francisco Chronicle* columnists Phil Matier and Andy Ross. "Where are the demonstrators for these kind of killings? Why is it that the only time 'black lives matter' is when police do the shooting?"[2]

To their credit, Matier and Ross took the question to Cat Brooks, a black leader in the Oakland area's relentless antipolice demonstrations. A committed alchemist, Brooks reassured the columnists that it did not matter whether the police or another black person did the shooting. "It is the system of oppression in our society that is responsible for the violence," she insisted. On the home page for the Onyx Organizing Committee she chairs, Brooks wrote about blacks in the Bay Area, the national capital of white guilt, as if she were writing about Jews in Nazi Germany. "Of course black people are being profiled," she observed, "the same way blacks are being pushed out, displaced from our homes, and locked out of job opportunities."[3] Scarier still, people seem to believe her and follow her lead.

For all her venom, Brooks served up an unusual dose of honesty in answering the question Walker and the columnists posed. Said Brooks, "I put out a press release on a police shooting, the phone rings off the hook. When I put one out on inner-community violence, we're lucky to get two calls." In attempting to explain why her white allies ignored black-on-black crime, Brooks speculated that such incidents "can't be directly tied to the struggle of class issues and to the issue of climate violence."[4]

As Brooks revealed, the media have a history of shielding their audience from stories that reflect badly on the way their fellow alchemists have treated black people. On April 19, 1993, for instance, the Clinton administration ordered a tank assault on a religious community in Waco, Texas. The media had convinced America that the members of that community were crazy, white, right-wing rednecks who deserved what they got. In fact, thirty-nine of the seventy-four people killed that day were racial minorities. Twenty-seven of the thirty-nine were black. Twenty of the dead were children. Neither Al Sharpton nor Jesse Jackson has ever said a word about the Waco dead. Hate to make their president look bad, after all.

The alchemists continue to manufacture incidents to keep blacks angry and resentful. One major such incident occurred just a few years ago when Obamacare was coming up for a vote by Congress. On that day, March 20, 2010, thousands of protesters, mostly white but not all, surrounded the Capitol. Now, usually members of Congress take a tunnel to get from their office building to the Capitol and back, but that afternoon a few members of the Black Caucus hoped to provoke an incident by walking through the crowd.

The crowd yelled, "Kill the bill" and other such things, but none of the many videos of the event picked up a single racial slur. That did not matter to Andre Carson of Indiana, one of the few Muslim members of Congress. When Carson reached the Capitol, he told reporters that he and Congressman John Lewis heard the "'n-word, n-word,' at least fifteen times, hundreds of people."[5] Think about this for a second. Today, white people almost never use the word *nigger,* even among themselves. It is a national scandal when one does. Most whites have never witnessed a white person calling a black person "nigger" or any other racial slur. The media know this, and yet some of them at least were willing to believe that "hundreds" of white people were yelling "nigger" at these two congressmen, one of whom, Lewis, was a veteran of the real civil rights movement.

On the way back from the Capitol to the office building, maybe a dozen other members of the Black Caucus accompanied Carson and Lewis. These included Jesse Jackson Jr. and Caucus head Emanuel Cleaver. Several held their phones out to record the walk. Again, they chose not to take the tunnel. Their goal was to provoke some incident by these "teabaggers," a nasty slur used casually by people who go ballistic when others slur them.

So trapped were these congressmen by their own hateful stereotypes that they may have actually believed Carson. They may have believed that nothing had changed since Selma, that hundreds of ordinary white people stood ready to call them "niggers." And when those white folks did just that, yes sir, these esteemed black leaders would spread the word far and wide that *nothing had changed.* You see, if nothing has changed, blacks absolutely need stand-up leaders like Sharpton and Jackson, Carson and Cleaver, to protect them against Republicans and the Tea Party and white people in general.

On the way back, with cameras rolling, nothing happened. Well, almost nothing. Without looking where he was going, Cleaver walked up the steps of the Cannon Office Building and right in front of a white man yelling, "Kill the bill" through cupped hands. As the video makes clear, Cleaver did not see the shouter, and the shouter did not see Cleaver. Cleaver later told the *Washington Post*, "The man . . . allowed his saliva to hit my face."[6] Visibly angry, Cleaver poked his finger in the man's face and then continued up the steps. A minute or so later, Cleaver came back with a black Capitol Police officer, but as the video again made clear, he failed to recognize the man, who was still shouting, "Kill the bill."

No matter. Immediately afterward, Cleaver's office put out a press release saying, "The man who spat on the congressman was arrested, but the congressman has chosen not to press charges."[7] This was all provably false. "There were no elements of a crime, and the individual wasn't able to be positively identified," Sgt. Kimberly Schneider of the US Capitol Police would tell Fox News.[8] The video supported the police. Cleaver's press release was then wrapped into a story by William Douglas, a black reporter for the McClatchy Newspapers, headlined, "Tea Party Protesters Scream 'Nigger' at Black Congressman."[9]

Publisher Andrew Breitbart offered a one-hundred-thousand-dollar reward to anyone who could produce a video of anyone using any racial slurs toward any of the congressmen coming or going—he got no takers, but the damage was done. The *Kansas City Star*, Cleaver's hometown paper, reported, "Some Tea Party supporter spat on Cleaver Saturday on Capitol Hill *because* the U.S. congressman is black."[10] Black *Washington Post* columnist Courtland Milloy told his readers what he felt about the protesters and how he expected them to feel as well: "I want to spit on them, take one of their 'Obama Plan—White Slavery' signs and knock every racist and homophobic tooth out of their Cro-Magnon heads."[11]

That fall Cleaver was facing a tough reelection against a white conservative supported by various Tea Parties. He made sure every one of his black constituents got the message about what these people were up to. The fact that no Tea Party ever addressed racial issues or committed inappropriate racial acts anywhere did not matter. The goal of the civil rights movement in the twenty-first century was to spread hatred and fear.

Black poet Langston Hughes once said, "A dream deferred is a dream denied," but he likely never would have guessed that today, *black* leaders would be the ones deferring and denying. With people like Jackson and Obama, our one hope is to self-mobilize. In the black community we have only ourselves to rely on. Out of respect for the values we once held dear and the strength we once had as a people, we are obligated to attempt with all our hearts to restore the values of our ancestors or die trying. We must now forget all our petty angers, our weaknesses, and our unfounded rage and come forward prepared for the great penance that lies ahead. And we must do so without self-pity. If we don't, the bars will always remain on the windows, and we will be caged within.

12

THE CLOWN PRINCE

t seems only fitting that the heir to Jesse Jackson's bloody shirt would be someone more outrageous and exploitative than he has been. Jackson's scandals did not bring him down. What did was the ambition of Al Sharpton, an even bigger scam artist than Jackson. If anything, Sharpton's childhood was more tortured than Jackson's.

Born in 1954, Sharpton lived a comfortable life for his first ten years. Even before the Civil Rights laws were passed, his father was a successful businessman.

In 1964, however, Sharpton's world came crashing in when his parents split up. That was all but inevitable after his half sister gave birth to his father's child. Sharpton tells this story in his 1996 autobiography, *Go and Tell Pharaoh*. "I had to watch my mother, whom I loved more than anyone, live with the fact that her daughter had stolen her husband, and that the two of them had given life of [sic] a child, out of wedlock," he writes. "To this day, I don't know how she lived with the humiliation."[1]

Sharpton used this story to justify his role in his first major public scandal, the Tawana Brawley case. Writes Sharpton, the case "stopped being Tawana, and started being me defending my mother and all the black women no one would fight for. I was not going to run away from her like my father had run away from my mother."[2] This is probably nonsense, but with Sharpton you never know.

In November 1987, in a small upstate New York town, the fifteen-year-old Brawley had gotten off her school bus after a day at school and then, instead of walking home from the bus stop, vanished into the night. Four days later, she showed up disoriented and covered in feces. As her black attorneys told the story, Brawley had been "kidnapped, raped, sodomized. 'KKK' and 'nigger' were inscribed on her body."[3] Brawley accused several white men of doing this to her. Then, as now, the media loved stories with black victims and white perpetrators, and this story exploded into the headlines. As Brawley's publicist, Sharpton helped put it there and keep it there.

For one very good reason—namely, that she had made the story up—Brawley refused to cooperate with law enforcement. One of those shut out was New York State's Jewish attorney general, Robert Abrams. When asked why Brawley failed to cooperate, Sharpton answered that doing so would be like "asking someone who watched someone killed in the gas chamber to sit down with Mr. Hitler."[4] After a few shifts in the story, Sharpton and Brawley's lawyers insisted that Steven Pagones, the assistant district attorney of Duchess County, was one of the girl's rapists. The case eventually fell apart when a security guard working for Brawley's lawyers testified that the lawyers and Sharpton knew Brawley was lying.[5] In July 1998, a jury awarded Pagones $345,000 from his accusers, $65,000 of it from Sharpton. Never one to pay his own bills, Sharpton got O. J. Simpson attorney Johnnie Cochran and friends to step up and settle the debt.

This was not even Sharpton's most destructive adventure in race-baiting. In 1991, Sharpton fueled the fires of lethal black-on-Jew violence in Crown Heights with the rallying cry, "If Jews want to get it on, tell them to pin their yarmulkes back and come over to my house."[6] In 1995, having learned nothing from Crown Heights, Sharpton led a protest against "white interloper" Fred Harari, a Jewish merchant in Harlem. Harari had evicted a black commercial tenant at the request of a neighboring black Pentecostal church. One of the protesters got carried away, shot several people in Freddie's Fashion Mart, and set the building on fire, killing eight in the process.

Perversely, none of this stopped Sharpton from seeking the Democratic nomination for president in 2004. By 2011, the still unrepentant Sharpton got his own nightly show on MSNBC. Scarier still, during the first six years of the Obama presidency, Sharpton visited the White House on seventy-two occasions, five of these being one-on-one meetings with the president, another twenty being meetings with staff members or senior advisers.[7] By the end of 2014, even the *New York Times* was admitting that Sharpton owed some $4.5 million in back taxes but that he carried on as though immune to "the sorts of obligation most people see as inevitable, like taxes, rent, and other bills."[8]

For all their deviousness, Jackson and Sharpton remain the public faces of the civil rights movement, now nearly fifty years into its bloody shirt phase. Today, if a white man says something that race hustlers find offensive, he is expected to go kiss the ring of one or both of these hucksters. All that this really accomplishes is to show the supplicant's weakness and strengthen the hands of Jackson and Sharpton.

You might remember the case of prominent radio talk show host Don Imus. In 2007, the veteran shock jock offhandedly called the girls' basketball team at Rutgers University a bunch of "nappy headed hos." This was not a very nice thing to say, but Imus made a career of saying not-very-nice things, and that never stopped prominent media people and politicians from appearing on his show. This time Sharpton took exception, and Imus promptly headed to the studios where Al Sharpton hosted his own radio show. You might recall that this was the same Al Sharpton who slurred the Jews in Crown Heights and mocked the ancient Athenian scholars as "Socrates and them Greek homos."[9]

As you might expect, Al Sharpton called Imus's comments "abominable" and "racist." Imus fell all over himself apologizing. "Our agenda is to be funny and sometimes we go too far. And this time we went way too far," whimpered Imus, but Sharpton was not in a forgiving mood.[10] Sharpton told Imus that his actions had "set a precedent." If Sharpton allowed him to escape unpunished, other white people might want to make fun of black people too. So Sharpton told Imus he planned to petition the FCC and Imus's sponsors and make sure dues were paid. Sure enough, that very same day, CBS radio suspended Imus for two weeks.[11] That move did not satisfy Sharpton and his fellow travelers. Two days later, CBS fired Imus. "He says he wants to be forgiven. I hope he continues in that process," said Sharpton. Meanwhile, Jesse "Hymietown" Jackson called Imus's termination "a victory for public decency."[12] Can anyone still be wondering why I say the civil rights movement is dead?

What black people refuse to see is that today they do not need these charlatans. Black people are not just free, they are freer than white people. Whites always have to watch what they say. Blacks do not. Black comedians, for instance, can tell jokes about white people right to their faces, and whites are expected to laugh. Thank goodness for black comedians. If not for them, no one would be able to point out the occasional absurdities of black culture. If a white person tried, he would be off the air quicker than you could say "Kramer from Seinfeld."

In time, women, Hispanics, gays, Muslims, and anyone else who fashioned themselves a "minority"—a ridiculous concept—caught on to the sensitivity game. They too wanted to be offended and reap the rewards. For political reasons, black leaders supported these other minorities, even if it meant selling out black citizens to do so. This has never been more obvious than in the support of black political leaders for illegal immigration. This only makes sense if black leaders see their primary allegiance not to black America, not to America in general, but to the Democratic Party. They look at people sneaking into the country, illegally taking jobs that poor blacks and whites might have otherwise had, and see only future Democratic voters.

For a while, here in Los Angeles, some decent black people rallied against this illegal activity. But their protests fizzled in part because the media did not want to hear them. Most just gave up and learned to accept things as they were. Like grateful slaves, too many black people still vote for those political leaders selling their jobs down the river. Sad but true, they are nearly as brainwashed as the residents of Jonestown.

It took a black sportscaster, Stephen A. Smith, to point out that Hispanics were being courted because neither political party could take their votes for granted. Black voters, however, had no such leverage, said Smith, "because one party knows they've got you under their thumb." Smith went so far as to suggest that blacks should try voting for Republicans in one election to show their independence.[13] Smith made few friends. Said one typical respondent, "And to think this shoe shining race traitor massa asskissin BYTchass sambo BUTler, is actually 'serious.' FK SAS foeEVah!"[14]

Sharpton, on the other hand, played this card as deviously as he has played all the others. On his website, he has posted an image from the *New York Daily News* showing him shaking hands with Obama under the headline, "Rev. Al Sharpton Joins President Obama's Immigration Reform Effort."[15] This article was posted well before Obama made waves with his executive orders on this subject. Sharpton was way ahead of the curve. Obama could not have opened the floodgates to our southern border without the blessing of Sharpton—or so he thought. In fact, as Sharpton knew, if he turned against Obama, the media would turn against him, and no one would know what he thought or why it mattered. It is a delicate game he plays.

Not surprisingly, in May 2012, as soon as Obama came out for gay marriage, so did Sharpton. A headline from that period reads, "'Hypocrites': Sharpton Blasts Black Pastors Who Won't Support Obama over His Gay Marriage Stance."[16] Although Sharpton had not yet mastered liberal spin on the issue—he compared homosexuality to Bill Clinton's adultery—he certainly knew where his bread was buttered. If he had to slander black pastors to make his point, so be it.

In early 2015, undercover filmmaker James O'Keefe exposed the way Sharpton was working the system. His reporters engaged in several discussions with black people who had encountered Sharpton in action and were disillusioned by what they had seen. One of them was Erica Snipes, the oldest daughter of Eric Garner, the New York street corner cigarette salesman who died of a heart attack when police tried to subdue him. After a Staten Island grand jury refused to prosecute the police, Al Sharpton swooped in and led the protests. He had earlier paid for the funeral.

When Snipes handed out fliers calling attention to her father's death, the local director of Sharpton's organization "started attacking" Snipes, demanding that she put Sharpton's logo on the fliers. "You think Al Sharpton is kind of like a crook in a sense?" O'Keefe's investigator asks Snipes in a video posted by Project Veritas. "He's about this," she replies, rubbing her fingers together. "He's about money with you?" the reporter asks. "Yeah," Snipes responds.[17] That's how the bloody shirt crew rolled fifty years after Selma.

13

KILLING THE MOCKINGBIRD

I f black Americans—all Americans, for that matter—are to save the nation, they have to reject the culture of blame. This culture leads to a false sense of entitlement, an unquenched fury, and an alienation from conscience and country. The blame mentality infects Americans of every race, putting us at odds with each other—black versus white, women versus men, children versus parents, poor versus rich—and dragging our nation to the brink.

I remember following the trial of Erik and Lyle Menendez here in Los Angeles some twenty years ago. These were two young men who had everything they wanted but wanted more. In the weeks after killing their affluent parents, but before they became suspects in the murder, they spent some seven hundred thousand dollars on all the material things their parents had denied them—cars, clothes, watches, and the like.[1] Once arrested, there was no accusation too depraved for them to lay on their dead parents to excuse their own cold-hearted greed. In a sick way, they reminded me of the boy in the old story who killed his parents and threw himself on the mercy of the court as an orphan. The Menendez brothers refused to accept blame for anything. Blame was for suckers. Their attorneys, of course, encouraged them.

Some years before that, in another high-profile case, then senator Ted Kennedy ducked and dodged mightily to avoid responsibility for the death of a young woman who drowned in a car that he had been driving. "There is no truth whatever to the widely circulated suspicions of immoral conduct that have been leveled at my behavior and hers regarding that evening," he said. "Nor was I driving under the influence of liquor," he insisted. "Although my doctors inform me that I suffered a cerebral concussion as well as shock, I do not seek to escape responsibility for my actions by placing the blame," he concluded, "on the physical and emotional trauma brought on by the accident."[2] Few believed him. Kennedy wore what some said was a phony neck brace for days following the drowning to establish his alibi. He was trying to escape responsibility by blaming his physical condition.

Refusing blame for bad behavior is deeply rooted throughout our shared culture. In black culture, however, refusing blame can launch a movement, especially in the hands of those self-serving "leaders" who have used the black community for their own personal gain. The blame mentality has never been more destructive than it was in Sanford, Florida, in the wake of the Trayvon Martin shooting. In the past, alchemists had specialized in declaring the obviously guilty innocent, especially if the accused were minorities. This practice dated back to the 1920s with the case of Nicola Sacco and Bartolomeo Vanzetti, two Italian anarchists justly accused of murder. In the years since, "civil rights" leaders have ignored the evidence and trumpeted the innocence of one thug after another—Indian FBI-killer Leonard Peltier, Philadelphia cop-killer Mumia Abu Jamal, and many more. Pathetically, in 1995, many in the civil rights community—and a whole lot of ordinary black people—cheered when the conspicuously guilty O. J. Simpson was acquitted by a largely black jury here in Los Angeles.

As real racial injustices grew more and more rare, Sharpton, Jackson, and crew had to look harder to find injustice and, if they could not find it, invent it. In September 2007, for instance, Sharpton and Jackson led a march in a tiny Louisiana town called Jena that drew some twenty thousand clueless marchers.[3] They were there to demand justice for the so-called Jena 6, all of them black and students at the local high school. The Jena 6 first made the news nearly a year earlier when one of them, Mychal Bell, sucker punched a white student and knocked him senseless. The other five then kicked and stomped the victim while he lay out cold.

Jackson and Sharpton knew the facts but came to protest the punishment. At the time they arrived, only Bell, who had been convicted of aggravated second-degree battery, was in jail. With the media's help, they tried to portray Jena justice as something right out of *Mississippi Burning*. It just did not take.

Their efforts fell flat in part because Mychal Bell had four prior arrests for violent crimes before he assaulted his fellow student. He did not make for an attractive poster boy. Nor did his thuggish friends.

What happened to George Zimmerman was of a different order. After the shooting, the civil rights community, aided by the White House and Obama's Justice Department, called for the head of a man that Obama and the DOJ, at least, knew was not guilty. It is one thing to call the guilty innocent. It is altogether scarier to call the innocent guilty.

In the movie *To Kill a Mockingbird*, liberals like to see themselves as Atticus Finch, the noble lawyer holding off the lynch mob with his courage and his shotgun. After the shooting death of Martin, liberals became the lynch mob, and those buffoons who pass themselves off as civil rights leaders were at the head of it, Sharpton and Jackson most conspicuously.

Jackson was in Europe on a political fund-raising gig when the Martin shooting surfaced, so Sharpton made his way to Sanford and took ownership of the protest before Jackson could hustle home. Upon his homecoming, Jackson tried to up the rhetorical ante. He told the media, "There was this feeling that we were kind of beyond racism. That's not true. [Obama's] victory has triggered tremendous backlash."[4] Jackson was trying to convince his audience that racism had intensified since Obama's election. "Blacks are under attack," he told anyone who would listen. Three days after arriving back in America, Jackson was down in Sanford with Sharpton, leading a march and vying with the Reverend Al to see whose shirt was bloodiest. By this time, Sharpton had an advantage. He had a daily talk show on MSNBC, and he used it to spew whatever madness came to mind. That madness was intimidating enough to persuade state officials to charge Zimmerman with second-degree murder.

While Sharpton, Jackson, and other alleged leaders of the movement, like Ben Jealous of the NAACP, were misbehaving in traditional ways, the fringe players of the movement were getting scary. The New Black Panther Party, for instance, offered a ten-thousand-dollar bounty for the capture of "child killer" George Zimmerman and passed out "Wanted Dead or Alive" posters.[5] Meanwhile, the New Black Liberation Militia threatened a citizen's arrest on Zimmerman. "We'll find him. We've got his mug shot and everything," boasted Najee Muhammad.[6]

Legitimately afraid for his life, Zimmerman left Florida to hide out with relatives in the Washington, DC, area. His mother, father, and grandmother also had to abandon their home and go into hiding. This was not easy. Zimmerman's father had been in the hospital for treatment of a heart attack and gotten out just a day before the shooting. His mother-in-law, who lived with the senior Zimmerman and his wife, had Alzheimer's. The so-called civil rights leaders, Obama and Attorney General Eric Holder included, did nothing about the threats, not even scold those making them.

Although Sharpton and Jackson had originally demanded only an arrest and a trial, they really wanted Zimmerman's head and were outraged when he was acquitted. "I do not accept the [verdict]," Jackson shouted from the rooftops. "Not one black lawyer on either side, not one black on the jury, not one male on the jury, and so something about it was stacked from the very beginning," he insisted.[7] The fact is that one out of the six jurors was black in a county in which only one out of ten citizens was black.

For Al Sharpton, the verdict was an "atrocity." He blamed the jurors. "What this jury has done," he said, "is establish a precedent that when you are young and fit a certain profile, you can be committing no crime . . . and be killed and someone can claim self-defense." Then without intending to, Sharpton admitted that without pressure from his mob, the State of Florida would never have indicted Zimmerman. Said Sharpton, "We had to march to even get a trial and even at trial, when he's exposed over and over again as a liar, he is acquitted."[8]

If liberals see themselves as Atticus Finch, they also see themselves as Juror No. 8, the Henry Fonda character in the classic film *Twelve Angry Men*, a man described by the screenwriter as one "who sees all sides of every question and constantly seeks the truth. A man of strength tempered with compassion. Above all, he is a man who wants justice to be done and will fight to see that it is."[9]

The one minority juror, Maddy, a Puerto Rican of African descent, was a chip off the Fonda block. "I was the juror that was going to give them the hung jury," Maddy said on ABC's *Good Morning America* after the trial. But after reviewing the evidence for sixteen hours, she voted to acquit Zimmerman. Said Maddy thoughtfully, "As the law was read to me, if you have no proof that he killed [Martin] intentionally, you can't say he's guilty."[10] This was not exactly the way the law was read to her, but it was a good approximation.

Many in the civil rights community did not appreciate Maddy's attempt to be fair. Maddy told the *Inside Edition* audience, "I've had death threats. On Facebook, someone wrote I'm gonna feel the same pain as Trayvon Martin's mom. Which means I'm gonna lose my son." Maddy is the mother of eight. The blowback cost her her job in a nursing home, her home, and many of her friends. "My whole life has fallen apart," she said.[11]

This was what the bloody shirt phase of the civil rights movement had come to in 2012. Where once its leaders protested injustice, now they were the agents of injustice. When, without provocation, an angry six-foot-tall black thug tried to beat senseless a Hispanic man nearly half a foot shorter, these leaders demanded the Hispanic man be arrested. When he wasn't convicted, they piled abuse on the female jurors, including the one minority juror who struggled to do the right thing in spite of her racial leanings. No one in the civil rights community came to Maddy's defense, not Jackson, not Sharpton, not the president, not the attorney general. As Maddy learned the hard way, the real civil rights movement, like the wicked witch, was not only merely dead; it was really most sincerely dead.

President Obama showed just how dead the movement was with his formal remarks on the occasion of a White House celebration of Black History Month in 2015. In his speech, he spoke of the "courage" protesters at Selma showed fifty years earlier in the face of "terrible violence" and then segued immediately to recognize "the third anniversary of Trayvon Martin's death." You see, the Selma protesters suffered to make sure their children would have a better future. So too did Trayvon's parents, who were in attendance. Said Obama of both, "Progress in this nation happens only because seemingly ordinary people find the courage to stand up for what is right."[12]

Just the day before, after dangling a sword over George Zimmerman's head for three years, the Department of Justice announced it was not going to charge Zimmerman, himself an Obama supporter and civil rights activist, with a hate crime. Trayvon's mother, Sybrina Fulton, was not happy. "Looks like this is our new history," she said. "This is like what is going on now, that they're not holding the person that shoots and kills our young people accountable for what they've done."[13]

If Fulton's words are an example of standing up for what's right, we are living in a strange new world. Let me recap the highlights. Fulton and her husband split when Trayvon was three. He spent most of the next twelve years with his father and stepmother until his father abandoned the stepmother. He bounced back to Sybrina's house, but she kicked him out a few months before his death. After his third suspension from school in one year, now forced to stay with his father's new girlfriend in a strange city, he got high, was wandering in the rain, got angry when Zimmerman took note of his suspicious behavior, and gratuitously attacked him. Refusing to accept any blame for her son's death, Fulton played along with the story line that her son was the victim of a corrupt criminal justice system. This was all bad enough, but what made it worse was that Obama saw fit to invite Fulton to the White House and honor her for her courage. Courage?

Zimmerman saw Obama's speech for the racist blame-shifting it was. "He took what should have been a clear-cut self-defense matter and, still to this day, on the anniversary of incident, he held a ceremony at the White House inviting the Martin-Fulton family and stating that they should take the day to reflect upon the fact that all children's lives matter," said Zimmerman of Obama. "Unfortunately for the president I'm also my parent's child and my life matters as well."[14]

"We don't set aside this month each year to isolate or segregate or put under a glass case black history," said Obama of Black History Month. "We set it aside to illuminate those threads—those living threads that African Americans have woven into the tight tapestry of this nation—to make it stronger, and more beautiful, and more just, and more free."[15] The thread that he just wove about Trayvon Martin was false and divisive. The jury rightly acquitted Zimmerman. Two-thirds of white Americans believed the jury got it right, and a smaller percentage of black Americans believed it as well.

"Trayvon Martin, God rest his soul, he did flip the switch and start beating the hell out of Mr. Zimmerman," said black basketball great Charles Barkley. "I agree with the verdict." He blamed the media for the way the case was misperceived. "Racism is wrong in any [way], shape or form," Barkley said. "A lot of black people are racist too. I think sometimes when people talk about racism, they say only white people are racist, but I think black people are too. I don't think the media has clean hands."[16]

How is it that an outspoken former NBA star could understand the Zimmerman case better than the president? For blacks like Barkley and the whites who followed the case, Obama's praise of Martin's parents was spit in their eye. How could they possibly take his presidency seriously when he was willing to equate the courageous marchers at Selma with the cowardly young thug in Sanford?

I thought I had seen everything, but I hadn't. The blaming-the-victim trend reached a new level of insanity in April 2015 when Kentucky circuit judge Olu Stevens lashed out at a three-year-old and her parents for harboring a stereotyped image of black men. Jordan and Tommy Gray had been home with their daughter, watching *SpongeBob*

SquarePants, when Marquis McAfee and Gregory Wallace, both black and twenty-seven, broke into their home and robbed them at gunpoint. In their victim impact statement, the Grays reported that the incident left their daughter permanently traumatized. "Whenever we are running errands, if we come across a black male, she holds me tight and begs me to leave," wrote Jordan, adding that it "has affected her friendships at school and our relationships with African-American friends."

Judge Stevens, who is black, sentenced Wallace to probation for a home invasion. Probation? His real wrath he reserved for the Grays. "I am offended," said Stevens from the bench. "I am deeply offended that they would be victimized by an individual and express some kind of fear of all black men." He clarified that he was not blaming the three-year-old but rather her parents for "accepting that kind of mentality and fostering those type of stereotypes."[17]

Judges are not supposed to make decisions based on whether they are "offended." They are supposed to follow the rule of law. Stevens was so blinded by his own racism, so intent on evening the score with white people, that he failed to see what the Jordans were saying. Theirs was a cry for sympathy. They were regretting their daughter's stereotyped view of black men. They were not fostering it. You cannot talk a three-year-old out of a trauma. The truth is, you could not talk a thirty-year-old out of that kind of trauma. Black-on-white violence is as traumatic for whites as white-on-black violence was for blacks in the pre–civil rights era. Blacks treasure their scars. Whites are not allowed to acknowledge them.

14

THE STARBUCKS SYNDROME

The blaming mentality could not exist in a vacuum. The fuel that gives it life is white guilt. This guilt was fully and comically on display in March 2015 when Starbucks management decided it would be a good idea if its baristas engaged customers in a discussion of race. According to plan, they would write "Race Together" on customers' cups to foster "an opportunity to begin to re-examine how we can create a more empathetic and inclusive society." In a *Time* magazine piece, business authors David Yoffie and Michael Cusumano called the move by Starbucks CEO Howard Schultz "brilliant."[1] Just about everyone else, left and right, white and black, called the move absurd. As *Adweek* observed, "The clumsy nature of reducing a serious, impossibly complex national conversation to a hashtag on a coffee cup has united Twitter users of all races in roundly denouncing the attempt."[2]

The idea would have made some sense if Starbucks management really wanted to hear honest exchanges. I was tempted to go to Starbucks to start one, but I knew the baristas were preprogrammed to recite the same lame talking points about white racism that the coffee shop crowd has been churning out since the sixties. I saw no point in hassling these young and clueless workers, especially if it meant holding up the people in line behind me.

Had I gone to Starbucks, I would have suggested the barista and I have a conversation about black racism. If my barista had been well trained, he or she likely would have told me there was no such thing as black racism, and that only the people who have power and control can be racist, and I would've had to set her straight. Anybody can be a racist. Racism is an irrational anger that inhabits your heart and controls you. For years, I have seen more of it among blacks than I have among whites.

In an article praising Schultz's idealism, basketball great Kareem Abdul-Jabbar served up the standard fare that we could have expected from a savvy barista. Wrote Abdul-Jabbar in *Time*, "Despite the killings of unarmed African-Americans, despite the evisceration of the Voting Rights Act, despite Oklahoma frat boys singing about lynching blacks, the majority of white Americans don't think racism is still a significant problem."[3] His article disappointed me. Abdul-Jabbar occasionally makes sense, but in this case, he saw the world no more clearly than a guilty white person might.

His article appeared the same day the *Washington Post* "Fact Checker" finally conceded, "'Hands up, don't shoot' did not happen in Ferguson." This was obvious to anyone paying attention months earlier, but people like Abdul-Jabbar apparently did not get the memo. In fact, the *Post* gave the "Hands up, don't shoot" a dreaded "four Pinocchios" for its flagrant dishonesty.[4] Then, too, no one "eviscerated" the Voting Rights Act. That's pure political propaganda. Requiring people to show the same ID to vote that they need to buy a can of beer is just pure common sense. And if Abdul-Jabbar asks us not to judge Islam by the Charlie Hebdo slayings in Paris[5]—or the thousands of other acts of violence committed in its name worldwide—should he be judging white America by the drunken chant of one Oklahoma fraternity?

More disappointing is that Abdul-Jabbar knows something about black racism, black-on-black violence, and black-on-Jewish violence. In 1973, at the peak of his basketball game, he bought a home in Washington, DC, to be used by his Islamic teacher, Hamaas Abdul Khaalis. Khaalis had denounced the head of the overtly racist Nation of Islam (NOI), Elijah Muhammad, as "a lying deceiver." That was true enough to merit a fatwa from the NOI. In one of the most barbaric mass slayings in recent American history, a Philadelphia-based NOI crew descended on Washington and slaughtered seven members of Khaalis's household, all of them black. This included drowning a newborn baby in a bathtub. Four years later, Khaalis, who was not at home during the slaughter, led a crew that took 150 people hostage in Washington, DC, many of them Jews who were beaten and stabbed by Khaalis's crew.[6] I am pretty sure a drunken frat boy chant does not really measure up to either of these assaults as a "significant problem."

That same month as the Starbucks escapade, March 2015, white guilt was turning the shooting death of Tony Robinson, a nineteen-year-old routinely described as "black and unarmed," into still another perverse morality play. The setting had a lot to do with it. If there is a loopier city in the Midwest than Madison, Wisconsin, I do not know what it is. For years people have been calling the city "the People's Republic of Madison," and with good reason. Having a very large university in the heart of the city explains much of the culture. As state capital, the city also is home to thousands of bureaucrats who like high taxes and the great job benefits that come with them.

More than twenty-five years ago, the University of Wisconsin in Madison prohibited "expressive behavior directed at individuals and intended to demean," as though that would magically eliminate hate and violence.[7] All it really eliminated was free speech on campus. It also empowered those who wanted to control speech to want to control more. "Progressives" can never be satisfied. They always want to "progress" in some new direction.

"Progress" in the Tony Robinson case meant sending the officer who shot him to prison for the rest of his life without knowing any of the facts as to why he shot him. "We demand that Matt Kenny be held accountable, be imprisoned, be locked up and charged with murder. And we won't stop until we get justice," said Alix Shabazz, twenty-two, an affiliate of a group called Young, Gifted, and Black.[8]

The facts that were known at the time Shabazz said this did not speak well for Tony Robinson. On the night of the shooting, the police received several 911 calls saying that an "agitated" Robinson was running around in the street, disrupting traffic and attacking pedestrians. Officer Matt Kenny took the call, went to the apartment where Robinson had holed up, and got punched in the head for his efforts. An uncle described Robinson as a "teddy bear," but he was one big mother of a teddy bear at six foot five. He was also clearly out of his head and "unarmed" only in that he did not carry a gun. To save his own life, Kenny shot and killed Robinson. There were no witnesses.

In the real world, people would have waited for the results of the investigation before rushing to judgment, but there is little real about Madison. Police chief Mike Koval made the first concession. He promptly visited the mother of the "victim" and apologized before the body was cold. "We need to start as any healing or any reconciliation should with an 'I'm sorry,' and I've done that privately," Koval told CNN, "and I'm attempting to do that publicly and that's the only way we can sort of begin the healing or the rift that may take years, if at all, to mend."[9] The groveling did not work.

The executive director of the Wisconsin Professional Police Association weighed in next. He tried to convince the world that "Madison, Wisconsin, is not Ferguson, Missouri," and that city cops had a strong relationship with the people they served.[10] No one paid any attention to him either.

Personally, I don't know why anyone needed to apologize, especially to the white mother of the "black teen." Despite her own whiteness, Andrea Irwin described her son as "another black kid shot by the police for no reason." The police obviously had a reason, but what struck me as more curious was that she would describe the boy she gave birth to and raised alone as "black." Playing the race card for what it was worth, she imposed the "one drop" rule on her own flesh and blood and wrote herself out of the equation.

"My son has never been a violent person, never,"[11] Irwin told the media, conveniently ignoring an earlier arrest for an armed home invasion and his attacks that provoked the 911 call. Like so many mothers of the young and thuggish, Irwin refused to accept any responsibility for her son's bad behavior. I am sure it never crossed her mind to apologize to the officer whose life her son had ruined. Like Trayvon's mother, Irwin may not have even known how far astray her son had wandered. Her multiple facial piercings and visible tattoos suggested she had priorities other than raising Tony.

As for Mr. Robinson, he played so little a role in his son's life that it took days for the media to find him for the loving couple "optics" that proved so appealing after the deaths of Trayvon Martin and Michael Brown. Like Martin and Brown before him, Tony Robinson bounced around from relative to relative, but in Madison that was not an issue. Its enlightened citizens seemed to believe the PC propaganda that "one kind of family is as good as another," despite the mountains of evidence to the contrary. That is the kind of propaganda that kills.

Matt Kenny had to be surprised by the rage directed toward him. To this point, he had been a perfectly PC Madison police officer. Just a year earlier, a photograph of him in uniform carrying a cake to help a colleague celebrate her same-sex "wedding" went viral and made Kenney something of a police icon in progressive circles. At crunch time, that cake carrying carried little weight. As Kenny discovered, there is no black in a rainbow, at least not in Madison.

Given all the guilt in Madison, any number of opportunistic groups rushed in to milk it. Thousands rallied day after day to exploit Robinson's death and air their personal gripes. In the progressive rent-a-mob tradition, many showed up by bus, happy to get a day off work or school. In a major traffic-stopping rally a week after the shooting, groups demanded a quick and thorough investigation, an end to the school-to-prison pipeline, and, of course, an increase in the minimum wage. "We've been collaborating with other community organizations to lift Madison businesses to a living wage," Michael Schuler of the First Unitarian Society told the media. What rally in Madison would have been complete without a little wage talk? "It's all the same fight," Bob Hudek of the SEIU Wisconsin State Council insisted.[12]

No, it was not all the same fight. Exploiting white guilt to demand a higher minimum wage may cost jobs, but it doesn't cost lives. The alleged school-to-prison pipeline is another thing. To his detriment, Robinson was spared that pipeline. At the time of his death, he should not have even been out on the streets. Just a year earlier, he and four of his homies broke into a house and got caught by Madison police on the way out. Robinson had in his possession a TV, an Xbox 360, and a BB-gun pistol that looked like the real thing. In any other city that crime would almost assuredly have sent him to prison and saved his life, but not in Madison, where white guilt often trumps common sense. Judge Josann Reynolds sentenced Robinson to three years' probation, and Robinson felt empowered to strike again. Ultimately, white guilt cost him his life.

Come to think of it, it was white guilt that cost Trayvon Martin *his* life as well. Trayvon had the misfortune of attending the Miami-Dade County Public Schools, one of the few districts with its own police department. To prove how enlightened they were, school district executives decided to subvert the school-to-prison pipeline by giving students in-school punishments rather than arresting them for criminal offenses. They did this even before Obama issued an executive order in July 2012 advising school districts to avoid "methods that result in disparate use of disciplinary tools." The White House claimed this new initiative would "improve educational outcomes for African Americans"—at least if it did not kill them first.[13]

On the night of February, 26, 2012, Trayvon Martin was enjoying the fruits of a similar policy. Instead of being back in Miami in a juvenile detention facility, he was wandering through the streets of Sanford, high and angry. On two occasions in the previous few months, school police had detained him for what should have been crimes, once for drugs and another time for possession of stolen female jewelry and a burglary tool. The police fudged his record in both cases to help the department lower arrest statistics for young black men.[14] Trayvon's high school did not even tell his parents the real reason their son had been suspended from school. The parents thought it was everyday mischief, and they left him pretty much to his own devices.

Fueled by marijuana and freed from the consequences of his behavior by white guilt, Trayvon was likely casing the residential community in which he was staying with his father's latest girlfriend when Zimmerman saw him on that rainy February night. Unlike Trayvon's parents, Zimmerman got to know the real Trayvon. He understood there was no room for white guilt when you're getting your head bashed against the sidewalk. As we've discussed, the outcome for Trayvon was fatal. The outcome for the school superintendent, however, was fabulous. A year after Trayvon's death, he was awarded the FBI Director's Community Leadership Award "in recognition of his work enhancing students' academic enrichment."[15]

Having learned nothing from Trayvon's death, the Obama Department of Justice took the Ferguson, Missouri, Police Department to the woodshed for arresting high school students who had committed crimes. The DOJ accused them of showing "insufficient appreciation for the negative educational and long-term outcomes that can result from treating disciplinary concerns as crimes."[16] Three years after Trayvon's death, the DOJ was insisting Ferguson adopt the very same strategy that had killed Trayvon. The media applauded the DOJ. White guilt kills.

15

OUTSIDE LOOKING IN

The man peering through the window of his ex-wife's condo on South Bundy had a secret that very few knew. His father, "Sweet Jimmy" Simpson, had decided that the gay scene then brewing down the hill in San Francisco's famed Castro district was much more enticing than his dreary life with Eunice and the four kids in the housing projects up above on Potrero Hill. So Jimmy "came out," which was bad enough, and then he took off, which was even worse. He left the management of his son, Orenthal James, in the hands of his wife, Eunice.

But try as she might, Eunice could not teach young O. J. to be a man.[1]

O. J. never talked publicly about his father's sexual proclivities. I can understand why. One of the worst traumas for a boy is to discover his father is gay. To make matters worse, Sweet Jimmy Simpson reportedly became a drag queen and later died of AIDS.

O. J. had to know what his father was up to, but he probably did not want to reflect on it. Given what the world learned of Simpson, it became clear he had little confidence in his own masculinity. He was hardly unique. The absence of fathers in the black community has left many a young boy having no one else to identify with but his mother or grandmother, and these women, intentionally or not, often turn their sons and grandsons against their fathers. These boys may not be "gay," but in identifying with the women in their family, they lack the strength and resolution to become the man society needs them to be.

Dr. David Gutmann, a psychology professor at Northwestern University, was the very rare academic to talk about what went wrong in

Simpson's early life. He believes that every boy needs a "true patriarch" in his life. I was fortunate to have one in my grandfather. At BOND we teach young men to become patriarchs. One fellow, Marquis, entered our counseling program because he had had enough of the empty bravado of false masculinity. He did well in the program and summed up his accomplishment. "I am so glad I am a man," he told me. "I love being a man"—not *the* man, a man.

Simpson, like so many young boys today, did not have a patriarch in his life, at least not when he needed it most. According to Guttman, it is the patriarch who shows a boy how to move beyond his mother's apron strings and into the world as a mature young man, one capable of disciplining himself and making decisions with long-term impact. Boys without such a patriarch find what Guttman calls "less trustworthy ways" to distance themselves from their mothers. "Physical distance," says Gutmann, "they achieve by flight: from the mother's home to the streets, to the fighting gangs that rule them and, at the end of the day, to the all-male fraternity of the penitentiary." They achieve social distance "by moving out of the mother's cultural world, and off her scale of values." In Simpson's case, he would bring that scale of values down with him.

In the '60s, as Simpson struggled to come of age, many other young black males were finding themselves without fathers as well. He roamed with several of them in a street gang known as the Persian Warriors. "These children," writes Guttman, "particularly need fathers who are different from their estimable mothers in equally admirable ways: tough without being macho brutes, stern without being petty tyrants, and yes, affectionate—but on the whole, less nurturing than their wives."[2] In California in the 1960s, there was a growing shortage of such men. Why their numbers were diminishing is a mystery only to the alchemists, whose formulas were responsible for the epidemic of fatherlessness.

To all the world, Simpson gave the impression that he could escape the traps that ensnare young black men. His immense athletic skills attracted attention when he was an adolescent, including that of baseball great Willie Mays. Mays mentored Simpson during his teen years and lured him from the gang life into which he was descending. In college and in the pros, Simpson had coaches who could set his goals and steer him toward them. With that daily discipline that all boys crave, Simpson flourished.

Still, there was a void in Simpson's life, and he knew it. "I resented his absence, especially when I became a teen-ager and was trying to find out who I was," he said of his father in a *Parents* magazine interview in 1977. "I really needed a man around then for guidance. I get along with my father now, but it's taken years for me to come to terms with my feelings."[3] As time would tell, he never did come to terms.

"The troubles of a poorly fathered son," says Gutmann, "can afflict not only his childhood and adolescence, but his later years as well." Never was this truer than in the case of O. J. At nineteen, Simpson married his high school sweetheart, a young black woman named Marguerite Whitley. He knew more or less what was expected of him as a husband and father, but he did not have the wherewithal to become the patriarch that all men aspire to be. A deeply Christian woman, Marguerite tried to keep her husband on the straight and narrow, but he was young and immature and the world was tempting. Still, Simpson never hit her. "If he did," Marguerite would later tell Barbara Walters, "he would have got a frying pan upside his head. There was just no way that I would allow that to happen to me."[4]

Three years after their marriage, the couple separated. They reconciled, but three years later Marguerite asked her lawyer to start divorce proceedings. By this time, the couple already had two children. The divorce did not go through, and the family moved back to California in 1977. Now thirty years old and at the top of his game, Simpson began casting about for someone younger and whiter than Marguerite and found her at a nightclub called the Daisy. The eighteen-year-old waitress, Nicole Brown, was bold and beautiful, as much a symbol perhaps of the white man's privilege as a new Ferrari or a gated home in Brentwood. Brown and Simpson began dating that year, the same year his third child, Aaren, was born. He made little effort to hide this relationship from his friends or even from Marguerite.

The year 1979 was Simpson's last as a professional athlete. It was not a happy one. His family was falling apart. His unhappy wife reportedly was threatening to hurt him. Divorce loomed. And most tragically of all, Aaren, not yet two, drowned in the family swimming pool. Simpson found no relief that year on the football field. With him sitting on the bench with injuries for much of the season, the San Francisco 49ers set a record for most games lost in which they held a lead—twelve. They would win only two games all season. At season's end, removed from the necessary disciplines of the locker room, Simpson was on his own. He was not ready. He never would be. Yet to all but the closest of observers, he gave no sign of the rage that abandoned children almost always feel.

In 1985, Simpson and Brown married. They would have two children together, Sydney and Justin, but their union would not be one of "wedded bliss."

Their troubles began well before their marriage. At some unspecified point before their wedding, Nicole sent O. J. a letter that was submitted in evidence during Simpson's civil trial for the wrongful deaths of Nicole and Ron Goldman. It speaks volumes about the kind of unresolved problems that abandonment causes. "I assumed that your recurring nasty attitude & mean streak was to cover up your cheating & a general disrespect for women & a lack of manners!"[5] Nicole wrote of the premarital years. She had assumed that once they were married his behavior would change.

It did. It got worse.

"I wanted to be a wonderful wife!" Nicole wrote. "I thought it was finally gonna be you & me—you wanted a baby (so you said) & I wanted a baby—then with each pound [I gained] you were terrible. You gave me dirty looks, looks of disgust—said mean things to me at times about my appearance[,] walked out on me & lied to me." Nicole apparently worked furiously to get back in shape after Sydney's birth, but it did no good. Simpson had selected her to be his trophy, the female equivalent of a Ferrari, the symbol of his status in the world. She had to look not just good but great, all the time. For a new mother, this was not possible. Simpson was less than understanding. Nicole wrote, "You beat the holy hell out of me & we lied at the X-ray lab & said I fell off a bike, Remember!??"[6] Nicole wanted more from Simpson than he was capable of delivering.

Like many young men who grew up as he did, Simpson had a love-hate relationship with women that traced back to his ambivalent relationship with his mother. He needed a woman to fill the void in his life, but never having seen a mature relationship between a man and a woman up close, he deeply resented the expectations his wife put upon him, and he cheated at will. A white wife like Nicole was particularly vulnerable because she had not been hardened by experience. She expected O. J. to be decent, but that just tempted him to flaunt his indecency.

At the same time, Simpson so feared the emptiness and unhappiness he felt when alone that he could never quite let the woman go. Nicole felt the whiplash. At one point in their marriage, she called the police "to save my life." As best she could, however, she kept the story out of the media, in part to preserve the image of "my wonderful life with the superstar that wonderful man, O. J. Simpson the father of my kids." Nicole believed the media would side with her husband.[7]

In 1992, the couple divorced. Justin Simpson was three. He would get to live the life of a fatherless boy much as O. J. had, but even more traumatically. Two years later, he would lose his mother as well. Her murder would shock everyone but Nicole and her closest confidantes. She saw it coming. Even after their divorce, Simpson continued to hound her, to haunt her life. Friends said he was still obsessed with her despite his having a steady girlfriend of his own. Even though they would date occasionally during this period, Nicole never lost her fear of Simpson. And with good reason. On the night of October 25, 1993, less than a year before her death, Simpson broke the back door of the house and stormed in. Nicole called the police. "My ex-husband has just broken into my house and he's ranting and raving outside the front yard," Nicole told the dispatcher. When asked if he was drunk, she answered, "No. But he's crazy."[8]

As Nicole explained, this was one of many times she had had to call the police. "Please leave," she begged Simpson, worried that the two children sleeping upstairs would be dragged into the middle of the disturbance. "I'm leaving with my two f***ing fists is when I'm leaving," Simpson can be heard saying. "You ain't got to worry about me any more."[9] Nicole obviously had a lot to worry about.

I have talked before about the emptiness of men like Simpson. Here he was, wealthy, well loved by the public, still in great physical shape, single, and capable of luring half the women in California with a snap of his fingers. And yet he was hollow inside, a man with a big house and no home, pushing fifty but living like a bachelor, not the patriarch all men aspire to be. Lacking confidence and still controlled by an anger he did not even understand, Simpson raged inside. Like so many black men, even ones held in high esteem by people of all races, he turned his anger toward white people.

It did not surprise me that he beat his white wife but not his black one. Nicole was a softer, more inviting target. A little more surprising was that he was more jealous of white men than black ones. The fact that white men might be seeing his ex-wife made him literally crazy. When he stormed Nicole's house that October night in 1993, he raged about a man called "Keith," some inconsequential white guy Nicole was seeing some time back. It made him wild with rage too when he saw Ron Goldman, a twenty five-year-old waiter at the nearby Mezzaluna restaurant, driving the white Ferrari he had given Nicole, now thirty-five, as a present.

On June 11, 1994, the last day of her life, Nicole and others in the Brown family attended a dance recital for Nicole's daughter, Sydney, now nine. When Simpson arrived, the Browns gave him the cold shoulder. Having arrived late, he could not a find a seat, and he brooded visibly. Even if he could not give voice to it, something about that recital must have reminded him he had failed as a father. He recognized again how estranged he had become from these white people with whom he had once been close. They did not invite him to dinner afterward with his children.

By all accounts that dinner was a happy one. The Browns were quietly celebrating the fact that Nicole had gotten O. J. out of her life. Or so she thought. Possibly as a pretext, Nicole had Goldman bring to her home some glasses her mother had left behind. While the children slept upstairs, she awaited Goldman below. What happened in the hours that followed has never been truthfully told, as only Simpson remains alive to tell the story.

From what I know of his history and the details of the case, I can imagine what happened. I can see Simpson lurking outside the home, seething with a fury he could not explain even to himself. He had plenty of money, a gorgeous white girlfriend, great health, tons of friends, but a festering anger that made everything else seem like nothing. Like so many men deprived of fathers, he was, in a way, always on the outside looking in. Unable or unwilling to see himself for who he was, he could only see who he was not. As comfortable as he seemed to be in the white world, he had been exposed, just as I had, to those same voices all his life telling him where to channel his anger. I never exploded quite as he did, but before I forgave my parents and purged my soul, I came close.

I imagine Simpson looking through the window and seeing Nicole entertaining a white man more than twenty years younger than he was, and he blew like a volcano, all that rage spewing out. Dr. Gutmann makes the case that Simpson gave the appearance of having matured, but as a desperate final attempt at asserting his masculinity, he turned as recklessly violent as a street thug and slashed both Goldman and Brown to death, nearly severing Nicole's head in the process. Knowing something about this kind of anger, I know that Simpson was not in his right mind when he killed them. I do believe, though, that in the days that followed, his remorse and guilt were real.

Four days after Nicole Simpson's body was discovered, O. J. Simpson was famously riding down the 405 in his white Bronco. The police were on his tail. His old pal Al Cowlings was at the wheel. And Simpson had a gun to his head while Cowlings negotiated his surrender with the police. At this point, the mama syndrome kicked in. Simpson had one request: to return to his Brentwood house for one last telephone call. He wanted to talk to his mother. This did not surprise me at all. In his world, mama was god. No matter what he did, she would forgive him, protect him, defend him. That is why a man-child like Simpson would never criticize mama. He may have quietly hated her, but he would tell the world he loved her. It is a complex, screwed-up relationship, but one that afflicts most males abandoned by their fathers and raised by their mothers.

Once the lawyers got hold of him, Simpson yielded to this new discipline. He was part of a team once again. He shut down his emotions and hit the line as hard as he had to in order to win. Knowing the composition of the jury, I knew how the verdict would fall. I could foresee as well the different way blacks and whites would react. Oprah Winfrey showed the verdict live to a studio audience, composed almost entirely of females. White America learned a lot that day. While the whites in Oprah's audience sat in stunned silence, the black women jumped to their feet and cheered without shame. To her credit, Oprah looked as horrified by this reaction as the white women in her audience.[10]

Although many black men cheered when they heard the verdict, it was the women who seemed most thrilled. If white women identified with Nicole, black women did not. By and large, they resent white women who "steal" their men with a strategic toss of their long, flowing locks, especially beautiful women like Nicole, with their fair skin and blonde hair. That verdict revealed to a lot of innocent white people how black people really feel. There were many friendships that did not survive the day.

For a moment I was optimistic. Maybe, I thought, white people, women especially, would finally have the courage to entertain honest discussions about the policies that were destroying the black family in America. It did not happen. Turtle-like, whites stuck their heads out of their shells, shook them in dismay, and pulled them back in. The fate of the black family would be left to the ideologues, the activists, and the race hustlers who had been working to destroy it for decades.

16

THE ABSENT BLACK FATHER "MYTH"

The moment of Simpson's acquittal was a rare one in media history. For just a moment, the alchemists lost control of the race narrative, but they did not lose it for long. Within days they were back to writing about race as though the Simpson trial never happened. If anything, they were working even harder to cover up the mess they'd helped make of black American life.

I could cite a thousand articles to make this point, but a 2014 article by Tara Culp-Ressler in the liberal online journal *ThinkProgress* does the job better than I could. The very title, "The Myth of the Absent Black Father,"[1] tells you where this article is heading. I deal with the unhappy products of that "myth" every day, the sad, broken young men who come to BOND for healing. It should not surprise you that Tara is a pretty young white girl from central Pennsylvania. She may even mean well. Many alchemists do. But as they say around here, the road to hell is paved with good intentions.

"Although black fathers are more likely to live separately from their children—the statistic that's usually trotted out to prove the parenting 'crisis'—many of them remain just as involved in their kids' lives," writes Ms. Culp-Ressler. "Pew estimates that 67 percent of black dads who don't live with their kids see them at least once a month, compared to 59 percent of white dads and just 32 percent of Hispanic dads."

Think about what Culp-Ressler said. She boasts that black fathers do a better job than white or Hispanic fathers because they are more likely to see them "at least once a month." True, there might be many more such absentee fathers, but she suggests that a father seeing the kids once a month somehow compensates for his not being in the home. Tara fails to mention that half of all black children live with their mothers only, with no father present, compared to just 8 percent of Asian children. Even more dramatic, black children are nearly *eight times* likelier than white kids to live in a home with a single mother.[2] And yet Culp-Ressler, and so many alchemists like her, tells us that the black fatherless issue is a "myth," and that there is "concrete evidence" to prove it's a myth. No, Tara, your evidence is not concrete. It is sand.

In mocking the alleged "crisis," a word she feels the need to put in quotes, Ms. Culp-Ressler has nothing to say about the effect that two parents have on a family's financial well-being. The fact is that black two-parent families outearn black single-parent families by about four to one. As might be expected, children in black single-parent homes are about five times more likely to live in poverty than black children living with both parents.[3] What statistics cannot measure is the effect on a boy's future of watching a father set the alarm clock each night, get up each morning, and go to work. Some boys have no idea that this is the way the world works.

Without a father, boys lack other skills as well. They likely know little about tools or crafts. They probably have never changed a tire or even hammered a nail. They may not know how to drive a car, and if they do, they probably don't know how to work a standard shift. If something breaks in their world, the mother calls the manager and hopes he shows up. When they finish school—if they finish school—these boys bring few if any skills to a potential job site and likely a poor work ethic as well. This failure to transmit a work ethic has been going on for generations. I had a grandfather to rely on, but many people today have not had a real man in their family, a provider and protector, since their ancestors left the South.

Tara Culp-Ressler gets so much backward you wonder whether she did it on purpose. Her handling of the Adrian Peterson case is an example of that very backwardness. In October 2013, the two-year-old son of

Peterson, a star Minnesota Vikings running back, died. He had been beaten to death by his mother's boyfriend. The *Headline News* article on his death, like all other mainstream reports, was sympathetic to Peterson. The article includes a tweet from basketball great LeBron James: "So Damn sad man! Makes no sense at all. Innocent kid with dreams gets taking away by a coward with no dreams at all! Smh #SickForAP."[4] And yet as Culp-Ressler interpreted events, the media were at fault. She scolds them, in fact, for "falling back on black stereotypes."

In truth, almost no one in 2013 mentioned just how messy Peterson's life was. Although unmarried and just twenty-eight at the time of his son's death, he reportedly had seven or so children. When asked the exact number, Petersen told the reporters at ESPN, "I know the truth, and I'm comfortable with that knowledge."[5] They didn't push or scold. Before things went bad, the media never mentioned Peterson's behavior as a problem, and the fans did not care as long as he was playing well. Alchemists had assured us time and again that families come in all kinds and shapes and that the problem in black families was a "myth."

True to form, Peterson grew up in an unstable home himself. His parents, both college athletes, never bothered marrying. Alchemists said they did not have to. When he was thirteen, his father was busted for his involvement in a crack cocaine ring and served seven years in prison. Peterson picked up a couple of half brothers along the way, one of whom would be murdered.

Not surprisingly, Peterson proved to be an even more unstable parent than his father. Just look at how his two-year-old son died. Like so many black children, the boy had multiple names, but Peterson wasn't one of them. Some called him Tyrese Ruffin after Bobby Ruffin, the man who helped raise him. Some called him Tyrese Doohen after his mom, Ann "Ashley" Doohen. Doohen had hooked up with Ruffin after Peterson abandoned her, and then dropped Ruffin for a guy named Joey Patterson.

Like so many "boyfriends," Patterson saw his girlfriend's kid as a nuisance and beat Tyrese to death. The first time Peterson met his son, he was still in a coma. "Daddy is sorry," Peterson said to the child, and the media sighed. Ms. Culp-Ressler described the boy as having "tragically passed away." No, Tara, he was murdered, and at the time the media gave Peterson a pass. They should not have.

Peterson did not get in real trouble with the law or the media until the fall of 2014, when he was charged with reckless or negligent injury to a child.[6] He might have skated even then except that all eyes were on the NFL as a result of an incident involving Baltimore Ravens star running back Ray Rice. In February 2014, Rice knocked out Janay Palmer, the mother of his daughter, in an Atlantic City casino elevator and then dragged her out of the elevator by her feet. Although the dragging part of the incident was shown early on, it was not until the video of the attack in the elevator went public that the NFL got serious about disciplining Rice and the public got upset with the NFL.

Soon thereafter, Rice married Palmer and publicly apologized. He told the media he was "working every day to be a father, a better husband and a better role model."[7] In all fairness, Rice did not have anyone to model himself on growing up. When he was just a year old, his father was killed in a drive-by shooting. A male cousin looked out for him after his father's death, but the cousin was killed in a car crash when Rice was eleven. Rice had no place to learn about responsible male adulthood and too many people telling him the lessons weren't worth learning. He had no idea how to treat women, no idea how to step up and be a man.

In the summer of 2014, Adrian Peterson married Ashley Brown, the mother of their three-year-old child. A few days after the Rice affair exploded in the media, Peterson was arrested for child abuse. He had given one of his two four-year-old sons—from two different mothers— a whupping with a small tree branch, usually called a switch. The boy apparently had pushed another one of Peterson's children.

Growing up when I did in Alabama, I felt the sting of a switch on my backside more than once. In fact, my grandmother would send me out to find a switch she could hit me with. The first time I had to find my own switch, I chose the thinnest one I could find before I realized the thin ones hurt more. I did not complain because I knew I deserved what I had coming. I also realized my grandmother did this out of love. It really did hurt her more than it hurt me, and I could see the pain in her eyes. Plus, she never drew blood.

Peterson, by contrast, hit the boy hard enough to leave cuts and bruises so extensive on his back, ankles, buttocks, genitals, and legs, that he was indicted by a grand jury in Montgomery County, Texas.[8] Even on my worst day, my grandmother never hit like that. More to the point, Peterson did not have the kind of connection to the boy he beat that I had with my grandmother. He was not married to or living with the boy's mother. He felt little more kinship with the child than boyfriend Joey Patterson had for little Tyrese, Peterson's dead son. For the record, Patterson is Asian. Doheen, the mother, is white. Peterson is black. The problem spans all races. It is not an NFL problem, as the media pretended it was. This is a cultural problem, one that is particularly severe in the black community because that is where fatherlessness has reached epidemic proportions. The absence of a father in a home can destroy a home. The absence of a father in multiple homes can destroy a community. But we're not supposed to talk about it.

During the hubbub about Rice and Peterson, the media chose to blame the NFL. They refused to ask how black NFL players were doing compared to black men of that age who were not in the NFL. The unfortunate truth is that the NFL players were doing much better. According to the Bureau of Justice statistics cited by the NAACP in its fact sheet, one in three black men can expect to end up in prison.[9] For NFL players, the number is probably more like one in three hundred. As violent as the game can be, football provides young men, many of them from fractured families, the kind of mentoring and discipline most young black men will never know.

At six foot four and weighing in at three hundred pounds, Ferguson's Michael Brown should have been playing football. If he had, he would likely be alive today. Compare his fate with that of Michael Oher, a youth of comparable size saved from a life of neglect first by a black coach and then by a white Christian family who adopted him and later told his story in the book and movie *The Blind Side*. As a result of this attention and care, Oher became a star left tackle in the NFL and a multimillionaire in the process.

Michael Oher excepted, the media pay much less attention to those black men who are doing the right thing. One of them—also named Adrian Peterson—was a running back for the Chicago Bears from 2002 to 2009. Although of lesser talent than his namesake, he is of greater character. Despite a speech defect, Peterson graduated from college; married his girlfriend, Angela; and raised four children with her as his wife. In June 2014, their six-year-old son, AJ, was diagnosed with inoperable brain cancer. For the next eight months, Peterson turned his full attention to AJ and cared for him as only a full-time father could. On February 17, 2015, Peterson wrote on Facebook: "#Ajsoars is in Heaven, where he belongs . . . #ajsoar #P3 #MyFirstSuperHero.'"[10] Imagine how different AJ's last eight months would have been if he had been one of the other Adrian Peterson's many and scattered children. A real father in the home does not just keep his son out of trouble. He provides love and support and security when trouble hits.

The NAACP has no sense of this. Its fact sheet cites a number of "contributing factors" as to why young black men are more likely to end up in prison. Given their Du Bois legacy, the editors of this sheet prefer to blame the criminal justice system.[11] Booker T. Washington would have focused his attention on the individual and the community. Once he did, he would have had no trouble either discovering the truth or telling it.

The death of Peterson's son Tyrese at the hand of an unrelated male speaks to a problem that alchemists stubbornly and perversely refuse to acknowledge, namely, the role that "boyfriends" play in child abuse. According to the federal government's Fourth National Incidence Study of Child Abuse and Neglect, children who live with their mother and her "boyfriend" are roughly eleven times more likely to suffer sexual, physical, or emotional abuse than those children who live with their married biological parents and six times more likely to suffer neglect.[12] These figures alone should silence those self-righteous knuckleheads who insist that all family types are equally good.

"We live in an increasingly diverse world, and that's true even for family structures," the Southern Poverty Law Center (SPLC) insists. The SPLC sees as a good thing the fact that "more children are being raised by single parents, by same-sex parents, by grandparents, [and] in blended families."[13] The SPLC thrives on attributing "hate" to people who tell the truth—even when children's lives are at risk. They insist that we "learn to appreciate, rather than fear, differences and to recognize bias and stereotypes when [we] see them." By their standards, and they are typical in educational circles, if I point out that children living with their mothers' boyfriends are in grave danger, and the danger factor goes through the roof when the boyfriend is left in charge, I am just perpetuating a stereotype. This is crazy.

The federal study came to another conclusion that the alchemists want us to ignore. Unmarried parents who cohabit are four times more likely than married parents to abuse their kids and three times more likely to neglect them. The bottom line is that children who live in a stable environment with married parents are much safer than children who don't. For all the talk of child safety—bicycle helmets, car seats, bullying campaigns, gun locks, cigarettes—why do progressive thought leaders scold anyone who talks about the most basic safety issue? The reason is that the nuclear family is the single greatest deterrent to socialism. A functioning nuclear family does not need much in the way of government help.

Although the problem in the United States is most severe in the black community because of the fatherlessness epidemic, wherever in the world children live with someone other than their married parents, they suffer. A family Court Reporter Survey for England and Wales, for instance, presented hard evidence that children were twenty to thirty-three times safer living with their biological married parents than in other family arrangements.[14]

Elsewhere, too, soft-headed leaders ask their citizens not to notice the numbers behind headlines such as "Couple Jailed for Life in One of Britain's Worst Child Abuse Cases." According to Australia's ABC News, a four-year-old boy died of head injuries after being systematically starved for months by—who?—a single woman and her drug-abusing boyfriend. Yet ABC assigned the larger blame to "the failure to act by Daniel's school and social services. . . . Teachers, health professionals and social services and police missed signs that Daniel was being ill-treated."[15] Not a word suggested that state-subsidized family breakdown had anything to do with the death.

Family instability comes in many shapes and forms. A former Muslim from Egypt, Nonie Darwish, has written about the problems in Islamic homes that are very similar to the kinds of problems I have seen. Darwish claims that polygamy has had much the same kind of devastating effect on the Muslim family that fatherlessness has had on black families. The reality, as she sees it, is that a man's loyalty, when divided between multiple wives, can never bring peace, stability, or trust to any of the family members involved, especially the children.

These anxious, oppressed mothers are responsible for raising their sons when young. They tend to shift their loyalties away from the unreliable husband to their firstborn son. "The son becomes her man and her defender," writes Darwish, "very often against his own father, whom he blames for marrying a second wife." My guess is that those sons also resent their mothers for alienating them from their fathers. Angry and unstable, they join, not street gangs, but ISIS or al-Qaeda to find their identity. Yet, just as the alchemists blame poverty at home for street crime, they blame poverty in the Muslim world for jihad. In neither case is poverty the problem. Darwish knows the real problem—and the solution. "None of this would be necessary if marriage was considered a holy covenant between one man and woman," she writes, "which would transfer the loyalty and trust to the basic nucleus of the family from where all trust comes: the husband and wife."[16]

17

FAKE AUTHENTICITY

"Let me tell you, the things that's about to happen, to these honkeys, these crackers, these pigs, these pink people, these people. It has been long overdue." So said Michelle Williams, chief of staff for an outfit called the New Black Panther Party, during an interview regarding the Trayvon Martin case. "My prize right now this evening," Williams continued, "is gonna be the bounty, the arrest, dead or alive, for George Zimmerman. You feel me?"[1]

Williams made these comments before the State of Florida even charged Zimmerman with a crime. He was a free man at the time, but understandably, given the threats, he was in hiding. So tolerant have the media become of threatening, bullying behavior by radical blacks—even death threats—that Williams got off with an apology. "Are they negative? Are they harsh?" she said to a 10 News reporter in Tampa of her earlier comments. "Yes, I will be the first to admit that. I have a passion when it comes to the justice system here in America. I have a passion when it comes to race."[2]

Harsh? Threatening to take someone's life is way worse than "harsh." It is criminal, but black "leaders" like Williams, or even slightly more civilized ones like Jesse Jackson or Al Sharpton, are held to a different standard than white leaders. If Zimmerman had said anything like what Williams did, before or after the shooting, he would have been sent to prison for a long, long time on a hate crime charge. Our black leaders, though, can call whites "crackers" as Williams did, or "hymies," as Jackson did, or "homos," as Sharpton did, and face nothing worse than a slap on the wrist, if that.

It didn't used to be this way. Growing up, I rarely heard racial slurs being uttered by either blacks or whites. I was only called "nigger" once in my whole life by white people, and that was forty years ago in Chicago. A friend and I were walking down the street when a carful of young toughs shouted "niggers" at us. I know we were supposed to be all upset, but it struck us as so stupid we both started laughing. Those black leaders who swoon at the notion that someone somewhere was called a racial slur of some sort are playing games. When they hear a racial slur—or even something that sounds like a slur—what they really hear is the *cha-ching* of a cash register. The object of the game is to make white people feel guilty and control them through their guilt.

No matter what young black people may try to tell you, most of them have never been called a "nigger" by a white person. They may not have even heard a white person use the word. Some black people will say that a white person called them some slur or another, but they will often make this claim to justify what they did next, like punch the white person out. I stopped believing these claims a long time ago. Today, there are more racial hoaxes than there are real white-on-black racial incidents.

That said, young blacks have heard the word *nigger* thousands of times. In fact, most of them have been called "nigger." The people doing the calling are, of course, black themselves. More and more, black people—Michelle Williams is a good example—have little hesitation about using racial slurs to talk about white people. I hear words like *redneck*, *cracker*, and *honky* frequently in LA. On national TV recently, a black basketball player said of a white player, "F*** that nigga" and got away with it. This coarsening of the language goes hand in glove with the coarsening of the culture.

Black leaders need to take some responsibility for the cultural breakdown. Too often they ignore bad behavior or even applaud it as "authentic," but it is not even that. As black economist Thomas Sowell observes, there is nothing authentically black about crude language, immoral behavior, and violence. "Violence was far more common in the South—and in those parts of Britain from which Southerners came," writes Sowell. "So was illegitimacy, lively music and dance, and a style of religious oratory marked by strident rhetoric, unbridled emotions, and flamboyant imagery. All of this would become part of the cultural legacy of blacks, who lived for centuries in the midst of the redneck culture of the South."[3]

Although most whites and blacks have abandoned the rough-and-tumble culture of the old South, the lifestyle, says Sowell, survives among the least educated blacks and those, black and white, who think imitating them is cool. He accuses the alchemists, in fact, of "aiding and abetting a counterproductive ghetto lifestyle that is essentially a remnant of the redneck culture which handicapped Southern whites and blacks alike for generations."

This trend began in the 1960s. Until then, blacks aspired to the same thing whites did—a good job, marriage, children, home ownership. Black parents fought to get their kids into good schools, and once in those schools, the kids worked hard to succeed. They dressed "sharp" when they went to school. They spent hours practicing sports or playing musical instruments. They did their homework. They knew they could grab a much bigger slice of the American dream than their parents had, and most young people went after it. When I return to Alabama, I see much of this same spirit still alive. I am amazed by how many more blacks I see working than I do in Los Angeles. I see too a much warmer, more natural relationship between blacks and whites than I see in LA and other big cities.

In America's cities, the most evil white supremacist could not have done a better job than the alchemists did in turning this all upside down. Today, as Sowell points out, "They denounce any criticism of the ghetto lifestyle or any attempt to change it." Teachers are not supposed to correct black youngsters who speak "black English," and no one is supposed to be judgmental about the whole lifestyle of "black rednecks." As she showed in her interview on Tampa TV, Michelle Williams is perfectly capable of speaking standard English. In her rants, though, she goes ghetto. She thinks speaking that way is authentic. As Sowell says, though, if it is authentically anything, it is authentically redneck.

One of the clearest indicators of how "redneck" black culture has gone is obvious to those who follow music. In his own backward way, white rapper Eminem has a better handle on the nature of the "authentic" black personality than do all the heads of all the sociology departments across the land. Born Marshall Mathers III, Eminem never knew his father. The man split before the boy was old enough to know he was gone. When Eminem tried to contact him, the letters would come back "Return To Sender." His drug-addled mother dragged him around the Midwest for the first eleven years of his life before settling in a largely black neighborhood on the east side of Detroit. He never forgave her.[4]

In Detroit, Eminem found relief from constant bullying by mastering rhyming skills and taking them public in local freestyle throw-downs. His loveless, disordered childhood and trailer park roots played well in the rap world and lent him an air of authenticity. In the climactic scene of *8 Mile*, a movie based on his life, he humiliates a would-be black gangster rapper in a throw-down. "This guy's a gangster?" Eminem asks before exposing his competitor for what he is: "His real name's Clarence. And Clarence lives at home with both parents." If that were not humiliating enough, Eminem tells the largely black audience that Clarence attends a prep school and his parents "have a real good marriage."[5]

Eminem gets it. Authenticity is accessible to anyone who wallows in his own sty, black or white. Jealous of kids with two parents, rappers like Eminem have interpreted a good family life as a sign of weakness, of whiteness. They have done the same with good grades, clean living, hard work, and marriage. "In that culture," confirms Sowell, "belligerence is considered being manly and crudity is considered cool, while being civilized is regarded as 'acting white.'"

I grew up listening to people like Diana Ross, James Brown, Otis Redding, the Temptations—the whole Motown lineup, for that matter. These people did not sing about how angry they were or who they wanted to humiliate or even kill. They sang about relationships, and almost always with respect for the one they loved. These relationships often ended in marriage. The song "You Send Me" by one of my favorites, Sam Cooke, had lyrics like "I find myself wanting to marry you and take you home."[6] The Dixie Cups sang, "Goin' to the chapel and we're gonna get married."[7] Al Green sang, "Let's stay together . . . whether good or bad, happy or sad."[8] Today, you have to look far and wide to find any reference to marriage in a song that is not some sort of punch line.

A more typical song today is Kanye West's "Monster," with charming lyrics like "So mommy best advice is to get on top of this" and "My presence is a present kiss my ass,"[9] and these are some of the cleaner lyrics. The video version is more troubling still. Critic Melinda Tankard Reist placed it in the "dead-bitches-are-the-best" theme with its "scenes of a murderous rampage with most of the dead being women. Dead women in lingerie swing from chains around their necks. Naked female corpses adorn the furniture. Two other female bodies are joined by West in bed."[10]

West has made a fortune imitating fake authentic blacks and selling their angry, misogynistic, antiwhite ghetto style to the culture at large. You would never guess it listening to his music or hearing him speak, but West's late mother had been chair of the English Department at Chicago State University before she retired. At age ten he attended school in Nanjing, China, and learned Chinese. In high school in Chicago, West got all As and Bs and received a scholarship to attend Chicago's American Academy of Art before dropping out to pursue his music career.[11] West's public persona, though, is gangster, or at least a bad imitation of the same. The song "We Don't Care" on his early album *College Dropout* set the tone: "We dont care what people say/ My Niggas/ drug dealin jus to get by stack ya money till it gets sky high."[12] This was easy enough for West to say. If his music thing did not work out, he had a nice home to return to. Not all his "Niggas" were so lucky.

West does have something in common with less fortunate blacks. His father, a former Black Panther, left home when he was three, the same age that the fathers of Michael Brown and Trayvon Martin also left home. This may be the reason why his music connects with real thugs. It may also account for why West, despite his spectacular success, has gone through life so visibly angry and projected so much of that anger toward white people.

For all his tough-guy talk, West was very much a captive of the mama syndrome. When his mother died in 2007 as a result of complications from cosmetic surgery—not your average black death—he fell apart. It would be a year before he could bring himself to talk about her death, and even then he did so out of desperation. "I'd rather talk it through than commit suicide," he told *People* magazine. "I'm super devastated."[13] He was thirty when she died.

His mother was still alive when West made his first big public angry splash. The occasion was the Live 8 concert tour to raise awareness of AIDS and global poverty. During the tour he told his audience, who may not have even known any better, that AIDS was a "man-made disease." In the world according to Kanye, the disease was "placed in Africa just like crack was placed in the black community to break up the Black Panthers." He repeated this theme in his 2005 hit "Heard 'Em Say." Wrote West, "And I know the government administered AIDS/ So I guess we just pray like the minister say." A few months later, during the post-Katrina concert for hurricane relief, he ignored the teleprompter and his startled cohost Mike Myers by blurting out, "They've given them permission to go down and shoot us." For those who may not have known who was giving permission, West announced, "George Bush doesn't care about black people."[14]

West's grudge toward white people wasn't limited to AIDS doctors and George Bush. At the 2009 MTV Video Music Awards, teenage Taylor Swift had just accepted the award for Best Female Video when West rushed the stage and grabbed the mike out of her hands. "I'm sorry," he said, "but Beyoncé had one of the best videos of all time!" Swift would later tell *People* magazine, "I was really excited because I'd just won the award, and then I was really excited because Kanye West was onstage.

And then I wasn't excited anymore after that."[15] West repeated the performance at the 2015 Grammys when he stormed the stage after the white singer Beck beat out Beyoncé for the Best Album award.

Not surprisingly, West is a big fan of President Obama, and Obama is a fan of West. The rapper openly supported Obama during the 2008 campaign and performed on an all-star CD titled *Yes We Can: Voices of a Grassroots Movement*. Obama seemed untroubled by West's comments on AIDS and George Bush, but when West's attack on Taylor Swift blew up in the media, Obama felt obliged to disown him, at least temporarily, much as he disowned Jeremiah Wright when the pastor became troublesome.

"The young lady seems like a perfectly nice person," Obama said of Swift in an interview with CNBC shortly after the incident. "She's getting her award. What's [West] doing up there? He's a jackass."[16] Apparently, they have since patched things up. In October 2014, Obama met with West and his celebrity wife, Kim Kardashian, and signed an autograph for them, "To Kanye & Kim—Thanks for the support and best wishes to your lovely daughter! Barack Obama." Said West of Obama a few months later, "He calls the home phone, by the way." There was no reason to disbelieve him.[17] Black leaders like Obama want a piece of that black redneck culture to authenticate themselves in the eyes of black America. Meanwhile, ghetto phonies like West have to keep dumbing the culture down for fear that his home boys will think he's acting white. "I am not a fan of books," said West to prove that point. "I would never want a book's autograph. I am a proud non-reader of books."[18] That much seems pretty obvious to anyone paying attention.

The late rap legend Tupac Shakur was much more convincing as a fake black redneck than West. With the words *thug life* tattooed on his belly, Tupac, born Lesane Parish Crooks, did his best to live up to that slogan during the twenty-five years he spent on this earth. He was arrested for several violent offenses, including an assault on black film director Allen Hughes. And, of course, every crime he committed only increased his star power in the crude alternative culture he was helping to create.[19]

Those crimes included a sexual assault on a nineteen-year-old fan. The starstruck young woman testified that she went to Shakur's hotel room, and there Shakur and several of his crew "set upon me like animals." In the wake of Shakur's arrest, the woman received threatening phone calls, suffered nightmares, and lived in constant fear while Shakur was "glorified by his peers and fans." At the sentencing hearing, she asked the court for justice, concluding, "He should not be allowed to use his so-called celebrity status to avoid the consequences of his actions." The judge obliged her by sentencing Shakur to prison for no less than a year and a half.[20]

Earlier, during the trial, an alleged robber, likely from a rival rap gang, shot Shakur five times. He'd recovered by the time of the sentencing and tearfully apologized to the young woman as well as to the "youth of America." But then, lest anyone think he was guilty of anything, he added, "I'm not apologizing for a crime." In black redneck culture, no one ever does anything wrong. Just ask the criminals' mothers. "I have no shame," said Shakur. "I don't feel shame." Shakur's female fans had no shame either. Many of those in attendance wept openly on hearing the sentencing. One of them leaned over the rail and kissed Shakur before a court officer restrained her.

The parallels between Shakur's background and West's are hard to overlook, but Shakur's was a little rougher. He first met his father, Billy Garland, when Garland visited Tupac in the hospital after his shooting. He likely came to stake his claim in Shakur's fortune. After Shakur's death, in fact, this absentee father took Shakur's mother to court, demanding his half of the pie. He didn't get it.

The mother was herself a product of a violent broken home. In the 2004 book *Afeni Shakur: Evolution of a Revolutionary*, Afeni offers a useful look at how family dysfunction can deform a child. "It's hard to hate your parents," she told the book's author, Jasmine Guy. "It's hard to live with that kind of hatred, because they are a part of you." As a girl, she "just hurt. Everything around me seemed hurtful." Like so many black kids brought up this way, she internalized this anger. "For most of my life I have been angry," she admitted. "I thought my mama was weak and my daddy was a dog."[21] Unable to face up to her own anger, Afeni took the natural step of projecting it outward. In the late 1960s, with Malcolm X and Martin Luther King dead, the Black Panthers seemed to offer the most complete avenue of escape.

Reading Afeni's book was, for me, like reading my own history. The pattern is so clear, and she acknowledged as much. "So the Panther Party for me, at that time, clarified my situation," Afeni told Guy. "They took my rage and channeled it against them [she points outside] instead of us [she holds her heart]. They educated my mind and gave me direction."[22] Looking back, I have to wonder why the media refused to see what was troubling people like Afeni Shakur and failed to hear their cries for help for what they were. Instead, they took their angry protests "against them" at face value and asked "them"—white Americans—to apologize for an anger they did not provoke.

Afeni has remained angry and bitter all her life. When radical politics failed to heal her hurt, she turned to crack cocaine, and that was no answer either. Like so many parents without a good role model, she was no better a mother to Tupac than her mother was to her, and Tupac suffered for it. Still, for all her problems, Afeni was better educated and brighter than the average ghetto parent. Although she chose not to attend, she was accepted to the Bronx High School of Science, New York City's most selective public school. Living in Baltimore as an adult, she steered Tupac to the Baltimore School for the Arts. There he took acting and dance classes, including ballet. In fact, he played the role of the Mouse King in the school's production of *The Nutcracker*, not your typical launching pad for a gangster rap artist.

From Baltimore, he moved with his fractured family to the soft suburbs of Marin County, California, and there his life took a turn very much like Trayvon Martin's. Shakur wrote about it with some insight in his song "Dear Mama," a song that moved me when I first heard it because it spoke to my own experience as well. As Shakur told the story, he was suspended from school and "kicked out on the streets" at seventeen. In commiserating with his baby sister, who had a different father than he did, they would "blame mama" when things went wrong. He acknowledged too that he got "no love from my daddy cause the coward wasn't there." Filled with anger toward both his parents, he started hanging out with drug dealers because at least "they showed a young brother love." In time, Shakur grew to appreciate Afeni—"And even as a crack fiend, mama/ You always was a black queen, mama"[23]— but he came to terms with "my anger" no better than his mother had.

Unable to understand this homegrown rage, Shakur, like so many other young black males, focused his anger on the white establishment and its representatives in the streets, the police. To do so, he did not have to join some outlaw organization. By the 1990s, when he came of age, the culture was much more accommodating. His brand of music was less about love than it was about hate. "Cops on my back, just cause I'm black," he rapped in "Souljah's Revenge." "Can't find peace on the streets/ til the niggaz get a piece, f**k police, hear them screamin." The song ends with the young "Souljah" getting pulled over by the police, shouting "Remember Rodney King," and blasting the "punk ass" cop.[24]

I was living in South Central Los Angeles when the Rodney King incident took place in 1991. For many years I had lived with the belief that every time the cops stopped me, they did so just to harass me because I was black. Once, in fact, they ordered a friend and me to lie facedown on the street while they searched my car. Nothing came of it. They said we matched the description of two suspects they were looking for. And let's face it: if you are young and black and live in a city, too many of the suspects do look like you, but back then I wasn't buying it. By the time of the King incident, my head was clear. I saw through the media propaganda and understood why the police did what they did. The cops weren't on King's back because he was black. They were on his back because he led them on a drunken high-speed chase through the San Fernando Valley and resisted arrest.

Rodney King was not a bad guy. He would go on to write a book called *The Riot Within: My Journey from Rebellion to Redemption*, in which he accepted his share of responsibility for the events of March 3, 1991. As King admitted, though, his life was pure "chaos" from an early age. He grew up in nearby Pasadena with his mother and an abusive, philandering, alcoholic father. He took to alcohol just as his father had, and his life spiraled quickly downhill after his father died. Two years before he became a household name, he threatened a Korean grocer with an iron bar and robbed his store. On parole at the time of the car chase and seriously inebriated, King rightly feared that if he were stopped for a DUI, he would lose not only his license but quite likely his freedom. The two fellows who rode with him had no such concerns and did what the cops told them to do. They avoided the beating.

All takedowns look bad on videotape, but the cops tried to subdue King, a huge guy, with every other technique in the book. They tased him twice and tried to swarm him without batons, but to no effect. Even after they'd used the batons to subdue him, King managed to lunge at the officers. This provoked the final beating caught on videotape and edited by the networks to take out the lunge. As would happen with Trayvon Martin and Michael Brown, the rap culture ran with the false narrative the media created and elevated Rodney King to martyr status.

When a jury acquitted the police in criminal court, the gangsters in my South Central neighborhood used the acquittal as an excuse to burn the city down. I kept my distance, but I could not avoid seeing the flames lighting up the nighttime sky. I felt ashamed for black Americans. They were hurting their cause, not helping it. A lot of them had no idea what was going on, and others simply did not care about the truth. They took joy in others' misery and were beyond shame.

Despite a $4 million cash settlement, King could never quite get his life in order. In the ensuing years he was arrested multiple times for driving under the influence—in several cases after causing accidents and once after knocking his wife down with his car. His businesses failed. His marriages failed. After the Trayvon Martin case exploded into the public in March 2012, King's publicist released a statement linking King's trumped-up legacy to Martin's. "The horrifying sound of a young black male screaming for his life on a 911 call reminded me of my horrifying scream on a videotape 20 years ago," King was quoted as saying. "At that time, I thought I was going to die. Very, very gratefully, I survived. Unfortunately, Trayvon Martin did not."[25] King did not survive much longer. Two months later, he drowned in his fiancee's swimming pool, his body toxic with alcohol, cocaine, PCP, and marijuana.

Tupac Shakur did not survive very long either. No sooner was he released from prison on the sexual assault charge than trouble came stalking him again. The anger that gnawed away at him and others in the rap world needed an outlet. To actually take on the cops and the establishment was a bridge too far. And he certainly wasn't going to fight mama. As so often happens, these would-be gangsters turned on each other. They had to prove they were the real thing and competed with each other to see who was most real, most "authentic," most red-neck. That kind of competition has a way of turning deadly, as Shakur learned the hard way.

The anger many "gangstas" feel toward their mothers is so intense that it sometimes drives them into less socially acceptable outlets. A number of these young men have confided to me that their rage has driven them to the point of participating in sex acts with other young men. This tragic scenario plays out in our nation's prison systems on a daily basis.

18

SELF-DESTRUCTION

On the night of September 7, 1995, Tupac Shakur attended a Mike Tyson fight at the MGM Grand in Las Vegas in the company of Marion "Suge" Knight, the impresario of a successful music production company with the ominous name, Death Row Records. Like Shakur, Tyson too was trying to bounce back from a prison stay. He too had sexually assaulted a young black woman, in this case the eighteen-year-old Desiree Washington, Miss Black Rhode Island.

The rape shocked almost no one who knew Tyson. His family life made Shakur's look like the Huxtables'. His mother and father never married, which is why he ended up with his mother's name. His father abandoned the family when Tyson was two, and his mother would spend the rest of her short life working bad jobs or on welfare. Like so many boys raised as he was, Tyson grew up angry at his father and with real mixed feelings about his mother. "I would be with my friends, and I'd see their mothers kiss them. I never had that," said Tyson later. "You'd think that if she let me sleep in her bed until I was 15, she would have liked me, but she was drunk all the time."[1]

Tyson took to the streets of Brooklyn early. Small for his age and saddled with a lisp, he was called "fairy boy" by the neighborhood thugs who tormented him. Growing up as I did with a cleft palate, I knew something about teasing, but in Tyson's world there was little discipline and no respect for the weak. It was *Lord of the Flies* Brooklyn-style. The youth ruled. When Tyson could take it no more, he fought back. It was then that he discovered his gift for fighting. By the time Tyson was eleven, he was living on the streets and terrorizing the neighbor-hood—mugging, robbing, and beating people almost at will. "I was a little kid looking for love and acceptance, and the streets were where I found it," he remembered.

At twelve, Tyson was arrested for possession of stolen property, which proved to be the best thing that ever happened to him. Sent upstate to a home for boys, he caught the eye of legendary boxing manager Cus D'Amato, who took Tyson under his wing and became the father Tyson never had. D'Amato was in his seventies then and not long for the world. He died when Tyson was just nineteen and not at all ready to be a man. Tyson never did manage to overcome his inse-curity or control his all-consuming rage. By the time he fought Bruce Seldon on that fateful night in 1996—and TKO'd him in the first round—Tyson had endured a disastrous, humiliating marriage, spent a few years in prison, and squandered his talents in almost as many ways as Tupac Shakur had.

Suge Knight met Shakur after the Tyson fight. He was driving a black BMW 750, and Tupac rode in the passenger seat. When they stopped for a light, a white Cadillac with California plates pulled up alongside them. An unknown black man exited the Cadillac, gun drawn. As Shakur tried to scramble into the backseat, the black man fired thir-teen shots, four of them hitting Shakur, the fatal two shots in the chest. He would die six days later. For the media, a star-studded murder of this magnitude was ripe for exploitation. The glitzy magazine *Vanity Fair*, for instance, celebrated Shakur's life and death in a lengthy article, "To Die Like a Gangsta."[2] He could not have asked for a better send-off. His legacy was sealed. Hundreds of young black men, maybe thousands, would die trying to live up to it.

One who died very quickly, and likely in retaliation in this phony and pointless East Coast–West Coast gangster war, went by the rap name the Notorious B.I.G., aka Biggie Smalls, aka Christopher Wallace. His story again fits the pattern of black self-destruction to a tee. His father had deceived Wallace's Jamaican mother, Voletta Wallace, into thinking he was single. He wasn't. "The hate just swelled and festered through my whole body," Voletta wrote of Wallace's father. By the time Wallace was two, his father had disappeared from his life altogether. "I never wanted Christopher to disrespect or hate his father on my behalf,"[3] Voletta would write, but that is much easier said than done.

To her credit, Voletta rejected the "welfare mentality" that she saw as a trap. She would work all her life to support her son, but that left little time to guide him. Like Shakur and West, Wallace was smarter and better educated than the average would-be rapper. This likely accounted for his success as a producer and performer. Like them too, he was angry and unfocused. He was selling drugs on the street by age twelve. "Hustlers were my heroes," he said. "Everything happened on the strip I grew up in. It didn't matter where you went, it was all in your face."[4] At seventeen, Wallace got busted for selling crack and would spend nine months in a North Carolina prison before making bail.

By this time, Wallace had dropped out of school and turned his attention to music. He also fathered a child out of wedlock and, as his career picked up, abandoned the baby's mother for Faith Evans, an R&B singer he married. Shortly after the wedding, Wallace released his first album, a semi-biographical best seller titled *Ready to Die*. Wallace had some obvious mother issues still to work out. From the album's title cut came some heartwarming lyrics, "My mother didn't give me what I want, what the f***?/ Now I got a glock, makin' motherf***ers duck."[5] Wallace was twenty-two at the time. He had three more years to live.

The six-foot-three, four-hundred-pound Wallace titled the most popular song on that album "Big Poppa." It speaks very clearly to the hateful, distrustful relationships so common among young black men and women who have grown up never seeing a stable, loving relationship between a husband and a wife. In the song, Wallace described these young women as "honies gettin' money playin' niggaz like dummies." As to the young men like himself, "Money hoes and clothes all a nigga knows."[6] Wallace wasn't fantasizing about the life he wanted. He was talking about the life he lived.

Wallace did not have much longer to live it. The East Coast–West Coast rap war heated up especially after Shakur survived his first shooting. He blamed it on Wallace and created the hit single "Hit 'Em Up," which was little more than an extended death threat disguised as a rap record. It was bad enough that Shakur threatened to kill Wallace in the song, but he began it with the lyrics, "I ain't got no motherf***in friends/ That's why I f***ed yo' b***, you fat motherf***er."[7] Just a generation ago, Sam Cooke was telling his girlfriend, "I find myself wanting to marry you and take you home." And now here was Shakur taunting a hip-hop rival in no uncertain terms, claiming he'd had sex with his wife.

Among the many things Shakur and Wallace had in common was the nature of their respective deaths. Each was riding in the passenger seat of a vehicle—Wallace, a Chevy Suburban in Los Angeles—when another vehicle pulled up alongside. In each case, an unknown black male reached over and opened fire. Wallace was a couple of months shy of his twenty-fifth birthday at the time of his death. Shakur had just turned twenty-five at the time of his.

As the culture so visibly collapsed around these young men, black leadership did nothing but talk. Some of them talked a good game, Jesse Jackson among them. In 1997, not long after the parallel murders, he told an interviewer on PBS that the lifestyle symbolized by Shakur and Wallace was "not morally sound." He explained, "When you begin to call yourself 'nigger with an attitude' and call yourself 'notorious' and call yourself 'bitch' and 'whore,' that's a level of demeaned degeneracy. That's a kind of surrender." This was all well and good to say, but the way to fight back that Jackson suggested was not. He argued that the young should use their energy to "demand" laptop computers, equal funding for public education, access to Wall Street, and—bizarrely, "a budget for African development and Caribbean development."[8]

Almost as an aside, he added that "young men who make babies" should take the trouble of raising them. He never mentioned marriage. Two years later, Jackson's mistress, Karin Stanford, gave birth very quietly to their daughter, Ashley. The story made the news two years after the birth. "I am father to a daughter who was born outside of my marriage," Jackson said when the story broke. "This is no time for evasions, denials or alibis. I fully accept responsibility and I am truly sorry for my actions."[9] We all make mistakes, me especially, but I made mine when I was eighteen. Jackson made his when he was an ordained reverend and in his fifties, posturing as the moral leader of black America. Worse, he proved to be a deadbeat dad. Periodically, over the years, tabloid readers would be treated to headlines like, "Babymama Drama: Messy Jesse Jackson Owes Nearly $12K in Child Support for His Outside Kid."[10]

And this was the man the alchemists had appointed our "leader."

19

SEX WAR

As Jesse Jackson's life shows, kids who grew up the way he did, in a fatherless home, have a very hard time creating a stable, loving home of their own. So many of them never learn to respect and appreciate women, including their mothers and other females of authority. The world got a look at this disrespect in action when Tupac Shakur went after C. Delores Tucker. At the time of their confrontation, Tucker was pushing sixty. A longtime civil rights activist, she marched with Martin Luther King and went on to serve as Pennsylvania secretary of state, the first black woman to do so.

Tucker had led many a crusade in her distinguished career but only one that caused a backlash from other black people. That was her campaign against what she called the "pornographic filth" of gangster rap, then in its heyday. Tucker made the case, which is hard to rebut, that hip-hop music degrades black women.[1] This bothered Tucker especially because she had been fighting to protect and promote the dignity of black women throughout her career. As Shakur's mother, Afeni, wrote in her memoir, black women were desperate for that kind of support. "All I wanted was protection. That's all every woman wants," Afeni wrote. Unfortunately, neither her son nor his father was ever capable of providing it. "All my life I have had to be the man," Afeni added. "Then what happens is I get in trouble for being the man."[2]

In 1994, Tucker took her fight to the NAACP and protested the organization's honoring of Tupac Shakur with an Image award. Forget about the degraded music for a moment; by the time the NAACP gave

Shakur this award, he had been already been arrested several times for violent offenses, including once for sexual assault. Tucker, who sat on the NAACP board, was confounded that this venerable organization could give Shakur any kind of award at all. Shakur was not pleased. Women were not supposed to get in his way. He retaliated with a song called "How U Want It," whose lyrics included the inflammatory line "Delores Tucker you a motherf***er/ instead of tryna help a nigga you destroy your brother."[3] Other prominent performers piled on, including The Game, Jay-Z, Lil' Kim, and Eminem, who rapped the memorable line, "Tell that C. Delores Tucker slut to suck a d***."[4]

For all their phony blackness, the big shots of the hip-hop world gave the white Eminem a pass on this grotesque insult to a righteous black woman. They saw in him a kindred soul, one who distrusted women as much as they did. He was big enough a star that even after the media started protesting violence against women, Eminem kept advocating violence and getting away with it. "Bitch I'll punch Lana Del Rey right in the face twice," he rapped in a 2014 video, "like Ray Rice in broad daylight."[5]

His stardom gave Eminem all the perch he needed to take revenge on his parents. In the biographical song "Cleanin Out My Closet," he makes his intentions clear. He trashes his "faggot father" for abandoning him as a baby. "I wonder if he even kissed me goodbye," he asks. "No I don't / on second thought I just f**kin' wished he would die." He expresses some regret for trashing his mother, but not much. "I bet ya probably sick of me now. ain't you momma/ I'm a make you look so ridiculous now."[6] In fact, Eminem condemned his mother so often that he began the song "My Mom" with the line, "My mom my mom I know you're probably tired of hearing about my mom." His audience apparently couldn't get enough of his mother hatred. Many of them probably felt the same way. "I know I should let bygones be bygones," he rapped, "But she's the reason why I am high what I'm high on."[7]

For this self-loathing rapper to insult Delores Tucker was just another day on the job. Tucker's enemies, however, went well beyond the world of hip-hop. In 1997, Tucker was instrumental in getting the US Senate to hold hearings on the content of rap music. Democratic senator Joe Lieberman singled out a few of the songs that he found troubling, like "Slap-a-hoe" by the group Dove Shack or the songs of a group called Cannibal Corpse that extolled the joys of raping a woman with a knife or masturbating with a dead woman's head. More troubling still was that major companies like Sony and Polygram were distributing this music. Hilary Rosen, CEO of the Recording Industry of America, nicely captured the alchemist response to the Senate hearing. "Popular music, after all, has often become the vehicle for young people to express the ways they differ from their parents,"[8] Rosen argued, refusing to see the difference between the Beatles' "I Want to Hold Your Hand" and the Dove Shack's "F*** Ya Mouth."

Then congressmen Jesse Jackson Jr. expressed his disappointment that the hearings seemed to be one-sided. He had wanted black Columbia University professor Eric Dyson to testify. "There was no balance at all in presenting an objective, scholarly or dispassionate investigation of the issues at hand," said Dyson. That was not all Dyson said. He added that Tucker had a "vicious and mean-spirited nature" and made the mistake of saying that within earshot of Tucker's husband, William Tucker. "You're just a disgrace and an embarrassment to yourself," Tucker told Dyson. "She has never called you a name or said a word about you."[9] Unlike Afeni Shakur, Delores had what every woman wanted—"protection." It gave her the courage to carry on.

Life is renewed through love, and real love is spiritual love, God's love passing through us. Rappers like Eminem, white or black, are not capable of writing love songs. All they can write—and do write—are hate songs. There is plenty of sex, but it is hateful, angry, exploitative sex. It has nothing to do with the kind of love the apostle Paul talked about. "Love your wives," he told the Ephesians, "just as Christ also loved the church and gave Himself up for her, so that He might sanctify her, having cleansed her by the washing of water with the word." In a strong, stable marriage, the children absorb the sanctified love between their mother and father and are nurtured by it. In the rap world, stable marriage is ridiculed and the children it produces are mocked. The results are becoming obvious to anyone who wants to see.

20

GENERATIONAL LOSS

In the video world, the term *generational loss* is used to describe what happens when you make copies of copies. Each subsequent generation loses something but adds nothing. "Generational loss" also describes what is happening to black women in America's cities. With each generation, young mothers are less and less capable of passing along to their daughters either useful skills or feminine virtues. This helps explain the increasingly prominent role of grandmothers or even great-grandmothers in black life.

For better or for worse, YouTube puts the results of this generational loss right in our faces. There on a daily basis we can see that the absence of fathers and the failings of mothers have damaged young women as badly as they have young men. To verify this, just Google "Girl Fights." As I was writing this, one particular fight proved to be so nasty it *almost* broke through the protective corridor the major media have constructed around the inner city. By shielding themselves from the realities of black life, the media can pretend these problems don't exist. The problem for them is that they can no longer control what people see. Violent fight videos surface every day on social media sites. They don't always involve black people, but they do much too often.

The incident in question took place inside a crowded Brooklyn McDonald's. All the participants and spectators were black, as was the fifteen-year-old victim at the center of the brawl. A group of girls punched the victim in the head, over and over.[1] That was one of many disturbing things about the attack. Another was that the attackers, all teens themselves, were so vicious and relentless. Some of these girls are generations removed from knowing a solid, nurturing, female role model. They don't know how a real woman behaves. Unable to attract males through their womanliness, they imitate them. Compounding the problem is that they are imitating boys who don't know how to be men, and so they funnel their anger into coarse and violent behavior. This is the girls' desperate way of getting recognition and respect, but it gets them nowhere.

Just as disturbing to me was that the spectators at McDonald's seemed to be enjoying themselves. Uneasy in their own skins, they lost themselves in the mob and delighted in the agony of others. I see this more and more. Misery loves company. If these poor souls cannot be happy, they don't want anyone to be happy.

For me, most troubling of all was that for ninety seconds—a lifetime in such an attack—no male, boy or man, stepped forward to intervene. When a few males finally did get involved, they exhibited so little authority that the girls continued to stomp the now helpless victim for ninety more seconds. This is a symptom of a larger problem that few dare discuss. Due to a man's separation from God, he lacks the strength to assume his rightful place as head of his wife, and she loses respect for his authority. For example, men have lost the authority to keep their own child, as women make the "choice" to kill their unborn children.

When I was a boy, men—as fathers and producers—commanded respect. Today, so many boys grow up without a real man to look up to; they end up imitating their mothers, with their piercings and tattoos and the attraction to "bling." If they act tough, it is to convince themselves and their friends that they are not the mama's boys they know themselves to be. What men don't understand is that it's the *spirit* of their mothers they must overcome to be a man. A real man at that McDonald's would not have waited ten seconds before wading in and pulling the girls apart. It wasn't fear that kept the male onlookers from doing this. The girls could not really hurt them—they knew that. It was a lack of confidence, a lack of self-respect, a lack of natural authority.

Thanks to the video, all the attackers were arrested. One was stopped with her mother as she attempted to flee to Jamaica. As is so often the case, the parents speaking on behalf of the victim and the accused were the mothers and grandmothers. The fathers were nowhere to be seen. The alleged ringleader, sixteen-year-old Aniah Ferguson, was a mother herself, but obviously not a good one. She had been arrested six times since turning sixteen eight months earlier. Those infractions included stabbing her brother, beating up her grandmother, and injuring a police officer during an arrest. There are too many Aniahs out there with too many issues, many of them traceable to the absence of fathers in their lives and the failures of their mothers. As obvious as these problems are, no one of importance in the media or in the civil rights community wants to talk about them.

Lucky for our civil rights "leaders," the Oklahoma frat boy video surfaced at the same time as the Brooklyn video.[2] Personally, I found the video funny—very stupid, but funny—worthy of a slap on the wrist maybe but not expulsion from school. I thought to myself, *Don't these white people know what's going to happen to them?* They apparently had no idea the mess they were singing their way into. Their video allowed the media to divert the national media's attention away from a large and growing problem to an anomalous, irrelevant one. Students held candlelight vigils about the Oklahoma incident. Editorialists blustered. One national bigwig after another weighed in.

Almost to a person, however, the national power players kept mum about the Brooklyn incident. Yes, there was a good deal of media attention in the New York area, and activists did respond, but they scarcely knew where to begin. Community advocate Tony Herbert told local ABC News that parents and other interested parties all over New York City and even Long Island were meeting to address the problem. "We're going to come together and we're going to get ahead of this curve and stop this violence," said Herbert. "We know there is a lack of programming, lack of funding, resources that these young people can plug into," Herbert added. "So what do we do? We engage those young people to have that access."[3] As much as I respect Herbert's good heart, he is saying the same things that community activists said fifty years ago. But the problem is not local, and it is not a lack of funding. The problem is a lack of fathers and mothers passing their anger on to the children. No amount of "programming" will change that.

In the comment sections on the McDonald's video, ordinary black people were making the kind of observations that Jesse Jackson or Al Sharpton should have been making if they really cared about the people they are supposed to represent. This first one came from honeybee31, a black woman raising a teenage daughter:

> This saddens, scares and bothers me at the same time. So the only time blacks want to march and scream foul play is when someone outside of their race commits an offense to them? What about the love and regard for your fellow man? What are we teaching these kids? Thats its ok so long as you're doing it to each other??? So long as "the authorities" arent violating your human rights, lets revert back to times when war raged on openly in the streets???? Wake up!!!! No one is going to respect us more than we respect ourselves. It starts with home.[4]

This second comes from Dennis DMan R, a male high school student who makes more sense on racial issues than his president:

> When has it ever been ok for 7 females to attack 1 female in such an ANIMALISTIC way? People standing by and recording instead of stopping and getting involved to stop the fight. We are in the STATE of MINDLESS, IGNORANT behavior, with a dash of denial. These youths supposed to be our FUTURE, all I see is the PAST. They call each other "NIGGAS," advocating not to "SNITCH" when they witness wrong doing, and think its ok to beat down one of their own like a lynch mob. I am so ashamed . . . I can't post anymore. . . . All I have to say "400 years . . . 400 tears." I guess the WHITE MAN made you attack this young sister too . . . SMDH [shaking my damn head] . . . make me want to vomit.[5]

Both of these respondents suggest the obvious: namely, that the powers that be prefer to blame white people for black problems rather than address those problems themselves. Although many of those who commented on social media sites had little to say worth repeating, one other theme did surface that deserves attention. "I can say that now I know why there are more black men who prefer to get into serious relationships with white women," said a self-identified Southern white female. "A woman is not designed to be like this. They are supposed to be feminine, loving, and nurturing to their families and everyone around them."[6]

Growing up in the South, I had the same impression about women. They could be tough—my grandmother certainly was—but they were bighearted enough to nurture a neighborhood. Men respond to that kind of woman. These are the women they want to marry, not the "animalistic" women who pride themselves on their fighting skills. "This generation is horrible," commented one young black woman. "The problem is babies (13–17 years of age) are having babies too."[7] She is much closer to the truth than the people on TV who are telling her what to think. These young women grow up angry and stressed out, and they transfer that anger to their children long before they learn how to understand it themselves, let alone cope with it.

In Alabama, I never saw anything like what I saw on that Brooklyn video. In fact, I never saw anything like that in Gary or even in Los Angeles, at least not when I first arrived. Without fathers in the home, these young women often suffer from a spiritual breakdown. They grow up hard and cynical, and they are getting harder and more cynical by the generation. They have sex to offer but little else. Men use them but don't want them. Some men turn to white women as an alternative, but these relations can be ripe with problems as well. Too often, the white women form relations with black men out of a false sense of compassion and an unthinking sense of superiority. They see themselves not as the equals of the men but as their saviors. If the woman is the major breadwinner in the family, the man will have a hard time establishing his sense of self-worth and independence. I have seen many such relationships built on guilt and exploitation.

There is another related problem to deal with. New York writer Ernest Baker put his finger on it in a recent article he wrote for *Gawker* about being seen with his white girlfriend. "It's nothing to walk past a random black woman on the street and get a death glare," wrote Baker, "and maybe even overhear something like, 'They're taking all of our men.'" One black woman walked right up to him and his girlfriend and asked point-blank why he was dating a white girl when she could not even get a man. "I totally get where black women are coming from," said a sympathetic Baker.[8]

Black women see the problem from another angle. "Black men don't like black women. Yes, I said it," wrote television journalist Courtney Carter. "I don't mean *all* black men, but it's true of many, and it's a growing problem." In a thoughtful *Huffington Post* article, Carter, an educated black woman, tried to explain why this is so, but she gave short shrift to the one explanation that is closest to the truth: "Black women have too much attitude/ghetto." Carter explained that she and many of her friends grew up in middle-class homes, and she said very clearly, "I am not ghetto," but she still does not see herself getting the respect she deserves.[9]

What Carter did not say is, "I don't have an attitude." Even affluent young black women can be angry and defiant. Unless they were surrounded by love as young girls, they too can develop an attitude from all the negative things they have been bombarded with at home, in school and in college, and from the media. In my experience, many well-educated black women are overly sensitive to the least slight from anyone, male or female, black or white. They have been taught from an early age that the system works against them—both for being black and for being female—and they are looking for proof that this is so.

In a 2015 *Playboy* magazine interview, rapper Azealia Banks showed just how thoroughly the alchemists have managed to poison the minds of black women, certainly this particular young black woman. "I hate everything about this country," she told *Playboy*. "Like, I hate fat white Americans. All the people who are crunched into the middle of America, the real fat and meat of America, are these racist conservative white people who live on their farms."[10]

At the time of the interview, Banks was twenty-three and precociously hateful. She traced her anger to an education that forced her to learn the following: "The white man gave you the vote. He Christianized you and taught you how to speak English. If it weren't for him, you'd still be living in a hut."

Banks went to school in New York City in the twenty-first century. I cannot imagine any teacher in liberal New York ever saying anything good about the white contribution to black culture. Then again, at least in retrospect, Banks hated her teachers enough to lie about them. She claimed to have written in her second-grade journal, "I cannot stand this white b**** teacher. F*** this white b****." The teacher reportedly called Bank's mother about this entry. The mother was a bit embarrassed because she was the one telling her daughter, "White people are of the devil. Stay away from them." It will not surprise you to learn that Banks grew up without a father. He died when she was two. Her mother was physically and verbally abusive. "Like she would hit me and my sisters with baseball bats," said Banks, "bang our heads up against walls, and she would always tell me I was ugly."[11] By age fourteen, Banks had left home to live with her sister.

Somewhere along the way, Banks learned to transfer her rage to the white man. And why not? It was the white man who'd deprived her of her African homeland. "When you rip a people from their land, from their customs, from their culture—there's still a piece of me that knows I'm not supposed to be speaking English, I'm not supposed to be worshipping Jesus Christ. All this sh** is unnatural to me." I suspect that posing nude in *Playboy* is not something that would go over well in her imagined native country, whether Christian or Muslim, but Banks was not thinking here. She was reacting to a lifetime of propaganda, much of it poisonous.

Whatever her physical appeal, Banks is almost unrecognizable as a woman. She prides herself on her hardness, her vulgarity, her bisexuality, and her rampant materialism. In telling *Playboy* why she prefers older men, she proves how little appeal the ordinary black man would hold for her or she for him. "The things in an older man's house are better—his furniture, even his knives and his pots. And they smell better," she said, as if her fixation on material things was admirable. Banks may posture as a "loud black bitch," but for all her pride in blackness, she has thoroughly estranged herself from the warm, nurturing women of her American and African past.[12] Far from being the opposite of an affluent white American, she has become a parody of one. She is not even close to the unique creation she imagines herself to be. Rather, she is a textbook case of why black men and black women are at war.

Too many young black women today grow up like Banks, in homes where anger is the norm and trust is unheard of. Given this kind of start, they focus on superficial things, like hair and skin color and even "furniture," and ignore the things that matter, like forgiveness, redemption, and love. A generous, unforced smile can make anyone beautiful, but only love can produce those smiles, and only security can produce love.

21

RACE WAR

More than any time in the past forty years, I fear for the future. President Obama, black political leaders, white agitators, and the media all seem intent on fomenting racial unrest. They have focused on incident after incident—the Capitol Hill protest, the Trayvon Martin shooting, the Michael Brown shooting, the Eric Garner death, the Tony Robinson shooting, the Freddie Gray death—lied to America about what happened, stirred up black anger with their lies, and then exploited the anger for ratings, cash, or ballots.

It took former Obama supporter George Zimmerman to point out what the media should have pointed out years before. Three years after the Martin shooting, and days after being cleared by the Department of Justice, Zimmerman said that Obama's involvement in his case "was clearly a dereliction of duty pitting Americans against each other solely based on race."[1] Exactly! And Zimmerman's was not the only case that Obama nosed his way into. I have got to believe this agitation has been planned. People who think the way Obama does always want power, and what better way to gain more of it than by using disorder as a cover.

The alchemists plot, I think, under a false premise. They believe that they still control the media. They think that the editorial voice of the *New York Times* is America's voice. They are confident that whites will respond as passively and as guiltily to a black uprising as the *Times'* readers would. I don't think they will. And there is one very obvious reason why.

Although the national media will not show the Brooklyn McDonald's video or the hundreds of other videos of young black people behaving badly, white people in the millions are watching those videos. Many show whites being attacked for no other reason than that they are white. Closed from legitimate channels of debate on racial matters, white people are going underground with their discontent, and the responses are not always what we might want them to be.

A week or so after the Brooklyn McDonald's video, a video out of Indianapolis surfaced. As the *Indianapolis Star* reported the incident, "A video of a young girl and her little brother being beat down by a female assailant surfaced early Sunday morning on the website LiveLeak.com."[2] The incident follows an all-too-familiar pattern. The reader learns that the fourteen-year-old attacker "throws the first punch." In fact, it was a sucker punch. This was not a fight. It was an attack. She knocks the victim down with the punch, and "continues to beat and kick her in the face." Several individuals watch the attack but, of course, "no one attempts to step in and break up the suspect's onslaught." The victim does not even know the name of her attacker. As the beating continues, she cries out, "What did I do? What did I do? No. What did I do? Please stop."

The victim finally manages to wrangle away and runs off with her five-year-old brother, but her attacker comes charging after her, tackles her, and "begins slugging and stomping the victim in the face." When the little brother—bless his heart!—steps in and swings at the attacker, she grabs him by his neck and flings him to the concrete sidewalk. At this point, the attacker backs off with the onlookers still laughing. She was subsequently arrested on another charge, the brass-knuckled beating of a second teen later that day—race, of course, unknown. The *Star* article concluded on this note, "By 8 p.m. Sunday, the video had been viewed more than 1 million times." To be clear, that is more than one million views in the first twelve hours.

Those who saw the video knew a few things *Star* readers did not. The most obvious was that the attacker was black, and the victim and her brother were white. The onlookers were black as well. So was the gleeful, cackling girl who shot the video and narrated it. To be fair, the *Star* was not the only media outlet to censor the obvious. Consider this absurd description of the attack from TV station Fox 59: "In the video, a girl wearing black is pulled to the ground by a girl wearing white."[3] That was helpful. Otherwise—what?—viewers would not have been able to tell them apart?

Viewers, however, are not as clueless as the media execs think they are. "If a white person did this to a black child," said one fellow on LiveLeak, "Obama would scramble the National Guard and CNN would headline it for the next three months."[4] He was likely not far from the truth. That the *Star* did not report so obvious a fact as the race of those involved had to disgust readers who also viewed the video. How could they take that paper seriously after so glaring and so typical an omission? By denying that basic a fact, the *Star* let its readers know there would be no public discussion of the problem at hand and, if there was, it would deal with "teen" violence.

The comments section on LiveLeak reveals the increasing anger among white people. "I'm so angry after watching that. That dirty f***** bitch needs to be hung from the nearest tree," reads one comment. "If that isn't a hate crime and felony then what is?" reads a second. And a third, "I really hope someone hangs that f***** from a tree one night. Swap the races and that would be national news and they'd be screaming for the death penalty!" There are two major takeaways from these comments. One is that white people don't buy the media spin anymore. They know that there is a glaring double standard in the way crime is being reported and even prosecuted. The second is that many are willing to express their anger in racially taboo terms. Although understandable, that is not healthy. As I know from my own life, anger is not something you control. It controls *you*. When we let anger control our souls, we all lose.

In the follow-up articles on the attack, we see all the symptoms of community collapse that I have been talking about for the last twenty-five years. The most obvious is that the spokesperson for the attacker's family is the grandmother. There is no father or grandfather in sight. "I was thinking my granddaughter went over the edge. That's how I felt," the grandmother told the local media. She visited her granddaughter in detention and recounted the conversation, "Grandma, I black out when this happens. I just black out."[5] No doubt this girl has as many mental health problems as she has excuses. The mother and grandmother traced her path through various government agencies, all to no avail. The media refused to see, however, that this girl was more the norm than the exception in the community that produced her.

The proof is that her friends cheered on this gratuitous attack. Scarier still, they were cheering because the victim was white. There was no other reason for the attack. "All the other people watching & laughing are just as guilty," wrote one Asian woman commenting on LiveLeak. Watching the video gave her flashbacks. As an Asian girl in an otherwise black and white neighborhood, it was inevitably the black girls who bullied her. For years nonblacks have had to stifle their complaints. Social media has given them voice. They may not express themselves charitably, but those who ignore that anger will pay for their ignorance.

If white anger is well concealed, black anger is not. The nightly news, almost every night, shows some manifestation of it—a march here, a mob action there, a riot somewhere else. Some talking head will be trotted out to explain why the anger is justified and what white America must do to atone. When asked, for instance, whether the police should crack down on mobs of black teens raising hell on the famed Country Club Plaza in his native Kansas City, Black Caucus chair Emanuel Cleaver said for the ages, "All we are going to do is make a lot of black kids angry and they are going to take out their anger somewhere else."[6] As to why those kids are angry, alchemists like Cleaver don't even bother with an explanation. You saw *Roots*, didn't you?

To understand how lethal this anger can be, it might pay to look at the phenomenon of the black mass murderer. You say, what? Black mass murderer? If you are like a lot of people, you think mass murder is a white thing. The media encourage you to do so. "Why Most Mass Murderers Are Privileged White Men," wrote Hugo Schwyzer in *Jezebel* in 2012.[7] This is a riff you hear occasionally from black comics as well, but the perception results from the way the media treat black serial killers, not from the reality on the ground.

An all-but-untold story is how black anger has been finding an outlet in unhinged acts of violence. Inevitably these killers blame white people for their rage. True to form, the media refuse to examine the deeper reasons for their rage, if they bother to discuss these crimes at all. For instance, in March 2015, J. C. X. Simon, sixty-nine, died an obscure death in a California prison cell. Thirty years earlier, he and three other "zebra killers" went on an openly racist killing spree that resulted in the shooting of at least twenty-one whites and Asians in San Francisco, fourteen of whom died.[8] Not one American in a thousand could tell you word one about the zebra murders, let alone about J. C. X. Simon. The Zodiac killer, by contrast, worked the same area, at roughly the same time, killed far fewer people, and drew hugely more media attention, including a feature film.

The media's natural impulse is to bury stories of black-on-white crime, even those with multiple victims. This the national media did successfully in December 2000 after brothers Reginald and Jonathan Carr raped, sexually humiliated, and shot five decent young men and women, killing four. Days earlier, the brothers had shot and killed another white woman. Despite the heinous nature of the crimes, the story of the "Wichita Massacre" barely left Wichita. The Kansas City media would not even talk about it. This was too bad if for no other reason than to show once again how paternal abandonment and abuse can fill the children left behind with murderous rage. The brothers' upbringing was textbook family breakdown.[9] Their targeting of white victims was hardly random. The media's indifference was not random either.

To get the attention of the media, black mass murderers must do something perverse, public, and undeniable. Jamaican-born Colin Ferguson did just that in December 1993 when he walked down the aisle of a Long Island Railroad car shooting twenty-five people, none of them black, killing six of them. After three brave passengers tackled him, the police found a note in his pocket. Under the heading, "reasons for this," he cited "racism by Caucasians and Uncle Tom Negroes."[10]

Throughout his troubled life, in fact, Ferguson had been accusing people of racism. He left Jamaica after his parents died and never found his stride. His relentless anger had cost him one job after another, and he inevitably lashed out at his employers. In 1993, however, even the *New York Times* wasn't buying his rationale. "While Mr. Ferguson blamed racism for all his misfortunes and shattered expectations," wrote the *Times*' Robert McFadden, "the examination of his past shows no evidence that he was ever a victim of discrimination."[11]

That lack of evidence did not trouble Ferguson's radical attorneys, Ronald Kuby and William Kunstler. They saw an opportunity to exploit white guilt and seized it, introducing a "black rage" defense to save their client. "Nobody is saying Colin Ferguson did a good thing," said Kuby. "We're just saying that he was not responsible for his own conduct. White racism is to blame."[12] The judge and jury did not see it that way—Ferguson was convicted and sent away for life—but the attorneys managed to shift the public debate away from Ferguson's guilt or innocence to society's. That shift did black people no good.

The next black mass murderer to show his head was arguably the most terrifying in recent American history. Born John Allen Williams in Louisiana, this killer went by the name John Allen Muhammad after joining the Nation of Islam in 1987. He would carry that name forward until the State of Virginia quietly executed him in 2009.

Muhammad's childhood is another textbook study in the effects of parental abandonment. Sari Horowitz and Michael Ruane, authors of *Sniper: The Hunt for the Killers Who Terrorized the Nation*, chronicled his early years in a chapter aptly titled "The Roots of Rage."[13] Those roots ran deep. Muhammad's father, a railroad porter, was scarcely around during the first few years of his son's life. Upon the death of his wife when Muhammad was three, he split altogether. From that point on, his aunts raised him.

Like so many young men in similar straits, Muhammad proved to be no better a father than his father was to him. He had one child out of wedlock, a second child with his first wife, Carol, and a third child with his second wife, Mildred. During much of that time he served in either the Army Reserves or in the regular army. A year after being discharged in 1994—honorably but with a few racially charged incidents along the way—he helped the Nation of Islam provide security for the Million Man March, an event attended by Barack Obama, among other luminaries.

Now on his own, Muhammad tried his hand at entrepreneurship but without success. Removed from the enforced discipline of the military, he quickly ran his car repair business into the ground and blamed everyone but himself, especially Mildred. After their divorce, she had to file a protection order against him. "You have become my enemy, and as my enemy, I will kill you," he told her.[14]

In 2000, Muhammad abducted his three children and flew to Antigua. There he supported himself, but just barely, with a variety of shadowy hustles. He spent about a year on the island. Before he left, though, he met a Jamaican woman and her fatherless teenage son, Lee Malvo. He took the needy Malvo under his wing and soon had him spouting verses from the Koran. Even before they headed back to the United States, Malvo was calling Muhammad "Dad."

A little over a year after returning to the United States, the heavily armed Muhammad was cruising the Washington, DC, area in a Chevy Caprice with Malvo, now seventeen and fully submissive, at his side. Unwilling to face his own failures as a son, father, and man, Muhammad transferred his wrath toward America. He would rage about its "slavery, hypocrisy and foreign policy," Malvo claimed at Muhammad's trial in 2006. According to Malvo, Muhammad planned to "terrorize" the area by killing six whites a day for thirty days. He was particularly keen on shooting pregnant white women.[15]

Muhammad did not get the body count he hoped, but for the month of October 2002, he did succeed in paralyzing metropolitan DC. Before the month was through, he and Malvo had shot thirteen random people, killing ten of them. Authorities would trace twelve shootings earlier in 2002 to the pair—seven of the victims died. For all the havoc he wreaked, Muhammad failed to secure the attention he craved. "Prediction: Muhammad's trial will make him as famous as McVeigh. All America will now know his name," columnist Pat Buchanan wrote shortly after their arrest.[16] Buchanan did not understand the media as well as he thought.

Up until the moment Muhammad and Malvo were apprehended, the media had been openly speculating—hoping, really—that the killers were white. When they proved to be black, with Muslim ties to boot, the media gave them as little attention as possible given the massive coverage they generated before their capture. The same media that had chronicled the pending execution of Oklahoma City bomber Timothy McVeigh day by day in 2001 all but ignored the execution of John Allen Muhammad in 2009. The alchemists could pull no useful spin from his death. "The motive for the attacks remains murky," wrote Dena Potter of the Associated Press.[17] Neither Potter nor anyone else in the media traced his motive to an irrational anger born out of abandonment and fueled by the alchemists who reassured him nothing was his fault. True to form, Muhammad protested his innocence to the end.

It was not until after Barack Obama was elected president that the pace of the killing picked up. This seemed ironic only to those who did not understand Obama's agenda. On August 3, 2010, thirty-four-year-old Omar Thornton headed into the family-owned Connecticut beer distributorship where he had worked for the last two years. He had cause to be anxious. Management had caught him on video stealing beer on more than one occasion. After a disciplinary hearing, Thornton handed in his resignation to avoid being terminated. Instead of leaving the building, however, he pulled two Ruger SR9 pistols from his lunchbox and started firing. After shooting ten of his coworkers, killing eight of them, he called 911. "You probably want to know why I shot this place up," said Thornton. "This place here is a racist place." Thornton made no bones about his motives. "They treat me bad over here," he continued, "and they treat all the other black employees bad over here too, so I just take it into my own hands and I handled the problem—I wish I coulda got more of the people."[18]

Thornton had the mama syndrome bad. Like O. J. Simpson after his murders, he made one personal call. It was to his mother, Lillie Holliday. "I killed the five racists that was there bothering me," he told her.[19] She took his claims of racism at face value. Among other insults he had allegedly experienced, Thornton claimed to have seen drawings on the wall of President Obama with his head in a noose. Holliday was unable to talk her son out of what he planned to do next—shoot and kill himself.

Despite the media's initial efforts, the racism angle did not play as well as Thornton and Holliday might have hoped. Every agency that examined the company's HR practices gave it a clean bill of health. Thornton had made no prior complaint to either management or the union about racial harassment. None of the other black employees had experienced any racism. And there was no doubt that the company had him dead to rights for stealing beer, a capital offense in a beer distributorship. With the racism well quickly running dry, the media collectively decided to bury the story. They much preferred the various narratives that white serial killers presented. Union officials wanted the story to die too. Said Teamsters honcho Christopher Roos, "It's got nothing to do with race. This is a disgruntled employee who shot a bunch of people."[20]

Of course, it had everything to do with race, just not in the way the media hoped it would. Holliday and other Thornton supporters kept the racial fires simmering through the OST (Omar Sheriff Thornton) Memorial Foundation. On the surface the foundation is dedicated to "raising awareness of and combating institutional racism in all of its forms." To reinforce that theme, one prominent visual contains images of the "legends" that inspired the foundation—Malcolm X, Martin Luther King, and back-to-Africa guru Marcus Garvey. Another visual shows lynched black men hanging from trees.

Race is obviously the prominent theme, but a closer look at the foundation shows it to be a tribute to an unhealthy relationship between a mother and her son. The foundation's updated cover image, for instance, has a photo of Thornton in the center—"MY ANGEL, MY EVERYTHING"—surrounded by what appears to be four photos of Holliday.[21] There is no mention of Thornton's father in the foundation literature or in any media accounts. The fact that Thornton and his mother have different last names suggests the father has not been in the picture—literally or otherwise—for a long time. The fact that Thornton formed no family of his own suggests the lack of a reliable role model in his life.

If the media had spent one-tenth the time on this Connecticut shooting that they did on the Sandy Hook shooting two years later, they might have helped their audiences understand what went wrong in the life of Omar Thornton. He was not the victim of racism—institutional or otherwise. If he was the victim of anything, it was of a disordered home life and of society's refusal to acknowledge the emotional fallout from that disorder. The pattern stares the media in the face—angry black man displaces his anger from his parents to the white man—but the media either avert their gaze or blame the white man. It is so much easier than telling the truth.

The media had another opportunity to avert their gaze just a few years later. In 2013, in Los Angeles, Christopher Dorner declared "unconventional and asymmetric warfare" on the Los Angeles Police Department. Before he took his own life, Dorner killed four people and wounded three others; six of the seven were police officers. Only one was black.

Born in 1979, Dorner grew up in largely white California neighborhoods and graduated from college. Despite his good fortune, he was an angry young man who funneled his anger—as the media encouraged him to—into racial grievances. In a manifesto of sorts that he wrote before his lethal rampage, he documented the racial insults he had endured or imagined all the way back to the first grade and right up through his time on the LAPD.[22] He also made frequent reference to his mother, who was biracial, but none to his father. In fact, I could find no reference at all to Dorner's father in any of the media accounts. That said, he congratulated several of his friends for being a "great father." He seems to have recognized what he missed in his own life.

In his relationships with women, Dorner showed all the classic symptoms of a man who never had a useful role model. One ex-girlfriend, a black woman, called him "severely emotionally and mentally disturbed." She went so far as to warn other would-be girlfriends about Dorner on a site called dontdatehimgirl.com. "Just be careful," wrote the woman, "because this guy is a police officer and he will probably think that he can get away with anything." Of note, she also claimed that Dorner hated himself for being black and wanted her to act more like a white woman.[23] Dorner married a fellow police officer in 2007, but that marriage lasted less than three weeks. And it was an incident with a white female training officer on the LAPD, also in 2007, that cost him his job.[24]

Much as I did before I saw the light, Dorner insisted on viewing all his troubles through a racial prism. Although the LAPD was subject to intrusive federal race and gender oversight during Dorner's tenure, the LAPD he saw was racist to the core. The "sole intent" of the white officers was to "victimize minorities who are uneducated, and unaware of criminal law, civil law, and civil rights," he wrote in his manifesto. As Dorner imagined, "The department has not changed since the Rampart and Rodney King days. It has gotten worse." The nation was doing no better than the department. Dorner "shed a tear" the night Obama was elected, and he bought the media line that Obama's critics attacked him only because he was black. "You," by which Dorner meant red state America, "call [Obama's] supporters, whether black, brown, yellow, or white, leeches, FSA, welfare recipients, and ni$&er [*sic*] lovers. You say this openly without any discretion."[25] This hateful mindlessness came to him courtesy of the mainstream media. Dorner cited people like MSNBC's Chris Matthews and Piers Morgan, then with CNN, for his political insights.

Yet for all his demons, Dorner had moments of real clarity. He concluded his manifesto with a thoughtful appeal for black self-improvement. The shame is that in rejecting Christ's love—"I am not a f***ing Christian"—he could not do for himself what he asked of others:

> Blacks must strive for more in life than bling, hoes, and cars. The current culture is an epidemic that leaves them with no discernible future. They're suffocating and don't even know it. MLK Jr. would be mortified at what he worked so hard for in our acceptance as equal beings and how unfortunately we stopped progressing and began digressing. Chicago's youth violence is a prime example of how our black communities values have declined. We can not address this nation's intolerant issues until we address our own communities morality issues first.[26]

Seven months after Dorner's killing spree, Aaron Alexis descended on the Washington Navy Yard, guns blazing, and killed thirteen people before being killed by police. Right up until the end, Alexis and Dorner led parallel lives. They were both black and male and were born within a month of each other in New York in 1979. Each of them graduated high school, attended college, joined the Navy Reserve, and assimilated at least superficially into the larger "white" world. Unfortunately, like Dorner and Thornton, Muhammad and Malvo, Alexis lacked a strong father figure in his life and learned to focus the resulting anger on racial grievances.

As was true in each of these cases, the media paid little attention to Alexis's family background. In reading multiple reports, I found the best evidence in the comments of a neighbor of Alexis's when he was growing up. According to *Newsday*, the neighbor remembered the family—"a mom, a daughter and two teenage boys"—living directly above her for two years. The father surfaced after the shooting to say that his son suffered from PTSD—the same ailment that the grandmother attributed to her granddaughter in the Indianapolis video—but had little else to offer.[27]

Unlike Dorner and Thornton, Alexis left no record of why he killed thirteen people, twelve of them his former colleagues. There is evidence, though, that Alexis directed his anger in much the same way others had. "He felt a lot of discrimination and racism with white people especially," said friend Kristi Suthamtewkal.[28] Like the others, Alexis refused to see his own emotional problems for what they were. When the navy discharged him after at least nine incidents of misconduct—including insubordination, unauthorized absences, drunkenness, and an arrest for disorderly conduct at an Atlanta nightclub—he blamed the navy. According to a friend, "He thought he never got a promotion because of the color of his skin."[29] Like several of the others, Alexis rejected Christianity, but he found no more peace in Buddhism than Muhammad did in Islam or Dorner did in the cobbled-together secular humanism he'd embraced.

In Oklahoma, Alton Nolen found a formal outlet for his hatred of white people as well. That hatred culminated in the beheading of a white, female coworker and the slashing of another at the food processing plant where they worked. Nolen had recently converted to Islam. Some saw his assault as something of a jihad, but his behavioral pattern almost perfectly mirrors that of the other murderers profiled.

As with the others, I could find no reference to a father in Nolen's life. The spokesperson for the family was the mother, Joyce Nolen. In an awkward video, she apologized to the families of the people her son attacked, but she insisted, "There's two sides to every story, and we're only hearing one." She added, "I am praying that justice will prevail, the whole story will come out, the whole story." She was suggesting, I suppose, that the victims somehow provoked the attack. Like the other mothers, she could not believe her son would do anything like this. "My son was raised up in a loving home," she insisted, but there was a big something missing from that home.[30]

Whatever was missing, it left Nolen an angry young man. That anger, I have seen, affects people in every aspect of their lives. Anger makes people irresponsible and inconsiderate. Angry people have no love and respect for themselves and or for their fellow man. They often have no functioning inner compass to override the anger. Consequently, angry people like Nolen—or Ferguson or Thornton or Dorner or Alexis—make for very poor employees. On the day of his rampage, Nolen was suspended for making insulting remarks about whites to his coworkers. "He was basically saying he didn't like white people and had an altercation with our second victim based on that," said the local district attorney. After being escorted out of the plant, Nolen drove home, grabbed a large kitchen knife, and came back slashing. If the company's CFO had not shot him, Nolen might have killed more people. He had every intention of doing just that.[31]

Like Nolen, Ismaaiyl Brinsley of Baltimore parked his antiwhite anger at the local mosque. He may well have been in the audience when the Nation of Islam's Louis Farrakhan came to Baltimore's Morgan State University in November 2014 to spread the same hateful venom that first infected me back in the late 1960s. Farrakhan spoke to a huge crowd at Morgan State, praising the rioters in Ferguson and elsewhere. He denounced the "cowardly punkified black leadership" of Eric Holder and Barack Obama for their rejection, however halfhearted, of the explosion of violence against "the white man's tyranny on black people." At the end of the speech, Farrakhan shouted, "We'll tear this goddamn country up." When he finished, the crowd leaped up cheering and chanting, "Allahu Akbar."[32]

Just a month later, Brinsley left Baltimore for New York to start tearing this country up. His anger ran deep. His father split when he was about nine. He quickly learned that if he got in trouble at school, his father would have to pay attention. So he got in trouble often, enough trouble that no one really wanted him around. He bounced from mother to father to sister to a home for troubled boys back to his sister again. "Ismaaiyl learned to live on a couch," wrote the *New York Times*. "He was so estranged at times from his mother that she wasn't certain where he went to high school." As a young adult, he wrote on Facebook, "SOMETIMES I FEEL LIKE A MOTHER-LESS CHILD." Opined the *Times*' reporters, "For some reason, Mr. Brinsley was feeling angry."[33] For some reason?

Brinsley's problems with his mother spilled over into his problem with women. Although he had two children out of wedlock, he never married. He had reportedly threatened to kill one woman and tried to punch out a Waffle House employee who asked him to leave. He began the final day of his life—December 20, 2014—by shooting a woman in Baltimore who had rejected him. After wounding her, he called his mother, Shakuwra Dabre, from a bus on the way to New York. "It's a wrap," he told her. "I already know it's a wrap."[34] Dabre was half-afraid he was coming for her.

He wasn't. The civil rights leadership and the media had given him a more heroic outlet for his wrath, the New York City Police. A few days before the shooting, marchers in New York were chanting, "What do we want? Dead cops. When do we want it? Now."[35] Enraged by the lies the media were spinning and inspired by the protests, Brinsley posted on Instagram, "I'm putting wings on pigs today. They take one of ours . . . let's take 2 of theirs." Brinsley surfaced in Brooklyn, saw a couple of cops sitting in a patrol car, and opened fire. He killed them both. One was Hispanic. One was Asian-American. Brinsley had failed at many things in his life. On this last day, he failed to even kill a white man. Before the police could apprehend him, he took his own life.[36]

Although the median age for murder is less than twenty-five, Brinsley was twenty-eight when he killed the New York cops. Nolen was thirty when he attacked his coworkers. Ferguson, Thornton, and Dorner were all in their early thirties as well when they launched their assaults. Muhammad was in his late thirties. I can tell you from my own experience that there is something about approaching thirty that makes a young man reassess his life. By this time, a man should have arrived or at least be on the way to his destination. He is not a child anymore. But these men were all children. They all had blown relationships with women. They all had lost jobs. They had all failed to master their anger and grow up. None of this set them apart from white mass murderers. What set them apart was that they had someone to blame other than themselves, and that someone was the white man or, in several cases, the white woman. Blame they did. And when they moved from blame to revenge, there was always someone, starting with their moms and ending with alchemists like Sharpton or Farrakhan, ready to reassure them they were right to do so. Racist anger, black or white, infantilizes anyone who harbors it. God changed my heart, and I was blessed to be able to let go and forgive. They were not. I chose to look within. They chose to look without, but their anger clouded their vision.

After the NYPD shooting, the civil rights leaders made a show of disowning Brinsley, but many of their followers took to social media to congratulate him. According to one blogger, Brinsley was a "Hero and African Freedom Fighter, who selflessly gave his life to Honor his Black Brothers."[37] In the streets of Ferguson, protesters honored the deaths of the two police officers with the hateful chant, "Pigs in a blanket; smell like bacon."[38] This was beginning to look an awful lot like a race war.

As I write, new evidence of an impending race war begins to surface. In Ferguson, Missouri, twenty-year-old Jeffery Williams confessed to shooting two police officers. Within days, however, Williams's attorney was saying that Williams only confessed after being beaten by the police and that he never fired a weapon. Not knowing how to handle so explosive a case, the media did their best to bury it.[39] Details about Williams's life were as sketchy as those about Brinsley's.

In New Orleans a black man named Richard White attacked two airport TSA agents with a machete before being shot by a female sheriff's deputy. White brought to the airport a bag containing six Molotov cocktails. Authorities were quick to write White off as "troubled," a line the media accepted without questioning, but no one seemed too eager to find out what troubled him.

In Boston, career criminal Angelo West shot Boston police officer John Moynihan in the face after being pulled over on a traffic stop. West was subsequently killed in a shoot-out with police. The neighbors weren't happy. A menacing crowd of them surrounded the crime scene, chanting, "Hands up, don't shoot" and "Ferguson, Ferguson." Two years earlier, Barack Obama had awarded Moynihan the nation's Top Cop Award at a White House ceremony for his heroic effort to save another cop's life after the Boston bombing. He had nothing to say about the shooting. "This is where we are now," one of the cops on the scene said. "Everyone has their own reality. Their own facts. The truth of the situation doesn't matter."[40]

In Illinois, cousins Hasan and Jonas Edmonds were caught plotting to attack the Joliet Armory and kill the soldiers within. Jonas was a loser. He never graduated from high school and served five years for armed robbery. Hasan, on the other hand, did graduate from high school and served in the National Guard for four years before being arrested. Little was revealed about Hasan's family background other than that his father was imprisoned for sexual assault when Hasan was still a child. That can do it. Like many of the others, the cousins attempted to legitimize their contempt for white America by becoming Muslims and would-be "freedom-fighters." Hasan and Jonas had been sending messages to an undercover FBI agent, sharing his desire to bring "the flames of war to the heart" of America and to "cause as much damage and mayhem as possible."[41]

These flames burn brighter every day.

In Baltimore, in late April 2015, the flames exploded. The excuse given for the sacking and burning of the city was the unexplained death of a poor soul named Freddie Gray while in police custody. Gray had lived a stereotypically fatherless life in inner-city Baltimore with a heroin-addicted mother who never went to high school. Gray had all the problems that kind of life entails, including mother issues. "I used to end up in my mother's bed," Gray said in a deposition for a lead paint case. "She always used to say like I used to sleep with her. She used to call me 'the mama's boy.'"[42] By the time of his death at age twenty-five, he had already been arrested eighteen times, including four times in the previous four months for assault, property destruction, burglary, and drugs—the staple of his arrest record.

At the time of Gray's death, Baltimore had a black mayor, a black police chief, a majority black city council, and a police force less than half white. All the excuses used in Ferguson were out the window. That did not stop the alchemists from blaming everyone but themselves. "I think there are police departments that have to do some soul searching," said Barack Obama. "I think there's some communities that have to do some soul searching. But I think we as a country have to do some soul searching. This is not new. It's been going on for decades."[43]

What has been going on for decades is the refusal of most black people to do any soul searching. All Obama did with his comments was create an environment for blacks to blame police. These were code words for "racism is real," and the problem is the white man. All that the Baltimore state's attorney did by indicting six police officers—three of them black—was to confirm that black people's problems are someone else's fault. In truth, nothing is going to change for the people in Baltimore—the people of America—until they take responsibility for their own lives.

22

PRODIGAL SONS

Here is a challenge for you. Go to Google Images and put in the name "Eminem." Now try to find a picture of him doing something other than scowling at the camera. That scowl is almost universal in inner cities. You see it on men and women, boys and girls. As Eminem proves, it has nothing to do with race and everything to do with anger. By this time, the pattern should be clear. The abandonment of a child by his father creates a void in that child's life that he will almost always fill in a negative way, and you can see it in his face.

Eminem is a millionaire many times over. He has all the women, all the cars, all the homes he could possibly want, but he has never learned to forgive. He knows he should "let bygones be bygones," as he raps in one song, but he does not know how. When I see him with his eternal scowl, I see beyond the "authentic" contempt for society to an empty heart within. I see myself as a young man. I see my son as a young man. I see the future of black America—and maybe white and Hispanic America as well—unless we can turn the hearts of our children back to their fathers.

That is one relationship in life that brings freedom and every other good thing. My broken relationship with my father negatively affected my whole life. Once the relationship was restored, my life was restored! The same is true for all men—black and white, yellow, and brown. They have to understand their role in life and the family. And they have to turn back to God, because they represent Christ on earth. Their role is to be the spiritual head of the family. Their love has to speak the truth. "Love is patient, love is kind," the apostle Paul told the Corinthians. "It does not envy, it does not boast, it is not proud. It does not dishonor others, it is not self-seeking, it is not easily angered, it keeps no record of wrongs. Love does not delight in evil but rejoices with the truth. It always protects, always trusts, always hopes, always perseveres. Love never fails." To the point: love is simply not hating. If men love like this, their wives and children will be richly blessed.

It is not easy, but it is possible for those deprived of that love as children to experience it as adults. Mothers have a role to play here. A woman needs to ask herself what responsibility she bears for driving her man away. Does she remind him of his mother? Is she mimicking that behavior? If the child's father does leave, she needs to remind her children that the father who left the home did not leave because of them. These kids need to know that their father loves them and wants to reconnect with them. Unfortunately, it is the rare single mother who is strong enough to share that message with her children. Too many such mothers would rather hurt the "baby daddy" than help the baby.

I learned a lot about this through experience. When the mother of my son married and moved to Brooklyn, she and her new husband left my son behind with his grandmother in Alabama. Once I had settled into life in Los Angeles, I returned to Alabama and brought my son out to live with me. That went well until I made the mistake of believing my son's mother when she told me that she just wanted him, then five years old, to come visit her. She was lying. She intended all along to keep my son with her in New York. I hired a lawyer, but we quickly saw how powerless I was to fight back. The official records had her name all over them, and the courts backed her.

My son's departure left a huge hole in my heart. I would call often to tell him I loved him, but I was fighting the poison his mother injected into his soul. She led him to believe that I abandoned him, that I did not care about him, that I did not love him. It will not surprise you to know that he grew up angry and unfocused.

If my boy had been with me many years later, after God had

changed my life, I would have been better prepared to show him the way out of the purgatory where he dwelled. Although it hurt, I had to let him go once more. We were two wounded souls. He went back to New York and repeated many of the mistakes I had made, including eventually fathering a child out of wedlock.

Some years after he left I found my way out of the darkness. In the light I could understand his behavior and mine much more clearly. What happened to him, I saw, had happened to me. I learned patience.

At eighteen, he decided to come live with me in Los Angeles. This had less to do with any affection he felt for me than it did his frustration with his mother and the life he was living in Brooklyn. From the day he arrived he communicated his anger with me in a hundred different ways. If I liked something, he hated it. If I didn't like something, he loved it. When I used my contacts to find him a job, he would take the job and misbehave until someone fired him. When I let him use my phone, he would run up the bills. He felt, perhaps rightly, that I owed him, but he wanted me to pay that debt in material things, money most obviously. By then I well understood I could not buy his love. He left for New York again.

From a distance, I communicated my love without pushing. And on his end, of his own accord, he demanded the truth from his mother about me. God's grace was moving us both, not in the same direction, but toward each other.

I remember the moment when it all happened. I was at my home in my bedroom getting ready for work when the phone rang. I sensed it was my son calling. I picked up. I was right. In those first seconds I found myself steeling my defenses—"No, your mother is lying; no, I cannot give you more money." We had had these kinds of conversations many times before, but from the sob in his voice I could tell this call was different. He had called to apologize. The apology was sincere and deeply felt. He had overcome the anger in his life. I felt like the man wandering in the desert who finally found a spring. His words poured over me. I cannot begin to describe how those words refreshed my soul. It was the most beautiful moment in my life.

In a flash I saw with fresh eyes the wisdom of the parable of the prodigal son. As Jesus tells the story, the younger son of a prosperous man takes his share of the estate, runs off, and wastes his inheritance in riotous living. When he comes to see the folly of his ways, he says to himself, "I will set out and go back to my father and say to him: Father, I have sinned against heaven and against you. I am no longer worthy to be called your son; make me like one of your hired servants."

The son knew little of forgiveness and the depth of paternal love. While he was still a long way off, "the father saw him and was filled with compassion for him; he ran to his son, threw his arms around him and kissed him."

The older brother was a little miffed that the father showered so much love on a son "who has squandered your property with prostitutes." The brother does not yet understand paternal love either. "We had to celebrate and be glad," says the father, "because this brother of yours was dead and is alive again; he was lost and is found." I know exactly how the father felt. Biblical wisdom never grows old. What was wise two thousand years ago remains wise today.

Today, my relationship with my son is stronger than ever. He got his life in order. And something that was missing is now part of me. We don't see eye to eye on everything, but on the serious issues, the moral issues, we are one. He calls to ask my advice. If he doesn't hear from me for a while, he calls to make sure I am okay. He insists that I visit him and his family and has even proposed that we vacation together. I'm blessed that God returned my son to me. And my son is blessed for having been returned to his father.

I tell the story of my son and me not to show how great we are but to show how great He is, how much love God has to share with anyone willing to put aside his anger and ask for forgiveness, even an old cotton-picking country boy like me.

23

THE ANTIDOTE

When I saw Michael Brown's endgame play out in the streets of Ferguson, Missouri, I wondered if there was any way his life could have been turned around. It would not have been easy. I know this from experience. Here at BOND, we have counseled any number of young men much like him. We are not always successful, but we have had enough success that I know what to say when a lost soul like Michael Brown comes through my door:

Son, the first thing you have to do is look within. This is where your education begins. Book learning is critical, but your spiritual self-education comes first. Look in the mirror and figure out who or what is looking back at you. Forget your size. God doesn't give a fig how big you are. Forget your looks. The girls may care, but God doesn't. As to your clothes or your tattoos or your bling—please! Those are all designed to disguise who you really are, not from others, but from yourself. They are the last things you need to concern yourself with.

Get beyond your appearance. People ask me what causes a person to stop and take that initial look. Often it is some kind of shock to the system—an arrest, a divorce, a death, a lost job, an addiction, an accident. Sometimes it is just a building sense of despair. In my case, it was because I was, like you, so lost, so unhappy, so deeply unsatisfied with my life I could cry. It was this suffering that caused me to ask God to let me see myself.

Richard Pryor had a similar experience. He looked within and saw what I saw—something cold and dark. We reacted differently. I think

I know why. Deep down, I knew that God loved me. I knew He could redeem me. I don't think Pryor had any such consolation. He had estranged himself from God's love. He had chosen the wrong side in the war between good and evil. In his misery, though, he sensed he had made a tragic error and allied himself with the Deceiver. So when he saw that devil, he set the devil on fire. I imagine Judas felt much the same before he hanged himself.

Michael Brown's relatives say he was struggling with his faith in the weeks before he died. It was not a struggle he was winning. The face that he presented to Officer Wilson, like the one Richard Pryor saw in the mirror, was that of a "demon."[1] Had he known where to turn, Michael might have found the spiritual assistance he needed. It is never too late. So as long as that divine spark burns within, there is help for you. Don't ever let the flame go out. Nurse it. Protect it. We as human beings will never become our best selves unless we seek God first.

You are, however, not going to find God in a building. You will find Him when you look at yourself and see the truth of what you've become through your anger. That is where self-knowledge begins. If you are to overcome your image of yourself as victim, you must see yourself for who you are. So much of what makes you feel victimized is anger. You are angry, but you don't know what you are angry about.

As we've discussed, I have found, and know from experience, that one of the greatest sources of anger is the lack of a father in the home. Heather Barwick, the woman we met in chapter 10, who was raised by two lesbians, put her finger on the problem: "My father's absence created a huge hole in me, and I ached every day for a dad." As Heather understood, those who turn away from their earthly father turn away from their spiritual Father as well. They can never learn to know and love God if their heart is filled with hate. We must all strive to forgive. It is God who allows us to forgive and reunite. What salvation is really all about is a return to the Father.

Young black men are particularly vulnerable to the temptation to hate. Son, you, like so many of your friends, have not had a father at home that you could identify with spiritually. You have had no reliable man to guide you, protect you, teach you, and discipline you when you needed it. You may not have seen a man like that in your neighborhood. Chances are that neither of your parents had a good father either. This means you may not even have had a strong grandfather in your life as I did. Your sisters suffer from this same problem, and it is just as severe, if not quite so deadly.

Fatherlessness is a problem for anyone who experiences it. Just ask Heather. As a young black man, you are vulnerable for another reason. Many of the people you trust—your relatives, your teachers, the president, maybe even your pastor—will discourage you from coming to terms with the anger you naturally feel. They will encourage you instead to direct that anger toward white people, America, even Christianity.

Tupac Shakur's mother, Afeni, who was deeply angry most of her life, understood how the process worked. She wrote of her time with the Black Panthers, "They took my rage and channeled it against them instead of us."[2] By "them" she meant those who pursued the American dream, black and white. By "us" she meant herself and her colleagues. By the time Afeni said this, she knew she had been lied to and abused. The "direction" the Panthers gave her was a pure dead end. She never did learn how to forgive. In not forgiving, she never learned how to love.

Son, a good church will help you nurture your relationship with God and grow in understanding of yourself, but be warned, not all churches are good. In the black community, too many pastors prefer judging white people to asking congregants to judge themselves. A preacher like Obama's pastor who says not, "God bless America," but "God damn America," should not have a pulpit, let alone a church.

That Jeremiah Wright would ask God to damn anyone is troubling enough. Even worse in the long run is that he gives his congregants an excuse not to examine their own consciences. They are encouraged to examine white people's consciences instead. It was Wright who said in Obama's presence, "White folks' greed runs a world in need." Yes, white folks are the problem. For Wright, they always are. His sermons have done almost nothing but remind his congregants of their grievances. Unfortunately, "victims" never accept blame, rarely forgive others, and do not grow up until they cast off the shackles of victimhood.

What you need, son, is love. Black or white, we all have that same need. But your anger separates you from God, and without God there can be no real love. To find your way back, you have to own up to your anger. Do not be afraid to pray. Do not be afraid to shut out the noise of the world. As the Bible tells us, "Be still, and know that I am God." If you are strong enough to forgive, you will be forgiven.

For you to get your spirit in order, however, you will have to get over your "blackness." This will not be easy with all those "respectable" people shoving your blackness down your throat. But as long as you see yourself as a black man first and a Christian and an American secondarily—if at all—your blackness will enslave you. It will dictate your thoughts, restrict your taste, limit your ambition, and direct your anger. You will find yourself doing things you don't like—and not doing things you do like—because the "brothers" expect you to. The weight of popular opinion in the black community has crushed many a good spirit. Don't let one of those spirits be yours.

Son, while you are learning about yourself, it is important to learn about the world. This is where a formal education comes into play. Follow your interests as long as you are comfortable following them, and don't let other people dictate what your interests are. When you get over your blackness, you will understand that to get good grades is not to "act white."

On the other hand, well-meaning people will tell you that you must attend college and find a major you can pass. This is all well and good if you have the disposition for higher education, but as Booker T. Washington reminded us, there is much to be said for mastering a marketable skill. A young black man with a plumber's license will likely have a better future than one who barely earned a sports management degree at the local state teachers' college. He will also have more self-respect. You don't want to sit in an office all day doing nothing of consequence only halfway well and wondering whether the company hired you to appease the Equal Opportunity crowd.

Son, with a marketable skill you are much better able to start thinking about a wife and children. They come in that order: wife first, children next. And once you are married, stay married. Jesus explained this order to the taunting Pharisees. "From the beginning of the creation God made them male and female," He said. "For this cause shall a man leave his father and mother, and cleave to his wife: and they two shall be one flesh. Wherefore they are no more two, but one flesh. What therefore God hath joined together, let not man put asunder." I cannot repeat this often enough: family breakdown is the great social and spiritual scourge of our time. Do not be part of that problem. There are few greater sins than abandoning your own children. If you only see your kids when you feel like it, you *have* abandoned them.

Being married is not enough. Without spiritual order in the family, children will be born into darkness. The apostle Paul shared with the Ephesians what that order should be: "Wives, submit yourselves unto your own husbands, as unto the Lord." As Paul went on to explain, the husband is the head of the wife in much the same way Christ is the head of man. This was a relationship based on mutual love and responsibility. Feminists often condemn this passage for seeming backward and undemocratic, but a family is not a democracy. At its best, it is an organic unit through which order and love flow.

This spiritual order reflects the natural instincts of men and women. Although as "liberated" as any woman could be, Afeni Shakur understood her heart. "All I wanted was protection," she wrote. "That's all every woman wants." By nature, men want to protect. They want responsibility. "Husbands, love your wives," Paul continued, "even as Christ also loved the church." By "the church," Paul meant "you," the man. In a family that lives by this creed, there is no abuse, no neglect, no intimidation, no fear. The husband grows strong. The wife blossoms. The children flourish.

Marriage offers material benefits as well as spiritual. A black single mother with children is more than four times likelier to live in poverty than a black married couple with children.[3] This only stands to reason. There are less tangible benefits as well. A married mother usually lives in a better home in a better neighborhood. Her children are safer. They go to better schools. She can drive her children and pick them up in her own car. She and her husband can travel, go on vacation, save for the future. She does not have to depend on unreliable boyfriends, uncles, or "whatever" for rides, loans, or "love." She has a sense of security that a single mother can barely imagine. I don't say this to criticize single mothers but rather to educate them as to what they are missing. Even if they have a child out of wedlock, they should not give up on marriage. First, though, they too have to look in the mirror and come to terms with who they are and what they need.

One more thing, son: work hard. Once you are over your blackness, you will see that black people are *not* the last hired and first fired. If anything today, the opposite is true. As much as I dislike affirmative action, I cannot fault you for taking advantage of it. What you don't want to do, though, is accept a position for which you are not suited just to fill someone's quota. You want an employer to hire you because of the skills and attitude you bring to the job.

Once hired, you will show up every day for work on time—enough of that "CP (Colored People) time" stuff. You will work as hard as the next man, maybe even harder because you want to get ahead on your own. Your colleagues will want to work with you. If you make a mistake, you will accept blame. You will take a sick day only when you are on your deathbed or very nearly so. You will tackle every task in good spirit. You will find the joy in every job, no matter how humble, and do it as well as you can. You will be grateful God has given you the health to do your work and that your employer has given you the opportunity. You will never, ever say, "I did not get promoted because I'm black." Your employer would not have hired you if he were scheming not to promote you. And if the employer does fire you, you will not sue. You will look hard in that mirror once again and ask yourself, "Where did I go wrong?"

If you follow these guidelines, you will not get fired. You will get promoted. You start saving your money and investing it. With savings comes freedom. Even if you get a bad boss—and they are out there; ask your white colleagues—you will have the freedom to walk away from the job. At some point, you will come to the understanding that an adult of a certain age should no longer have to ask permission. When you do, you will realize it is time to start your own business. And when you have to hire your own employees, you will look at the black workers who apply and see exactly what white employers do. I take no joy in telling you that my black entrepreneur friends are reluctant to hire them. They will not be reluctant to hire you. I will gladly write you a recommendation.

* * *

I know this all sounds simple. It sounds simple because, in a way, it is. The antidote to our communal despair is within reach of every single American, black or white, and its formula is as simple as the one described above. God wants us to be free. Freedom begins for black Americans when we throw off the shackles of anger, hate, dependency, debt, and "blackness." Freedom ends for us in self-awareness, love, mercy, happiness, and forgiveness. Forgiveness, remember, is a spiritual gift God can give us only when we admit we are wrong.

At BOND we work on one soul at a time. This is, of necessity, a slow process. I am old enough and wise enough to know that I may not be the one to liberate black America. That said, I am hopeful enough to think black America will one day be liberated. And I am brash enough to think that those who will free black America just might begin by reading this book. It will take some especially strong people to throw off so much entrenched evil, but if they succeed, the rewards will be astonishing.

I imagine a South Central in which every child lives with both parents and those parents love and protect their children. I see these kids walking safely to the neighborhood school in the morning and eagerly tackling their studies without fear of disruption. I see them skipping home after school and being greeted at the doors by their mothers. And upon seeing her, I see these little black kids with smiles as big as their heads. This is the way millions of American kids live their lives right now. It should be the way all American kids live their lives going forward. Remember: our battle is not a physical one. It is a spiritual battle between good and evil. The Kingdom of Heaven is within. Be still. Go within and find your Father.

AFTERWORD

I pray that the nation avoids any serious racial strife in the months and years to come, but I see no efforts by anyone in power to speak honestly about the issues at hand, let alone address the underlying problems. Walter Scott of South Carolina had many of those problems. At the time the fifty-year-old Scott was shot by Officer Michael Slager, he had an outstanding warrant for failure to pay child support. Although he had not paid for the care of his four children in three years, he was driving a Mercedes. He obviously did not have his priorities in order. He had been arrested about ten times previously, many of those for child support issues. For some reason, he chose to run after Slager stopped him for a broken taillight. Slager caught up with the heavyset Scott, and the two men reportedly struggled. Officer Slager told the police dispatcher, "He grabbed my Taser." Scott broke free and bolted. Slager, in turn, shot Scott in the back.

Why either man did what he did I do not know. Each appears to have made a tragic error. There are thousands of interactions between black men and white police officers each week, and some of them are bound to go bad. This one certainly did. In the aftermath, however, all the talk was about what Officer Slager did wrong. I had a chance to address that issue the week following the shooting on the Fox News channel. I appeared with black civil rights attorney Leo Terrell.

"In America you are innocent until proven guilty," I said, "and right now, Sean [Hannity], white officers are under attack by angry black folks in this country, and when they're stopped by these officers, they're not listening, they're not obeying the authority of the police officers."[1] This, to me, was the larger problem. Why were so many black people so angry that they put their own lives in jeopardy?

Terrell could not contain himself. "Jesse Lee Peterson is the only man on the face of this earth who is talking about everything else but the unlawful shooting of this man," he shouted. In a sense, he was right. The shooting was so out of the ordinary that it dominated the news. Scott's resisting arrest was so commonplace it did not seem worthy of Terrell's time. But Scott's behavior was a symptom of a cultural disease that is crippling black America. And I was not supposed to address that? Apparently not.

"You are an embarrassment to the world right now!" said Terrell. "The whole world is looking at how stupid you are!" I answered, "All that I'm saying is that we should wait for due process because I don't think Americans understand how angry and brainwashed these young black folks are." For years civil rights attorneys had fought to secure the right to due process embedded in our Constitution. "No person shall be held to answer for a capital, or otherwise infamous crime," reads the Fifth Amendment, ". . . nor be deprived of life, liberty, or property, without due process of law." Yet when I suggested that even a white police officer deserved due process as well, Terrell exploded. "Come to me right now or I'm gone," he fumed, "because I'm not going to sit here and listen to this hate."

The Internet warriors were even more hateful. "Uncle Tom!!!" wrote one. "May you burn in hell for being an Oreo! Placate the white man while putting down your own people." Wrote another, "The coonery you represented on the Hannity Show tonight is beyond unbelievable. I hope it was a sick joke. Any person, especially [a] person of color working for or with [this] guy should question their own sanity."

Yes, that is how strange our world has become. To ask for a civil discussion of the larger issues is provocative. To ask that an accused murderer be allowed due process is hateful. To ask that we look at the underlying problems that led to Scott's criminal action is an "embarrassment." This is what the alchemists have wrought. "I'm done, I'm done, I'm done, I'm done," Terrell mumbled before ripping out his earpiece and walking off set.

Well, Leo, I am not done. I am in earnest—I will not equivocate—I will not excuse—I will not retreat a single inch . . .

AND I WILL BE HEARD.

NOTES

CHAPTER 1: DEATH ON CANFIELD DRIVE

1. The following account is taken largely from Heather Mac Donald, "Justice Is Blind," *Weekly Standard*, March 30, 2015, http://www.weeklystandard.com/author/heather-mac-donald.

2. John Richardson, "Michael Brown Sr. and the Agony of the Black Father in America," *Esquire*, January 5, 2015, http://www.esquire.com/news-politics/interviews/a30808/michael-brown-father-interview-0115/.

3. Jesse Bogan et al., "Why did the Michael Brown shooting happen here?" *St. Louis Post-Dispatch*, August 17, 2014, http://www.stltoday.com/news/local/metro/why-did-the-michael-brown-shooting-happen-here/article_678334ce-500a-5689-8658-f548207cf253.html.

4. Transcripts, *Anderson Cooper 360 Degrees*, CNN, June 28, 2013, http://transcripts.cnn.com/TRANSCRIPTS/1306/28/acd.01.html. No longer accessible.

5. Tracy Martin, Facebook account, October 27, 2010, cached by "sundance" in "Trayvon Martin—perhaps the Inconsistencies from Tracy and Sybrina are more easily explained . . . ," *The Last Refuge* (blog), June 23, 2012, http://theconservativetreehouse.com/2012/06/23/trayvon-martin-perhaps-the-inconsistencies-from-tracy-and-sybrina-are-more-easily-explained/.

6. Elizabeth Chuck et al., "Zimmerman defense releases texts about guns, fighting from Trayvon Martin's phone," NBC News, May 23, 2013, http://usnews.nbcnews.com/_news/2013/05/23/18449794-zimmerman-defense-releases-texts-about-guns-fighting-from-trayvon-martins-phone?lite.

7. "Martin Family Lawyer Likens Trayvon to Medgar Evers and Emmett Till," *RealClearPolitics*, July 14, 2013, http://www.realclearpolitics.com/video/2013/07/14/martin_family_lawyer_likens_trayvon_to_medgar_evers_and_emmett_till_.html.

8. "Eric Holder Likens Michael Brown to Emmett Till: 'The Struggle Goes On," *RealClearPolitics*, November 17, 2014, http://www.realclearpolitics.com/video/2014/11/17/eric_holder_likens_michael_brown_to_emmett_till_the_struggle_goes_on.html.

9. "Brown's mother: 'How could your conscience be clear?,'" *CBS This Morning*, November 26, 2014, http://www.cbsnews.com/news/ferguson-michael-brown-family-speaks-out-on-shooting-officer-wilson-grand-jury-decision/.

10. "Trayvon Martin's Mom: 'If They Refuse to Hear Us, We Will Make Them Feel Us'," *Time*, August 18, 2014, http://time.com/3136685/trayvon-sybrina-fulton-ferguson/.

11. "Mike Brown Never Had a Step-Dad—Police Report Shows Lesley McSpadden and Louis Head Not Married—However, Both Participated in Physical Attack During October Robbery . . . ," *The Last Refuge*, December 1, 2014, http://theconservativetreehouse.com/2014/12/01/mike-brown-never-had-a-step-dad-police-report-shows-lesley-mcspadden-and-louis-head-not-married-however-both-participated-in-physical-attack-during-october-robbery/.

CHAPTER 2: THE ALCHEMISTS

1. In an October 2008 campaign visit to Missouri, Obama told voters, "We are five days away from fundamentally transforming the United States of America." See Tim Ryan, "In context: What Obama said about 'fundamentally transforming' the nation," Politifact.com, May 11, 2015, http://www.politifact.com/truth-o-meter/article/2014/feb/06/what-barack-obama-has-said-about-fundamentally-tra/.

2. *The Liberator*: Inaugural Editorial by William Lloyd Garrison, January 1, 1831, on America's Civil War website, http://static.sewanee.edu/faculty/Willis/Civil_War/documents/Liberator.html.

CHAPTER 3: BEFORE THE FALL

1. Jack Cashill, *Sucker Punch: The Hard Left Hook That Dazed Ali and Killed King's Dream* (Nashville: Thomas Nelson, 2006), 130.

2. William Nack, "The Fight's Over, Joe," *Sports Illustrated*, September 30, 1996, http://www.si.com/vault/1996/09/30/208924/the-fights-over-joe-more-than-two-decades-after-they-last-met-in-the-ring-joe-frazier-is-still-taking-shots-at-muhammad-ali-but-this-time-its-a-war-of-words.

3. Joe Frazier and Phil Berger, *Smokin' Joe: The Autobiography of a Heavyweight Champion of the World, Smokin' Joe Frazier* (New York: Macmillan, 1996).

4. Cavan Sieczkowski, "'Duck Dynasty' Star Phil Robertson Claims Black People Were 'Happy' Pre-Civil Rights," *Huffington Post*, December 19, 2013, http://www.huffingtonpost.com/2013/12/19/phil-robertson-black-people_n_4473474.html.

5. Isabel Wilkerson, *The Warmth of Other Sons, The Epic Story of America's Great Migration* (New York: Random House, 2011).

CHAPTER 4: FALL FROM GRACE

1. Jeffrey Goldberg, "The Color of Suspicion," *New York Times*, June 20, 1999, http://www.nytimes.com/1999/06/20/magazine/the-color-of-suspicion.html?pagewanted=all&src=pm.

2. Peter Guralnick, *Dream Boogie: The Triumph of Sam Cooke*, repr. ed. (New York: Back Bay/Little, Brown, 2006), 186.

3. Ibid., 188.

4. Walter Williams, "Black Unemployment," *Townhall.com*, April 10, 2013, http://townhall.com/columnists/walterewilliams/2013/04/10/black-unemployment-n1561096.

5. United States Department of Labor, "Databases, Tables & Calculators by Subject," Bureau of Labor Statistics website, accessed May 8, 2015, http://data.bls.gov/timeseries/LNU04000000?years_option=all_years&periods_option=specific_periods&periods=Annual+Data.

6. Deanese Williams-Harris, "Gary's first woman mayor: 'Gary is open for business,'" *Chicago Tribune*, November 9, 2011, http://articles.chicagotribune.com/2011-11-09/news/chi-gary-residents-elect-their-first-woman-mayor-20111109_1_mayor-rudy-clay-land-based-casino-gary-airport.

CHAPTER 5: THE ROAD TO DAMASCUS

1. Wendy Leigh, *Arnold: An Unauthorized Biography* (Chicago: Congdon & Weed, 1990), 91.
2. "Farrakhan helped build climate for Malcolm X's death, historian says," Stanford News Service, January 17, 1995, http://news.stanford.edu/pr/95/950117Arc5411.html.
3. The statistics that follow are from the California Crime Index, Office of the Attorney General— California Department of Justice, https://oag.ca.gov/crime.
4. "Texas Police Probe Recidivist Road Rager," Smoking Gun, February 12, 2015, http://www. thesmokinggun.com/documents/stupid/austin-texas-road-rager-546930.
5. "Interview with Andrew Young," *Frontline*, PBS.org, accessed May 11, 2015, http://www.pbs.org/wgbh/pages/frontline/jesse/interviews/young.html.

CHAPTER 6: THE CHAINS OF BLACKNESS

1. The Official Kwanzaa Website, accessed May 12, 2015, http://www.officialkwanzaawebsite.org/index.shtml.
2. Maulana Karenga, "The Values of Kwanzaa: The Nguzo Saba (The Seven Principles)," official Kwanzaa website, http://www.officialkwanzaawebsite.org/7principles.shtml.
3. Quoted in "Maulana Karenga," Discover the Networks, accessed May 12, 2015, http://www. discoverthenetworks.org/printindividualProfile.asp?indid=2222.
4. "Karenga Tortured Women Followers," Wife Tells Court," *Los Angeles Times*, May 13, 1971. Archived at http://pqasb.pqarchiver.com/latimes/doc/156710021.html?FMT=ABS&FMTS=AB S:AI&type=historic&date=May%2013,%201971&desc=Karenga%20Tortured%20Women%20 Followers,%20Wife%20Tells%20Court.
5. "Maulana Karenga," Discover the Networks.
6. "Statement from the President and the First Lady on Kwanzaa," website of the White House, Office of the Press Secretary, December 26, 2014, https://www.whitehouse.gov/the-press-office/2014/12/26/statement-president-and-first-lady-kwanzaa.
7. Quotes, *Guess Who's Coming to Dinner*, IMDB.com, accessed May 12, 2015, http://www.imdb. com/title/tt0061735/quotes.
8. See Heather Foster, "Honoring the African American Experience: The White House Celebrates Black History Month," *The White House Blog*, March 3, 2015, https://www.whitehouse.gov/blog/2015/03/02/honoring-african-american-experience-white-house-celebrates-black-history-month.
9. "The Empire Taraji P. Henson Built," *Uptown*, February 11, 2015, http://uptownmagazine. com/2015/02/empire-taraji-p-henson-interview/4/.
10. Alyssa Norwin, "'Empire' Star Taraji P. Henson's Tragic Lover," *Star*, March 26, 2015, http:// starmagazine.com/2015/03/26/taraji-henson-boyfriend-death/.
11. "History of Jazz," Black History in America, on the Scholastic website, accessed May 12, 2015, http://teacher.scholastic.com/activities/bhistory/history_of_jazz.htm.

CHAPTER 7: THE ONE-DROP LEGACY

1. Alex Haley, *The Autobiography of Malcolm X*, repr. ed (New York: Ballantine, 1992), 437.
2. Gordon Parks, "The Violent End of the Man Called Malcolm," *Life*, March 5, 1965.
3. Adam White, "Malcolm X, Not Madison: Welcome to the Eric Holder Book Club," *Weekly Standard*, February 27, 2015, http://www.weeklystandard.com/keyword/Malcolm-X.

4. Haley, *The Autobiography of Malcolm X*, 2.
5. Manning Marable, *Malcolm X: A Life of Reinvention* (New York: Penguin, 2011), 33.
6. Haley, *The Autobiography of Malcolm X*, 3.
7. Robert Stulberg, "The Final Speech of Malcolm X," *Columbia Spectator*, February 18, 1965, cached at http://spectatorarchive.library.columbia.edu/cgi-bin/columbia?a=d&d=cs19690220-01.2.11&e=————-en-20—1—txt-txIN-ezra+koenig————-.
8. John Egerton, "Heritage of a Heavyweight," *New York Times*, September 28, 1980, https://www.nytimes.com/books/98/10/25/specials/ali-heritage.html.
9. Haley, *The Autobiography of Malcolm X*, 3.
10. Ibid., 9.
11. Ibid., 22.
12. Ibid., 4.
13. Thomas Hauser, *Muhammad Ali: His Life and Times* (New York: Open Road Media, 2012), 110.
14. George Davis, "Tiger Woods: Black Life in Cablinasia," *Psychology Today*, December 15, 2009, https://www.psychologytoday.com/blog/modern-melting-pot/200912/tiger-woods-black-life-in-cablinasia.
15. Maureen Dowd, "Tiger's Double Bogey," *New York Times*, April 19, 1997, http://www.nytimes.com/1997/04/19/opinion/tiger-s-double-bogey.html.
16. Halle Berry, Academy Award Acceptance Speech, March 24, 2002, Academy Awards Acceptance Speech Database, http://aaspeechesdb.oscars.org/link/074-3/.

CHAPTER 8: THE FORBIDDEN FRUIT

1. W. E. B. Du Bois, "The Talented Tenth," excerpted on the website of the Gilder Lehrman Center at Yale University, accessed May 12, 2015, http://www.yale.edu/glc/archive/1148.htm.
2. Jonathan Alter, *The Promise: President Obama, Year One* (New York: Simon & Schuster, 2010), 64.
3. Barack Obama, in an interview with Larry King on CNN's *Larry King Live*, aired October 19, 2006. Transcript available on CNN.com at http://transcripts.cnn.com/TRANSCRIPTS/0610/19/lkl.01.html.
4. "Barack Obama's Speech on Race," *New York Times*, March 18, 2008, http://www.nytimes.com/2008/03/18/us/politics/18text-obama.html?pagewanted=all&_r=0.
5. Barack Obama, *Dreams from My Father: A Story of Race and Inheritance* (New York: Crown, 2007), 293.
6. "Barack Obama's Speech on Race."
7. Ibid.
8. Xuan Thai and Ted Barnett, "Biden's description of Obama draws scrutiny," CNN.com, February 9, 2007, http://www.cnn.com/2007/POLITICS/01/31/biden.obama/.
9. Abby Goodnough, "Harvard Professor Jailed; Officer Is Accused of Bias," *New York Times*, July 20, 2009, http://www.nytimes.com/2009/07/21/us/21gates.html.
10. Associated Press, "Friends and police rally behind Sgt. James Crowley, who arrested Harvard professor," *MetroWest Daily News*, July 24, 2009, http://www.metrowestdailynews.com/x905592581/Friends-and-police-rally-behind-Sgt-James-Crowley-who-arrested-Harvard-professor.
11. Jospeh Williams, "Trayvon Martin shooting: Black leaders press White House," Politico, March 22, 2012, http://www.politico.com/news/stories/0312/74385.html.
12. Stephanie Condon, "Obama: 'If I had a son, he'd look like Trayvon,'" CBS News, March 23, 2012, http://www.cbsnews.com/news/obama-if-i-had-a-son-hed-look-like-trayvon/.
13. Du Bois, "The Talented Tenth."

14. Booker T. Washington, *Up from Slavery: An Autobiography* (New York: Doubleday, Page, 1901), 53.
15. Ibid., 54.
16. "Booker T. Washington Delivers the 1895 Atlanta Compromise Speech," History Matters, http://historymatters.gmu.edu/d/39/. The quotes that follow are also from this speech.
17. June O'Neill et al., *The Economic Progress of Black Men in America* (United States Commission on Civil Rights, 1986), https://www.law.umaryland.edu/marshall/usccr/documents/e1858e471986.pdf, 1.
18. Matthew Yglesias, "The Strange Case of Woodrow Wilson," *ThinkProgress*, December 11, 2009, http://thinkprogress.org/yglesias/2009/12/11/195405/the-strange-case-of-woodrow-wilson/.
19. "Application for Membership in the Communist Party by W.E.B. DuBois," October 1, 1961, Communist Party USA, http://www.cpusa.org/application-to-join-the-cpusa-by-w-e-b-du-bois-1961/.
20. O'Neill et al., *The Economic Progress of Black Men in America*, 6, 48.
21. Frances Fox Piven and Richard Cloward, "The Weight of the Poor: A Strategy to End Poverty," *Nation*, May 2, 1966, http://www.thenation.com/article/weight-poor-strategy-end-poverty#.
22. Ann Brenoff, "Pew Analysis of Jobs Report Shows That More Young People Are Saying 'No' to the Workforce," *Huffington Post*, December 14, 2014, http://www.huffingtonpost.com/2014/11/14/youth-unemployment_n_6158238.html.
23. "Benjamin Carson interview," Academy of Achievement, June 7, 2002, embedded at http://www.achievement.org/autodoc/page/car1int-1. All subsequent quotes are from the two interviews at this site.
24. Barack Obama in a public reading, video posted by RichardAnthony in "BREAKING: Shocking 1995 Video Surfaces of Barack Obama Revealing Who He REALLY Is," April 15, 2015, on the website of UFP News, http://universalfreepress.com/breaking-shocking-1995-video-surfaces-of-barack-obama-revealing-who-he-really-is/#.
25. Obama, *Dreams from My Father*, 70.
26. Ibid., 85, 86, 89.
27. Ibid., 91.
28. Ibid., 293.
29. Ibid, 198.

CHAPTER 9: TARNISHED ANGELS

1. David Henry and Joe Henry, *Furious Cool: Richard Pryor and the World That Made Him* (New York: Algonquin, 2014), 230.
2. Ibid., 230, 244.
3. Ibid., 270.
4. Ibid., 256.
5. Ibid., 214.
6. Jeff Hobbs, *The Short and Tragic Life of Robert Peace: A Brilliant Young Man Who Left Newark for the Ivy League* (New York: Simon & Schuster, 2014), 57–58.
7. Ibid., 151, 173.
8. Anand Giridharadas, "Man Down: The Short and Tragic Life of Robert P. Peace," *New York Times*, September 18, 2014, http://www.nytimes.com/2014/09/21/books/review/the-short-and-tragic-life-of-robert-peace-by-jeff-hobbs.html.

9. Henry and Henry, *Furious Cool*, 169.

10. *The Liberator*: Inaugural Editorial by William Lloyd Garrison, January 1, 1831, on America's Civil War website, http://static.sewanee.edu/faculty/Willis/Civil_War/documents/Liberator.html.

11. Henry and Henry, *Furious Cool*, 169.

12. Julie Bosman, "Obama Sharply Assails Absent Black Fathers," *New York Times*, June 16, 2008, http://www.nytimes.com/2008/06/16/us/politics/15cnd-obama.html.

13. "Obama's Father Day Speech" (transcript), June 27, 2008, CNN Election Center 2008, http://www.cnn.com/2008/POLITICS/06/27/obama.fathers.ay/index.html.

14. "Jesse Jackson used racial epithet," LiveLeak, July 16, 2008, http://www.liveleak.com/view?i=aae_1216262864; see also "Jesse Jackson Says He Wants to Cut Obama's 'Nuts Out,'" *New York Post*, July 9, 2008, http://nypost.com/2008/07/09/jesse-jackson-says-he-wants-to-cut-obamas-nuts-out/.

15. Suzanne Goldenberg, "US election 2008: 'I want to cut his nuts out'—Jackson gaffe turns focus on Obama's move to the right," *Guardian*, July 10, 2008, http://www.theguardian.com/world/2008/jul/11/barackobama.uselections2008.

CHAPTER 10: BLOODY SHIRTS

1. Eric Hoffer, *The Temper of Our Time* (New York: Harper & Row, 1967), 33.

2. Hampton Sides, *Hellhound on His Trail: The Electrifying Account of the Largest Manhunt in American History* (New York: Anchor, 2011), 235.

3. Ibid., 219.

4. Jack Kraft, "Rev. Abernathy Says the Dream Continues to Live," *Morning Call*, April 19, 1988, http://articles.mcall.com/1988-04-19/news/2634460_1_abernathy-rev-jackson-jesse-jackson.

5. Clarence Page, "Life's Not Easy for Jackson Critics," *Chicago Tribune*, April 17, 1988, http://articles.chicagotribune.com/1988-04-17/news/8803090887_1_jesse-jackson-jackson-critics-louis-farrakhan.

6. Louis Farrakhan, Million Man March speech, October 16, 1995, transcript posted at the website of Voices of Democracy: The U.S. Oratory Project, http://voicesofdemocracy.umd.edu/farrakhan-million-man-march-speech-text/.

7. "Jesse Jackson's 'Hymietown' Remark—1984," *Washington Post*, accessed May 13, 2015, http://www.washingtonpost.com/wp-srv/politics/special/clinton/frenzy/jackson.htm.

8. David Barboza, "Toyota Earmarks $8 Billion for Diversification Efforts," *Business Day* (*New York Times* blog), August 10, 2001, http://www.nytimes.com/2001/08/10/business/10JESS.html.

9. These details are confirmed in "Jesse Jackson Exposed: A Judicial Watch Special Report," 2006, http://www.judicialwatch.org/archive/2006/jackson-report.pdf.

10. Lynn Sweet, "Obama's cites 'Joshua generation' in 2007 Selma speech. Transcript," *Chicago Sun Times*, March 7, 2015, http://chicago.suntimes.com/lynn-sweet-politics/7/71/421587/obamas-cites-joshua-generation-2007-selma-speech-transcript.

11. Maya Rhodan, "Transcript: Read Full Text of President Barack Obama's Speech in Selma," *Time*, March 7, 2015, http://time.com/3736357/barack-obama-selma-speech-transcript/.

12. Dr. Susan Berry, "Black Pastors Coalition Leader: Obama's Comparison of Civil Rights and Gay Marriage Struggles a 'Disgrace to the Black Community,'" Breitbart, March 10 2015, http://www.breitbart.com/big-government/2015/03/10/black-pastors-coalition-leader-obamas-comparison-of-civil-rights-and-gay-marriage-struggles-a-disgrace-to-the-black-community/.

13. Heather Barwick, "Dear Gay Community: Your Kids Are Hurting," *Federalist*, March 17, 2015, http://thefederalist.com/2015/03/17/dear-gay-community-your-kids-are-hurting/.

14. Katie Yoder, "MSNBC's Harris-Perry: Today's Selma March Is for 'Reproductive Rights,'" *NewsBusters*, March 9, 2015, http://newsbusters.org/blogs/katie-yoder/2015/03/09/msnbcs-harris-perry-todays-selma-march-reproductive-rights.

CHAPTER 11: FEAR AND LOATHING

1. The following story about Jones is summarized from Jack Cashill, *What's the Matter with California? Cultural Rumbles from the Golden State and Why the Rest of Us Should Be Shaking* (New York: Simon & Schuster, 2008), 142–46.

2. Phil Matier and Andy Ross, "A death too close for funeral assistant working to stop violence," *San Francisco Chronicle*, March 15, 2015, http://www.sfchronicle.com/bayarea/matier-ross/article/A-death-too-close-for-funeral-assistant-working-6135834.php.

3. Ibid.

4. Ibid.

5. Larry O'Connor, Breitbart Big-Journalism, April 12, 2010, http://www.breitbart.com/big-journalism/2010/04/12/were-reporters-used-to-spread-n-word-narrative/.

6. Courtland Milloy, "Courtland Milloy: Congressmen show grace, restraint in the face of disrespect," *Washington Post*, March 24, 2010, http://www.washingtonpost.com/wp-dyn/content/article/2010/03/23/AR2010032304018.html.

7. Douglas, "Tea party protesters scream 'nigger' at black congressman." McClatchy Newspapers, March 20, 2010, http://www.mcclatchydc.com/2010/03/20/90772/rep-john-lewis-charges-protesters.html.

8. "Tea Party Protesters Dispute Reports of Slurs, Spitting Against Dem Lawmakers," Fox News, March 22, 2010, http://www.foxnews.com/story/2010/03/22/tea-party-protesters-dispute-reports-slurs-spitting-against-dem-lawmakers/.

9. Douglas, "Tea party protesters scream 'nigger' at black congressman."

10. Jack Cashill, "Anatomy of a Racial Smear," *American Thinker*, March 24, 2010, http://www.americanthinker.com/articles/2010/03/anatomy_of_a_racial_smear_1.html, emphasis added.

11. Milloy, "Congressmen show grace, restraint in the face of disrespect."

CHAPTER 12: THE CLOWN PRINCE

1. Al Sharpton, *Go and Tell Pharaoh: The Autobiography of the Reverend Al Sharpton* (New York: Doubleday, 1996), 28.

2. Ibid., 125.

3. "Brawley Case: Stubborn Puzzle, Silent Victim," *New York Times*, February 29, 1988, http://www.nytimes.com/1988/02/29/nyregion/brawley-case-stubborn-puzzle-silent-victim.html.

4. James Barron, "Cuomo Won't Remove Abrams in Brawley Case," *New York Times*, February 23, 1988, http://www.nytimes.com/1988/02/23/nyregion/cuomo-won-t-remove-abrams-in-brawley-case.html.

5. William Saletan, "The Worst of Al Sharpton," *Slate*, September 8, 2003, http://www.slate.com/articles/news_and_politics/ballot_box/2003/09/the_worst_of_al_sharpton.html.

6. Jake Tapper, "The skeletons and suits in Al Sharpton's closet," *Salon*, June 20, 2003, http://www.salon.com/2003/06/21/sharpton_7/

7. Jennifer Hickey, "WaPo Fact Checker: Giuliani Right on Sharpton Visits to WH," *Newsmax*,

December 30, 2014, http://www.newsmax.com/US/Rudy-Giuliani-Al-Sharpton-White-House/2014/12/30/id/615632/.

8. Russ Buettner, "As Sharpton Rose, So Did His Unpaid Taxes," *New York Times*, November 18, 2014, http://www.nytimes.com/2014/11/19/nyregion/questions-about-al-sharptons-finances-accompany-his-rise-in-influence.html?_r=0.

9. Jake Tapper, "The skeletons and suits in Al Sharpton's closet," *Salon*, June 20, 2003. http://www.salon.com/2003/06/21/sharpton_7/.

10. Deepti Hajela, "Imus takes his lumps on Sharpton's show," *USA Today*, April 9, 2007, http://usatoday30.usatoday.com/life/theater/2007-04-09-739667894_x.htm.

11. Bill Carter, "Radio Host Is Suspended over Racial Remarks," *New York Times*, April 10, 2007, http://www.nytimes.com/2007/04/10/business/media/10imus.html.

12. Judy Faber, "CBS Fires Don Imus over Racial Slur," CBS News, April 12, 2007, http://www.cbsnews.com/news/cbs-fires-don-imus-over-racial-slur/.

13. Chris Cillizza, "Stephen A. Smith wants all black people to vote Republican in 2016. Um, okay," *Washington Post*, March 19, 2015, http://www.washingtonpost.com/blogs/the-fix/wp/2015/03/19/stephen-a-smith-wants-all-black-people-to-vote-republican-in-2016-um-ok/.

14. Comment posted by Taurusingr in response to EURPublisher01, "Stephen A. Smith: All Blacks Should Vote GOP for One Election," Lee Bailey's Eurweb, March 19, 2015, http://www.eurweb.com/2015/03/stephen-a-smith-all-blacks-should-vote-gop-for-one-election-watch/.

15. Thomas M. DeFrank, "Rev. Al Sharpton joins President Obama's immigration reform effort," *New York Daily News*, April 20, 2011, http://www.nydailynews.com/news/politics/rev-al-sharpton-joins-president-obama-immigration-reform-effort-article-1.113516.

16. Billy Hallowell, "'Hypocrites': Sharpton Blasts Black Pastors Who Won't Support Obama over His Gay Marriage Stance," *The Blaze*, May 17, 2012, http://www.theblaze.com/stories/2012/05/17/hypocrites-sharpton-blasts-black-pastors-who-wont-support-obama-over-his-gay-marriage-stance/.

17. "Eric Garner and Trayvon Martin Families, Michael Brown's Lawyer, and Others Accuse Al Sharpton of Exploiting Their Tragedies in New James O'Keefe Video," Project Veritas, February 24, 2015, http://projectveritas.com/posts/news-blog-media-video/eric-garner-and-trayvon-martin-families-michael-brown's-lawyer-and.

CHAPTER 13: KILLING THE MOCKINGBIRD

1. Dominick Dunne, "The Menendez Murder Trial," *Vanity Fair*, October 1993, http://www.vanityfair.com/magazine/1993/10/dunne199310.

2. Edward Kennedy, "Address to the People of Massachusetts on Chappaquiddick," *American Rhetoric*, July 25, 1969, http://www.americanrhetoric.com/speeches/tedkennedychappaquiddick.htm.

3. CNN, "Thousands 'march for justice' in Jena, court orders hearing on teen," CNN.com, September 20, 2007, http://bit.ly/14rWgd3.

4. Rene Lynch, "Trayvon Martin case: 'Blacks are under attack,' says Jesse Jackson," *Los Angeles Times*, March 23, 2012, http://articles.latimes.com/2012/mar/23/nation/la-na-nn-trayvon-martin-case-jesse-jackson-20120323.

5. John Perazzo, "The New Black Panthers' Bounty on George Zimmerman," *Frontpage Mag*, March 29, 2012, http://www.frontpagemag.com/2012/john-perazzo/trayvon-martin-and-collective-racial-guilt/.

6. "Black militia group wants to arrest Trayvon Martin shooter," The Grio, March 19, 2012, http://thegrio.com/2012/03/19/black-militia-group-wants-to-arrest-trayvon-martin-shooter/.

7. "Jesse Jackson: 'I Do Not Accept' Zimmerman Verdict," Lakeshore Public Media, July 15, 2013,

http://lakeshorepublicmedia.org/stories/jesse-jackson-i-do-not-accept-zimmerman-verdict/.

8. Jack Mirkinson, "Al Sharpton: George Zimmerman Verdict 'An Atrocity,'" *Huffington Post*, September 12, 2013, http://www.huffingtonpost.com/2013/07/13/al-sharpton-george-zimmerman-verdict_n_3593001.html.

9. "Characters: Twelve Angry Men," website of the Utah Shakespeare Festival, accessed May 13, 2015, http://www.bard.org/characters-twelve-angry-men.

10. Nicole Flatow, "Only Minority Juror Says George Zimmerman 'Got Away With Murder,'" *ThinkProgress*, July 25, 2013, http://thinkprogress.org/justice/2013/07/25/2357791/only-minority-juror-says-zimmerman-got-away-with-murder/.

11. "Zimmerman Juror Says Serving on Jury Ruined Her Life," *Inside Edition*, October 31, 2013, http://www.insideedition.com/headlines/7269-zimmerman-juror-says-serving-on-jury-ruined-her-life.

12. White House Office of the Press Secretary, "Remarks by the President at Black History Month Reception," the White House website, https://www.whitehouse.gov/the-press-office/2015/02/26/remarks-president-black-history-month-reception.

13. NewsOne Now, "Sybrina Fulton, Mother of Trayvon Martin, Responds to DOJ Decision Not to Charge George Zimmerman," NewsOne, February 25, 2015, http://newsone.com/3093705/sybrina-fulton-mother-of-trayvon-martin-responds-to-doj-decision-not-to-charge-george-zimmerman-video/.

14. Joe Tacopino, "George Zimmerman Blames Obama for Racial Tension After Trayvon Martin Shooting," Fox News, March 24, 2015, http://nation.foxnews.com/2015/03/24/george-zimmerman-blames-obama-racial-tension-after-trayvon-martin-shooting.

15. White House Office of the Press Secretary, "Remarks by the President at Black History Month Reception."

16. Matt Wilstein, "Charles Barkley 'Agrees' with Zimmerman Verdict, Hits Media for Giving 'Racists' A 'Platform to Vent Ignorance,'" *Mediaite*, July 18, 2013, http://www.mediaite.com/tv/charles-barkley-agrees-with-zimmerman-verdict-hits-media-for-giving-racists-a-platform-to-vent-ignorance/.

17. James Beattie, "Watch: Judge 'Offended' by 3-Year-Old Girl's 'Racism' So He Does Something Insane," *Western Journalism*, April 13, 2015, http://www.westernjournalism.com/watch-judge-gives-man-probation-armed-robbery/.

CHAPTER 14: THE STARBUCKS SYNDROME

1. David Yoffe and Michael Cusamnao, "Starbucks 'Race Together' Brilliant," *Time*, March 18, 2015, http://time.com/3749221/starbucks-howard-schultz-race-together-initiative/.

2. "The Internet Is United in Despising Starbucks' 'Race Together' Cup Campaign," *AdWeek*, March 18, 2015, http://www.adweek.com/adfreak/internet-united-despising-starbucks-race-together-cup-campaign-163540.

3. Kareem Abdul-Jabbar, "Starbucks' Flawed but Wonderful Plan to Tackle Race," *Time*, March 18, 2015, http://time.com/3749633/kareem-abdul-jabbar-starbucks-racetogether/.

4. Michelle Ye Hee Lee, "'Hands up, don't shoot' did not happen in Ferguson," *Washington Post*, March 19, 2015, http://www.washingtonpost.com/blogs/fact-checker/wp/2015/03/19/hands-up-dont-shoot-did-not-happen-in-ferguson/.

5. Kareem Abdul-Jabbar, "These Terrorist Attacks Are Not About Religion," *Time*, January 9, 2015, http://time.com/3662152/kareem-abdul-jabbar-paris-charlie-hebdo-terrorist-attacks-are-not-about-religion/.

6. Mark Jones, "The Hanafi Siege of 1977," *Boundary Stones,* March 14, 2014, http://blogs.weta.org/boundarystones/2014/03/14/hanafi-siege-1977.

7. "CAMPUS LIFE: Wisconsin; Regents Approve a Disputed Ban on Discrimination," *Time,* June 18, 1989, http://www.nytimes.com/1989/06/18/style/campus-life-wisconsin-regents-approve-a-disputed-ban-on-discrimination.html.

8. Jeff Glaze, "Heartbroken and afraid, Tony Robinson's mother speaks at vigil," *Wisconsin State Journal,* March 17, 2015, http://host.madison.com/news/local/crime_and_courts/heartbroken-and-afraid-tony-robinson-s-mother-speaks-at-vigil/article_3818d7ae-ae90-50d0-b22b-4ce456c71fe5.html.

9. Ashley Fantz, "Madison police leaders: This won't be Ferguson," CNN.com, March 9, 2015, http://www.cnn.com/2015/03/09/us/madison-ferguson-differences/.

10. Ibid.

11. "Family, friends peacefully remember Tony Robinson," CBS News, March 9, 2015, https://www.facebook.com/CBSEveningNews/posts/10153234666859073?comment_id=10153234839669073&offset=0&total_comments=93.

12. Pat Schneider, "1,000 protesters block East Washington Ave. in march for justice for Tony Robinson," *Cap Times,* March 11, 2015, http://host.madison.com/ct/news/local/writers/pat_schneider/protesters-block-east-washington-ave-in-march-for-justice-for/article_dc79819b-0ff0-5f42-a3eb-5c8f71a26c66.html.

13. The White House, Office of the Press Secretary, "President Obama Signs New Initiative to Improve Educational Outcomes for African Americans," whitehouse.gov, July 26, 2012, https://www.whitehouse.gov/the-press-office/2012/07/26/president-obama-signs-new-initiative-improve-educational-outcomes-africa.

14. "Affidavit from Commander Deanna Fox Williams," Miami-Dade Schools Police Department, http://www.scribd.com/doc/135692728/Affidavit-From-Commander-Deanna-Fox-Williams.

15. FBI Miami, "Miami Dade County Public Schools Superintendent Alberto M. Carvalho to Receive FBI Director's 2014 Community Leadership Award," FBI website, December 10, 2014, http://www.fbi.gov/miami/press-releases/2014/miami-dade-county-public-schools-superintendent-alberto-m.-carvalho-to-receive-fbi-directors-2014-community-leadership-award.

16. Jessica Bock, "DOJ: Ferguson school resource officers too quick to use force," *St. Louis Post-Dispatch,* March 4, 2015, http://www.stltoday.com/news/local/education/doj-ferguson-school-resource-officers-too-quick-to-use-force/article_e5d7a423-aa4e-5689-91b4-cabb698000e6.html.

CHAPTER 15: OUTSIDE LOOKING IN

1. David Gutmann, "In the Absence of Fathers," *First Things,* February 1995, http://www.firstthings.com/article/1995/02/004-in-the-absence-of-fathers.

2. Ibid.

3. "Meet O. J. Simpson: Home Is Always Where the Heart Is," *Parents' Magazine,* February 1977, 42–43.

4. Bianca Floyd, "For Marguerite Whitley Simpson Thomas," *Meanderings,* June 1995, http://newsavanna.com/meanderings/me206/me20601.html.

5. "Nicole Brown Simpson's Letter to O.J. Simpson," n.d., http://law2.umkc.edu/faculty/projects/ftrials/Simpson/brownletter.html, accessed May 18, 2015.

6. Ibid.

7. Ibid.

8. Ibid.

9. "Nicole's 911 Call of 1993," http://walraven.org/simpson/911-1993.html, accessed May 18, 2015.

10. "Audience Members React to the O. J. Simpson Verdict," *The Oprah Winfrey Show*, October 1995, http://www.oprah.com/oprahshow/Audience-Members-React-to-the-OJ-Simpson-Verdict-Video.

CHAPTER 16: THE ABSENT BLACK FATHER "MYTH"

1. All Culp-Ressler quotes in this chapter are from Tara Culp-Ressler, "The Myth of the Absent Black Father," *ThinkProgress*, January 16, 2014, http://thinkprogress.org/health/2014/01/16/3175831/myth-absent-black-father/.

2. "Census Bureau Reports 64 Percent Increase in Number of Children Living with a Grandparent over Last Two Decades" (press release), United States Census Bureau, June 29, 2011, http://www.census.gov/newsroom/releases/archives/children/cb11-117.html; African American Family Facts, First Things First, http://firstthings.org/african-american-family-facts, accessed May 18, 2015.

3. Stephan Thernstrom and Abigail Thernstrom, *America in Black and White: One Nation, Indivisible* (New York: Simon & Schuster, 2009), 344.

4. Makenzie Bowker, "Adrian Peterson's son dies after alleged assault," HLN, October 12, 2013, http://www.hlntv.com/video/2013/10/12/adrian-peterson-minnesota-vikings-son-death.

5. "C.J.: Asked on TV 1-on-1, Adrian Peterson won't say how many kids he has," *Star Tribune*, October 25, 2013, http://www.startribune.com/entertainment/228979291.html.

6. The State of Texas, Montgomery County District Clerk's Office, Criminal Inquiry Screen, accessed May 18, 2015, http://www.co.montgomery.tx.us/dclerk/kiosk/UNIDATADETAIL2.ASP?Type=CRIMINAL&Cause=14-09-10024-CR.

7. Louis Bien, "A complete timeline of the Ray Rice assault case," *SB Nation*, November 28, 2014, http://www.sbnation.com/nfl/2014/5/23/5744964/ray-rice-arrest-assault-statement-apology-ravens.

8. The State of Texas, Montgomery County District Clerk's Office, Criminal Inquiry Screen, accessed May 18, 2015, http://www.co.montgomery.tx.us/dclerk/kiosk/UNIDATADETAIL2.ASP?Type=CRIMINAL&Cause=14-09-10024-CR.

9. NAACP "Criminal Justice Fact Sheet," NAACP.com, http://www.naacp.org/pages/criminal-justice-fact-sheet, accessed May 18, 2015.

10. Marissa Payne, "Ex-Bears player Adrian Peterson loses young son to cancer," *Washington Post*, February 17, 2015, http://www.washingtonpost.com/blogs/early-lead/wp/2015/02/17/ex-bears-player-adrian-peterson-loses-young-son-to-cancer/.

11. NAACP "Criminal Justice Fact Sheet."

12. "National Incidence Study of Child Abuse and Neglect (NIS-4), 2004–2009," Office of Planning, Research and Evaluation, http://www.acf.hhs.gov/programs/opre/research/project/national-incidence-study-of-child-abuse-and-neglect-nis-4-2004-2009.

13. Southern Poverty Law Center, "My Family Rocks," Teaching Tolerance, http://www.tolerance.org/lesson/my-family-rocks, accessed May 18, 2015.

14. Patrick F. Fagan, "The Child Abuse Crisis: The Disintegration of Marriage, Family, and the American Community," Heritage Foundation, May 15, 1997, http://www.heritage.org/research/reports/1997/05/bg1115-the-child-abuse-crisis.

15. "Couple jailed for life in one of Britain's worst child abuse cases," ABC.net, August 2, 2103, http://www.abc.net.au/news/2013-08-03/uk-jails-parents-for-starving-boy-to-death/4862950.

16. Nonie Darwish, *Now They Call Me Infidel: Why I Renounced Jihad for America, Israel, and the War on Terror* (New York: Penguin, 2006), 136.

CHAPTER 17: FAKE AUTHENTICITY

1. Erica Ritz, "'Suited, Booted, and Armed,'" *The Blaze,* April 8, 2012, http://www.theblaze.com/stories/2012/04/08/suited-booted-and-armed-unbelievable-audio-from-the-new-black-panthers/.

2. "Full Interview: Michelle Williams" (video), accessed May 18, 2015, 10 News Tampa, http://www.wtsp.com/video/1557353015001/1/Full-Interview-Michelle-Williams.

3. All Sowell quotations in this chapter are from Thomas Sowell, "Black rednecks and white liberals," Townhall.com, May 5, 2005, http://townhall.com/columnists/thomassowell/2005/05/05/black_rednecks_and_white_liberals/page/full.

4. "Eminem," Biography, *Rolling Stone,* http://www.rollingstone.com/music/artists/eminem/biography.

5. "8 Mile: Final Battle," Genius, http://genius.com/Eminem-8-mile-final-battle-lyrics.

6. Sam Cooke, "You Send Me," from the album *Portrait of a Legend 1951–1964* (Remastered). Lyrics available from MetroLyrics, at http://www.metrolyrics.com/you-send-me-lyrics-sam-cooke.html.

7. Jeff Barry, Ellie Greenwich, and Phil Spector, "Chapel of Love," recorded by the Dixie Cups, 1964. Lyrics available from MetroLyrics at http://www.metrolyrics.com/chapel-of-love-lyrics-the-dixie-cups.html.

8. Al Green, Willie Mitchell, and Al Jackson Jr., "Let's Stay Together," from the Al Green album *Let's Stay Together,* Memphis, Royal Recording Studio, 1972.

9. Kanye West et al., "Monster," from the album *My Beautiful Dark Twisted Fantasy,* New York: Roc-A-Fella Records, 2010. Lyrics available from MetroLyrics, http://www.metrolyrics.com/monster-lyrics-kanye-west.html.

10. Melinda Tankard Reist, "So decapitated women are fine with you Kanye West," *MTR,* http://melindatankardreist.com/2011/01/so-decapitated-women-are-fine-with-you-kanye-west/.

11. "Kanye West," Biography, *Rolling Stone,* http://www.rollingstone.com/music/artists/kanye-west/biography.

12. "We Don't Care," from the album *College Dropout,* New York: Roc-A-Fella Records, 2004. Lyrics available from Genius, at http://genius.com/Kanye-west-we-dont-care-lyrics.

13. Ann Clark, "Kanye West: I'm Looking for the 'Right Girl,'" *People,* November 12, 2008, http://www.people.com/people/article/0,,20239777,00.html.

14. "Top Ten Most Outrageous Kanye West Moments," *Time,* accessed May 18, 2015, http://content.time.com/time/specials/packages/article/0,28804,1922188_1922187_1923051,00.html.

15. Ibid.

16. Kia Makarechi, "Obama: Kanye Is a Jackass, but He's Talented," *Huffington Post,* April 12, 2012, http://www.huffingtonpost.com/2012/04/12/obama-kanye-jay-z-jackass_n_1420683.html.

17. Kaitlan Collins, "Kanye West: 'Obama Calls the Home Phone,'" *Daily Caller,* March 3, 2015, http://dailycaller.com/2015/03/03/kanye-west-obama-calls-the-home-phone/.

18. Mark Egan, "'Proud non-reader' Kanye West turns author," Reuters, May 26, 2009, http://www.reuters.com/article/2009/05/26/us-kanyewest-idUSTRE54P5L820090526.

19. "Tupac Shakur," Biography.com, http://www.biography.com/people/tupac-shakur-206528.

20. George James, "Rapper Faces Prison Term for Sex Abuse," *New York Times,* February 8, 1995, http://www.nytimes.com/1995/02/08/nyregion/rapper-faces-prison-term-for-sex-abuse.html.

21. Afeni Shakur, *Evolution of a Revolutionary* (New York: Simon & Schuster, 2010), 35.

22. Ibid., 62.

23. Tupac Shakur et al., "Dear Mama," from the album *Me Against the World,* Santa Monica: Interscope Records, 1995. Lyrics available from MetroLyrics, at http://www.metrolyrics.com/dear-mama-lyrics-2pac.html.

24. Tupac Shakur, "Souljah's Revenge," from the album *Strictly 4 My Niggaz*, Santa Monica: Interscope, 1993. Lyrics available from A–Z Lyrics, at http://www.azlyrics.com/lyrics/2pac/souljahsrevenge. html.

25. "Southern California, This Just In," *Los Angeles Times*, April 11, 2012, http://latimesblogs.latimes. com/lanow/2012/04/rodney-king-speaks-out-on-trayvon-martin.html.

CHAPTER 18: SELF-DESTRUCTION

1. Mike Tyson, "My Life as a Young Thug," *New York Magazine*, October 20, 2013, http://nymag. com/nymag/features/mike-tyson-2013-10/index1.html.

2. Robert Samanson, "To Die Like a Gangsta," *Vanity Fair*, March 1997, http://www.vanityfair.com/ culture/1997/03/tupac-shakur-rap-death.

3. Voletta Wallace, with Tremell McKenzie, *Biggie: Voletta Wallace Remembers Her Son, Christopher Wallace, aka Notorious B.I.G.*, Google ebook (New York: Simon & Schuster, 2005), 44.

4. "Biggie Smalls," Biography, http://www.biography.com/people/biggie-smalls-20866735.

5. Christopher Wallace, "Ready to Die," from the album *Ready to Die*, New York: Bad Boy Records, 1994. Lyrics, available from MetroLyrics, at http://www.metrolyrics.com/ready-to-die-lyrics-notorious-big.html.

6. Christopher Jasper et al., "Big Poppa," from *Ready to Die*. Lyrics available from A–Z Lyrics, at http://www.azlyrics.com/lyrics/notoriousbig/bigpoppa.html.

7. Duane S. Hitchings et al, "Hit Em Up" from the album *All Eyez on Me*, Los Angeles, Death Row Records, 1996. Lyrics available from MetroLyrics, http://www.metrolyrics.com/hit-em-up-lyrics-2pac.html.

8. "Interview: Jesse Jackson," *Frontline*, PBS.org, spring 1997, http://www.pbs.org/wgbh/pages/ frontline/shows/race/interviews/jackson.html.

9. Reuters, "Jackson Admits He Has Daughter Out of Wedlock," *Los Angeles Times*, January 18, 2001, http://articles.latimes.com/2001/jan/18/news/mn-13818.

10. *Bossip* staff, "Babymama Drama: Messy Jesse Jackson Owes Nearly $12 K in Child Support for His Outside Kid," *Bossip*, January 19, 2012, http://bossip.com/528982/babymama-drama-messy-jesse-jackson30346/.

CHAPTER 19: SEX WAR

1. Tanya Barrientos and David O'Reilly, "She's Fighting the Enemy Within: C. Delores Tucker Is Taking On Black Gangsta Rappers Under the Banner of Dr. King," philly.com, January 20, 1994, http://articles.philly.com/1994-01-20/living/25822345_1_national-political-congress-black-women-delores-tucker.

2. Afeni Shakur, *Evolution of a Revolutionary* (New York: Simon & Schuster, 2010), 37.

3. Tupac Shakur et al., "How Do U Want It" from the album *All Eyez on Me*, Los Angeles, Death Row Records, 1996. Lyrics available from Genius, at http://genius.com/24047.

4. "Rap Game," by D12, featuring 50 Cent, 1995. Lyrics available from knowyoursong.com, http:// www.knowyoursong.com/Rap-Gamefeat-50-Cent-by-D12-Lyrics.html/Tell-That-C-Delores-Tucker-Slut-To-Suck-A-Dick-line-41.html.

5. Jessica Goodman, "Eminem Raps That He'll 'Punch Lana Del Rey Right in the Face Twice Like Ray Rice,'" *Huffington Post*, November 11, 2014, http://www.huffingtonpost.com/2014/11/11/ eminem-lana-del-rey_n_6138712.html.

6. M. Mathers and J. Bass, "Cleanin Out My Closet," from the album *The Eminem Show*, New York: Shady Records, 200. Lyrics available from Genius, http://genius.com/Eminem-cleanin-out-my-closet-lyrics.

7. M. Mathers et al., "My Mom," from the album *Relapse*, New York: Shady/Santa Monica: Aftermath/Interscope, 2009. Lyrics available from A–Z Lyrics, at http://www.azlyrics.com/lyrics/eminem/mymom.html.

8. James Kuhnhenn, "Clash over Pop Music Renewed at a Hearing on Violent Lyrics Senators Said There Was a Link to Youth Violence. A Critic and C. Delores Tucker's Husband Were at Odds," philly.com, November 7, 1997, http://articles.philly.com/1997-11-07/news/25545019_1_violent-lyrics-rap-senate-hearing.

9. Ibid.

CHAPTER 20: GENERATIONAL LOSS

1. "Brooklyn Girl beaten by gang as crowd does nothing in McDonalds," YouTube video, March 12, 2015, posted by Wewwooff, https://www.youtube.com/watch?v=8eX-t6laaf8.

2. "Video 'shows University of Oklahoma fraternity's racist chant,'" YouTube video, 2:14, March 9, 2015, https://www.youtube.com/watch?v=0f8lr3B628c.

3. Dray Clark, "Final Suspect, 15, in Brutal Brooklyn McDonald's Brawl Arrested," Eyewitness News, March 20, 2015, http://7online.com/news/brutal-mcdonalds-brawl-video-now-sparking-community-action/554045/.

4. Ibid., comments.

5. Desire Thompson, "Police to Investigate Massive Brawl Involving Teens in Brooklyn McDonald's," NewsOne, March 12, 2015, comments, http://newsone.com/3097840/massive-brawl-fight-teens-brooklyn-mcdonalds-video/.

6. Clark, "Final Suspect, 15, in Brutal Brooklyn McDonald's Brawl Arrested," comments.

7. Thompson, "Police to Investigate Massive Brawl Involving Teens in Brooklyn McDonald's," comments.

8. Ernest Baker, "The Reality of Dating White Women When You're Black," *Gawker*, June 3, 2014, http://gawker.com/the-reality-of-dating-white-women-when-youre-black-1585401039.

9. Courtney Carter, "Black Men Don't Like Black Women," *Huffington Post*, December 14, 2014, http://www.huffingtonpost.com/courtney-carter/black-men-dont-like-black_b_5973030.html.

10. Rob Tannenbaum, "Azealia Banks: Wild and Uncensored for Playboy," *Playboy*, March 16, 2015, http://bit.ly/1xscXB7.

11. Ibid.

12. Ibid.

CHAPTER 21: RACE WAR

1. "George Zimmerman says his conscience is clear, accuses Obama of bias," *Los Angeles Times*, April 9, 2015, http://touch.latimes.com/#section/-1/article/p2p-83131474/.

2. Michael Anthony Adams, "Video shows beating of young girl and her little brother," *IndianapolisStar*, March 16, 2015, http://www.indystar.com/story/news/crime/2015/03/15/video-surfaces-showing-beating-of-woman-and-child/24811775/.

3. Rebecca Bennett and Eric Levy, "Violent video shows girl beating another female, kid brother," Fox 59, March 15, 2015, http://fox59.com/2015/03/15/woman-caught-on-video-beating-another-woman-and-a-child/.

4. "Teen beats young girl and then attacks a child," LiveLeak, March 15, 2015, http://www.liveleak. com/view?i=b97_1426395661&comments=1&selected_view_mode=desktop.

5. Katie Delong, "My granddaughter went over the edge": Family of teen arrested after brutal fight caught on camera says she has PTSD," Fox 6 Now, March 17, 2015, http://fox6now.com/2015/03/17/ my-granddaughter-went-over-the-edge-family-of-teen-arrested-after-brutal-fight-caught-on-camera-says-she-has-ptsd/.

6. Garrett Haake, "Cleaver: All plaza curfew will do is 'make a lot of black kids angry,'" KSHB 41, May 5, 2013, http://www.kshb.com/money/angies-list/cleaver-all-plaza-curfew-will-do-is-make-a-lot-of-black-kids-angry.

7. Hugo Schwyzer, "Why Most Mass Murderers Are Privileged White Men," *Jezebel*, July 24, 2012, http://jezebel.com/5928584/why-most-mass-murderers-are-privileged-white-men.

8. Lee Romney, "'Zebra Killer' J. C. X. Simon found dead in San Quentin prison cell," *Los Angeles Times*, March 13, 2015, http://touch.latimes.com/#section/-1/article/p2p-83053956/.

9. Ron Sylvester, "Carrs knew violence and instability as children," *Wichita Eagle*, November 10, 2002, https://groups.google.com/forum/#!topic/alt.true-crime/7hOf5DgdxNY.

10. Richard Perez-Pena, "Woman in '92 Subway Dispute with L.I.R.R. Suspect Says All the Signs Were There," *New York Times*, December 13, 1993, http://www.nytimes.com/1993/12/13/nyregion/woman-in-92-subway-dispute-with-lirr-suspect-says-all-the-signs-were-there.html.

11. Robert McFadden, "A Tormented Life—A special report; A Long Slide from Privilege Ends in Slaughter on a Train," *New York Times*, December 12, 1993, http://www.nytimes.com/1993/12/12/ nyregion/tormented-life-special-report-long-slide-privilege-ends-slaughter-train.html.

12. Nicolaus Mills, "The Shame of 'Black Rage' Defense," *Chicago Tribune*, June 6, 1994, http://articles. chicagotribune.com/1994-06-06/news/9406060097_1_kunstler-and-kuby-william-kunstler-colin-ferguson.

13. Sari Horowitz and Michael Ruane, *Sniper: The Hunt for the Killers Who Terrorized the Nation* (New York: Random House, 2003).

14. Stephen Kiehl, "Muhammad's ex-wife recalls death threat," *Baltimore Sun*, November 20, 2003, http://touch.baltimoresun.com/#section/-1/article/p2p-10300901/.

15. Harry Mount, "The sniper's plan: kill six whites a day for 30 days," *Telegraph* (UK), May 25, 2006, http://www.telegraph.co.uk/news/worldnews/northamerica/usa/1519411/The-snipers-plan-kill-six-whites-a-day-for-30-days.html.

16. Pat Buchanan, "The Beltway Sniper and the Media," American Cause, October 30, 2002, http:// www.theamericancause.org/patthebeltwaysniper.htm.

17. Associated Press, "DC sniper keeps silence before execution; John Allen Muhammad also charged with Montgomery murder," AL.com, http://blog.al.com/live/2009/11/dc_sniper_keeps_silence_ before.html.

18. *Murderpedia*, s.v. "Omar S. Thornton," http://www.murderpedia.org/male.T/t/thornton-omar.htm, accessed May 19, 2015.

19. Kevin Hayes, "Omar Thornton: 'I Killed the Five Racists,'" CBS News, August 4, 2010, http:// www.cbsnews.com/news/omar-thornton-i-killed-the-five-racists/.

20. Ibid.

21. "OST Memorial Foundation," Facebook, https://www.facebook.com/OstMemorialFoundation, accessed May 19, 2015.

22. "Christopher Dorner's Manifesto," KTLA 5, February 12, 2013, http://ktla.com/2013/02/12/ read-christopher-dorners-so-called-manifesto/.

23. "Ex Reported Christopher Dorner on DontDateHimGirl.com, Called Him 'Paranoid' and 'Twisted,'" *Laist*, February 9, 2013, http://laist.com/2013/02/09/exes_call_christopher_dorner_parano.php.

24. Sharon McNary, "LAPD manhunt: Christopher Dorner's promising career ended with angry manifesto, fugitive status," 89.3 KPCC, February 8, 2013, http://www.scpr.org/news/2013/02/08/35876/lapd-manhunt-racism-fuels-christopher-dorner-ex-la/.

25. "Christopher Dorner's Manifesto."

26. Ibid.

27. Zachary Dowdy and Nicole Fuller, "Aaron Alexis's family 'shocked' by Navy Yard rampage," *Newsday*, http://www.newsday.com/news/nation/aaron-alexis-family-shocked-by-navy-yard-rampage-1.6088413.

28. "Navy Shooter Complained of 'White Racism,'" WND, September 18, 2013, http://www.wnd.com/2013/09/navy-shooter-complained-of-white-racism/.

29. "Vet in Navy Yard shooting had troubled past," Fox News, September 17, 2013, http://www.foxnews.com/us/2013/09/17/vet-in-navy-yard-shooting-fired-gun-into-neighbor-apartment-in-fort-worth-in/.

30. Michael Pearson, "Who is Oklahoma beheading suspect Alton Nolen?," CNN.com, September 30, 2014, http://www.cnn.com/2014/09/29/justice/oklahoma-beheading-suspect/.

31. Timothy Williams and Michael Schmidt, "Oklahoma Man Is Charged in Beheading of Co-Worker," *New York Times*, September 30, 2014, http://www.nytimes.com/2014/10/01/us/oklahoma-man-charged-with-murder-in-beheading-of-co-worker.html?_r=0.

32. Doug Donovan, "Speaking at Morgan, Farrakhan predicts violence in Ferguson," *Baltimore Sun*, November 22, 2014, http://touch.baltimoresun.com/#section/-1/article/p2p-82064370/.

33. Kim Barker et al., "Many Identities of New York Officers' Killer in a Life of Wrong Turns," *New York Times*, January 2, 2015, http://www.nytimes.com/2015/01/03/nyregion/ismaaiyl-brinsleys-many-identities-fueled-life-of-wrong-turns.html.

34. Ibid.

35. "Video Shows NYC Protesters Chanting for 'Dead Cops,'" News 4 New York, December 15, 2014, http://www.nbcnewyork.com/news/local/Eric-Garner-Manhattan-Dead-Cops-Video-Millions-March-Protest-285805731.html.

36. Barker et al., "Many Identities of New York Officers' Killer in a Life of Wrong Turns."

37. "The Grandfather," https://twitter.com/africa_4u/status/546905221990203393.

38. Paul Joseph Watson, "Ferguson Protester Who Met with DOJ Taunts Police with NYPD Cop Killer Quote," *Infowars*, December 22, 2014, http://www.infowars.com/ferguson-protester-who-met-with-doj-taunts-police-with-nypd-cop-killer-quote/.

39. Jason Sickles, "Ferguson shooting suspect gave false confession, lawyer says," Yahoo! News, March 17, 2015, http://news.yahoo.com/ferguson-shooting-suspect-gave-false-confession-lawyer-says-230410789.html.

40. Mike Barnicle, "A Boston Cop-Shooting and Our Post-Truth Era," *Daily Beast*, March 29, 2015, http://www.thedailybeast.com/articles/2015/03/29/a-boston-cop-shooting-and-our-post-truth-era.html.

41. Jason Howerton, "Revealed: Chicago-Area Cousins' Alleged Plot to Bring 'Flames of War to the Heart' of America and 'Cause as Much Damage and Mayhem as Possible,'" *TheBlaze*, March 26, 2015, http://www.theblaze.com/stories/2015/03/26/revealed-chicago-area-cousins-plan-to-bring-flames-of-war-to-the-heart-of-america-and-cause-as-much-damage-and-mayhem-as-possible/.

42. Jean Marbella, "Beginning of Freddie Gray's life as sad as its end, court case shows," *Baltimore Sun*, April 23, 2015, http://touch.baltimoresun.com/#section/-1/article/p2p-83373966/.
43. John Fritze, "Obama calls for national 'soul searching' over Freddie Gray's death," *Baltimore Sun*, April 28, 2015, http://touch.baltimoresun.com/#section/-1/article/p2p-83404797/.

CHAPTER 23: THE ANTIDOTE

1. Sabrina Siddiqui, "Darren Wilson Testimony: Michael Brown Looked Like 'a Demon,'" *Huffington Post*, November 25, 2014, http://www.huffingtonpost.com/2014/11/25/darren-wilson-testimony_n_6216620.html.
2. Encyclopedia.com, s.v. "Shakur, Afeni," http://www.encyclopedia.com/doc/1G2-3027700050.html, accessed May 19, 2015.
3. "Poverty," BlackDemographics.com, accessed May 19, 2015, http://blackdemographics.com/households/poverty/.

AFTERWORD

1. Jonathon Seidl, "'Hannity' Guest Storms Off Set During Explosive Talk about Killer Cop: 'You Are an Embarrassment to the World!'" *TheBlaze*, April 10, 2015, http://www.theblaze.com/stories/2015/04/10/hannity-guest-storms-off-set-during-explosive-talk-about-killer-cop-you-are-an-embarrassment-to-the-world/.

INDEX